# Thinking Goes to School

# Thinking Goes to School

## Piaget's Theory in Practice

**Hans G. Furth and Harry Wachs**

New York
**Oxford University Press**
1974

Photographs by J. M. Singer and R. Even
Copyright © 1974 by Oxford University Press, Inc.
Library of Congress Catalogue Card Number: 73-87607
Printed in the United States of America

To my parents, Hermoine R. Wachs and Sam Wachs,
and my wife, Ruth, and our children.

H. W.

To Jean Deveau and all others who love children.

H. G. F.

# Preface

This is one of those books that was written more by the sheer force of circumstances than by the authors' desire to add to the already existing multitude of innovative educational proposals.

The first set of circumstances occurred in the mid 60's when one of us discussed with his colleague Bruce Ross the application of Piaget's theories to educational practice. Somewhat naively we thought that one short article could easily revolutionize the field of education. At that time also, with colleague Jim Youniss, we first introduced a "thinking game," the symbol-picture logic, to deaf children.

The second set of circumstances began at a restaurant overlooking the Lake of Geneva, where in 1967 the authors and their families met for the first time and shared ideas, inspired by the presence of the Genevan scholars. Here was sparked our joint interest in basing the obviously needed educational innovations on the solid rock of an all-encompassing developmental theory. This was followed a few years later by an opportunity, offered by the school district of Charleston, West Virginia, with a telephone call from Pittsburgh to Washington: "Here is your chance to turn your book *Piaget for teachers* into a reality."

Then came the two years of cooperative work at the Charleston school which we describe in these pages. And so the one short article and the one thinking game have become for one of us a fourth book in a series of books enlarging on Piaget's theory— and for the other, an expression of twenty years of clinical study and practical experience with all types of children. We share a sober realization that the most pervasive arguments of a book and the most decisive demonstrations of science alone will not bring about desirable educational changes: this can be done only by committed and courageous persons, parents, teachers at all levels, administrators, civic and political leaders.

We present the variety of concrete activities in Part III not without some trepidation. The idea of a curriculum with cumulative performance objectives is so strongly advocated in teacher training that there is always the risk of seeing the thinking games in this book treated as tasks to be accomplished. We trust that the preceding parts will provide sufficient theoretical insight so that our fear of being misunderstood will prove unfounded. We particularly urge the reader to grasp the significance of raising or lowering the demands of a task according to the developmental level of the child. This assures that the child works successfully at his appropriate high level—to ask less or more would be equally harmful in the long run.

To the many persons who during the years encouraged our work—our colleagues, students, and friends—our thanks for sharing your thinking with us. Special mention is here made of the personnel and children of the Charleston school district and of our friend Carol Even whose professional experience in dramatic play with children added another dimension to the book.

Both of our families were most helpful and unselfishly endured our periods of isolation while writing. Sherri and Hallie contributed their efforts in numerous ways. To Ruth and Madeleine we want to express our gratitude for their unbiased critical appraisals, helpful suggestions, and constant encouragement. In particular, we owe an immense debt to Ruth for her untiring arrangement of schedules.

We are indebted to the administrative staff at the Catholic University Center for Research in Thinking and Language and at the Pennsylvania Vision Institute for the hours of typing and editing. Thanks also to the Pennsylvania Vision Institute clinic staff, past and present, who helped develop many of the thinking games, specifically E. Eugene Handley, Donald A. Deets, and D. Michael Simon.

There is no need to parcel out our own respective contributions to the book except to point out the obvious. The psychologist was mainly responsible for the theoretical framework and the overall organization of the project while the clinician's practical experience is evident in the multitude of thinking games and their application to the classroom. Nevertheless, this was truly a cooperative effort where the final shape of ideas arose from group collaboration. Neither of us feels possessive of our ideas. Indeed, nothing would be dearer to our hearts than to see the spark of our educational philosophy catch on and become a flaming fire through which the schools could preserve and foster the creative impulse of human development. Of this living fire, embracing the mind, the heart, and the body, the poet Blake has written:

> Unless the eye catch fire
>     The God will not be seen
> Unless the ear catch fire
>     The God will not be heard
> Unless the tongue catch fire
>     The God will not be named
> Unless the heart catch fire
>     The God will not be loved
> Unless the mind catch fire
>     The God will not be known

H.F., H.W.

# Acknowledgments

**Mark Atkinson**   Cover artist, student at Potomac School, McLean, Virginia.

**Richard Even**   Photography, chapter 13.

**James Henkelman**   Critical reading of chapter 12.

**Sally Siegel**   Critical reading and editing of the introduction and chapters 6 through 11.

**Joseph Singer**   Photography, chapters 6 through 11.

**Phyllis Theroux**   Critical reading of chapter 1 and chapter 14 of which she had the last word.

**Esther Tucker**   Critical reading of chapter 3.

**Victor Vasarely**   Graciously permitting reprint of his painting in Figure 23.

# Contents

# List of Thinking Games

**Thinking Goes to School**

# Introduction

When I was One
I had just begun.
When I was Two
I was nearly new.
When I was Three
I was hardly Me.
When I was Four
I was not much more.
When I was Five
I was just alive.
But now I am Six, I'm as clever as clever.
So I think I'll be six now for ever and ever.

A. A. Milne*

Anyone interested in the intellectual health of children should find *Thinking Goes to School* of value, for its purpose is to show how we can prepare our children to develop their full potential as "thinking" human beings. Because each child should be viewed as an individual we have not attempted to describe a rigid curriculum into which all children must fit; we have rather described a philosophy and a program which can be adjusted to fit all children. The games and play sequences are designed to develop the child's thinking ability. We assume the primary school age child thinks and wants to go on thinking "for ever and ever." Our pur-

* From the book *Now We Are Six* by A. A. Milne. Decorations by E. H. Shepard. Copyright 1927 by E. P. Dutton & Co., Inc. Renewal 1955 by A. A. Milne. Published by E. P. Dutton & Co., Inc. and used with their permission. Also reprinted by permission of The Canadian Publishers, McClelland and Stewart Ltd, Toronto; and by Methuen & Co. Ltd, London, and C. R. Milne.

3

pose is to help him achieve this. The activities or games described in this book provide a general foundation which should help the child to deal successfully with specific academic subjects. They can be played at home or at school; they require no elaborate or expensive equipment. They do require the presence of intelligent, patient, and perceptive adults who are willing to create situations in which children can grow. Although a program designed for kindergarten through the third grade is described in some detail, it is flexible and suitable, depending on the child, for chronological ages four through ten. While we dedicate the book to children, it is written for parents, teachers, and all those devoted to the successful development of children. Thinking environments, happy places for children to live and learn, should be created not only in our schools but also in our homes and places of work.

In these pages thinking environments will be called a "School for Thinking"; it is the term we use for what we hope will be the trend of the future in education. Specifically we refer to a project carried out over a period of two years at the Tyler Thinking School in Charleston, West Virginia. This project was not the type of "open classroom" in which children reigned and did whatever they felt like doing—or did nothing at all. There was freedom, but it was *freedom within structure*.

An environment was created midway between the open-ended school where children are left to do as they want and the sort of highly structured program where every response of the child is programmed as true or false. We describe this in some detail not because we see it as a model to be slavishly imitated but rather to provide a springboard for creative thought. It is an example which, it is hoped, will inspire many models.

We devote Chapter 1 to Piaget's theory. While familiarity with this theory is helpful, an expert understanding is not necessary for those interested in creating Schools for Thinking. For over half a century this Swiss scholar has been actively engaged in the study of the development of children's thinking. In brief, the growing child is constantly constructing his understanding of himself and his world. The workings of the child's developing mind are beginning to be understood, and systematic observations have demonstrated what happens during the process of restructuring—when the young child from his present developmental stage is reaching a new, more advanced, stage of thinking. The theory also clarifies how the activities and strategies developed by the thinking child are acquired through experience. The purpose of the School for Thinking is to implement Piaget's theory by providing the child with experiences best designed to develop his thinking.

In Chapter 2 we discuss how we became involved in the development of the Tyler Thinking School. One of us (HGF) wanted to put into practice a philosophy of education he had been developing and writing about; the other (HW) was interested in extending the work of his child development clinic, the Pennsylvania Vision Institute, into the classroom. Although both of us had begun our work with children who needed remedial help, we had grown increasingly interested in prevention. Rather than treating failure, we wanted to prevent failure. Our long-range objectives were fivefold: (1) to develop the habit of creative independent thinking; (2) to develop within the child a positive self-image; (3) to develop attitudes of social cooperation and moral responsibility; (4) to develop a knowledge and appreciation of persons, things, and events in the environment; and (5) to develop competence in the basic skill areas of reading, writing, and arithmetic.

These objectives are discussed more fully in Chapter 3 where we describe the underlying principles of a School for Thinking. We stress the importance of providing a multitude of stimulating activities so that a child has opportunities to develop and exercise behavior both in areas for which he has strong predispositions and in areas where he may be less gifted. We emphasize individual differences and make instructive use of them as they are crucial aspects of the program. Teachers may recognize some of our activities from prereading and remedial reading programs. However, the School for Thinking treats reading as one of many thinking activities in which the child is permitted to engage only if he has adequately developed the prerequisite skills; in the meantime, it provides the child with a rich variety of these prerequisite activities. Unnecessary educational failures are thereby avoided but, at the same time, no child is held back in reading.

In learning to read a child must know how to match sound patterns of the spoken language and phoneme sequences transcribed as letters. The correspondence between acoustic patterns and phonemic elements is far from simple or straightforward. For the young child who knows his language very well but does not read, the phoneme "t" in the three words "Tom, bat, stay" is not one invariant element but rather corresponds to three different speech and auditory processes. A speech spectogram of these words would show three different patterns with no clear boundaries of phonemes. To extract the invariance of the phoneme "t" from these different experiences means to analyze and interpret sounds. Knowing how to do this is primarily a developmental process of thinking and not a mere matter of learning a piece of information and memorizing it. Similar things can be said about the process of visual thinking which is necessary for the recognition and meaningful coordination of graphic squiggles. A child in school who is given ample opportunities to work successfully on these prerequisites can then readily apply his developed thinking capacity to the specific task of learning to read.

In our general rationale for classroom activities, we stress the importance of thinking for its own sake, freedom within structure, and developmentally appropriate activities. Emphasis on the activity rather than on imitation of the teacher frees the teacher from the impossible role of being the object of, the cause of, and the reason for all children's attention at the same time. While we recognize the educational value of directed classroom teaching and instructional television programs, we know that all children are not equally ready to benefit from the same situation at the same time. In addition, physical participation in activities is necessary for the child's healthy intellectual development; passive observation is not enough. Group play is particularly important in that it builds—if properly structured—cooperation rather than competition. The School for Thinking becomes challenging for the teacher as well as for the children.

The structure of the classroom is described in Chapter 4,

and we have drawn freely from our experience at Tyler for illustration. Activities are often referred to as "games" in the spirit of child's play for its own sake. But child's play, characterized by the child's spontaneous involvement, *is* thinking. It also has an important intellectual and biological function, and it advances the child's mental, physical, and emotional growth.

In Chapter 5 we discuss our school's primary goal—intellectual health. Thinking is the healthy use of the child's intelligence. But over and above this desirable goal we accomplish a far broader aim since intelligence permeates all human behavior and is inseparably intertwined with action, emotion, and social relations. While knowing facts is important, it is less important than knowing how to think, if for no other reason than the rapid change in our technological society that continually makes many facts obsolete. We discourage mere repetition and rote memorization because they often lead to boredom, which is a symptom of nonthinking. The child, encouraged to participate in problem-solving play that is neither too easy nor too difficult for him, is not bored because he is thinking at a personally challenging level. He is encouraged by his own success, not by a feeling of inferiority or superiority to others.

In Chapters 6 through 13 we describe body and sense, logic, and drama games which develop thinking strategies applicable to a wide range of more traditional academic subjects. These special activities do not usually form a normal part of the daily routine in elementary school. Many of them could fall under what is often called perceptual-motor training. What do these activities have to do with the development of thinking and how do they fit into the program? As an answer to the first question, consider a child who is learning to read. A child who does not have the habit of coordinating visual attention across a horizontal sequence should not have to acquire this coordination at the same time he is trying to learn to read. The child would then be in danger of failing in both. But once he has control of the general skill of vision coordination he can give his undivided attention to what is specific in learning to read.

According to Piaget all thinking develops from the coordination of external actions. Coordination of body movements and sense inputs are therefore a prerequisite to the application of body and sense activities to specific problems and tasks. In the young child thinking is still closely tied to such activities, and they are given a prominent place in our primary classroom. From our experience with five- to six-year-old children we know that regardless of background they find the majority of body and sense thinking games of this book not only not childish, but on the contrary difficult and challenging. Therefore, these activities stimulate intellectual development.

We are not, however, emphasizing perceptual-motor skills in the manner they are presently taught and understood. In our philosophy, we make it clear that it is not the muscles or the senses that need training, but the thinking which controls specific muscle or sense activities. Body and sense games are planned to exercise the developing thinking of the child; similarly drama or mathematical games are focused on the underlying social or mathematical thinking and not on theatrical performance or the memorizing of mathematical rules. In other words, all games are done with the accent on thinking and not on performance. Children quickly get the message that what counts in the classroom is not an arbitrary level of performance but the overall atmosphere of being "as clever as clever."

In sum, this book is a description of how to structure a first or second grade classroom to bring about an atmosphere for thinking. Our theory gives us the optimistic trust that all but the most seriously deficient children are capable of a level of thinking that should assure a successful mastery of whatever society decrees to be learned in the first three or four grades of school. These first grades of elementary school coincide with the child's entry into a psychological reality (his first capacity for adult-like thinking) and into the first formal setting where standards of learning are socially imposed. This, then, is an intellectually critical period. It could quite easily be a most exciting and fruitful period which encourages the child to continue his expanding capacity for thinking in the service of learning and in this way become a knowledgeable and socially responsible adult.

# I. Theory

# 1. Piaget's Theory Applied to the School for Thinking

Piaget's theory deals with the nature and development of thinking. Its main function for our purpose is to provide a criterion for thinking. It is the standard against which the activities in the classroom can be weighed and by which these activities can be theoretically justified.

What is unique in Piaget's theory and what relevance has it to education? Unfortunately, on the topic of thinking, scholars at large have not been overly explicit. A mere listing of Piagetian themes could be recognized as familiar clichés: "Thinking is based on experience." "Intelligence is the product of the innate potential interacting with the environment." "A little child knows more than he can verbalize."

While these statements are fully in accord with Piaget's theory—and this is the decisive difference—they are to be understood in a much more precise and selective sense than is usually the case. To clarify Piaget's theory and its significance for education we show in what way these verbal statements are interpreted by Piaget and to what extent different interpretations of these same statements lead to diametrically opposed opinions. In other words, the importance and the difficulty of thinking is illustrated in this very exercise of going beyond the words of a theory to their full meaning in reality.

Before turning our attention to some of Piaget's revolutionary positions on developmental psychology, think of the mother who is doing well with her infant without being theoretically knowledgeable of what she is doing and why she is doing it. Similarly, the thinking mechanisms which the child has and the School for Thinking activates by the games described in Part III, are to be *used* in connection with a task at hand; they are not primarily objects to *know*. For example, the child does not know and does not need to know that he has mechanisms of comprehending probability (Piaget calls them operations) when he guesses the more likely color of marbles he draws from a bag. But the probability thinking games demonstrate that he has and can use the mechanisms intelligently. As the child grows into an adult he will become capable of reflecting on these mechanisms and can then formulate specific mathematical rules of probability. Similarly, the teacher in the School for Thinking need not know the details of an adequate theory of thinking and its development; he uses the theory implicitly in his everyday classroom activities. The structure of the school provides the support and the objective setting which gives him the opportunity and the challenge to do so. To know some parts of Piaget's theory is helpful if and when the teacher develops some theoretical interest. Moreover, a teacher will have occasions to discuss and verbally justify the thinking activities of the school, both in terms of what is being done and perhaps also of what is not being done.

## Development versus learning

Piaget's theory is unique in its formulation of educational goals. This is because it separates two processes that are related but conceptually quite different: development and learning. Development has to do with *general* mechanisms of action and of thinking; it pertains to intelligence in its widest and fullest sense. Everything that can be called characteristic of human intelligence comes about chiefly through the process of development as distinct from the process of learning. Learning deals with the acquisition of *specific* skills and facts and the memorizing of *specific* information.

Piaget's theory states clearly that the general development of intelligence is the basis on which any specific learning rests. Learning can only take place on condition that the child has general mechanisms to which he can assimilate the information contained in learning. In this sense intelligence is the most necessary instrument of learning: A child's learning of geographical names would be quite senseless if he did not have a general comprehension of spatial, historical, and social relations. One should not teach that Boise is the capital of Idaho to a child who confuses the concepts of state and city. A child's learning of mathematical formulas would be quite useless if he did not have a general comprehension of the number system. A child's learning of any facts depends in part on the child's general capacity to relate these specific facts to other facts in a meaningful manner. In all these examples intelligent comprehension is the most vital ingredient of the total learning process. Consequently, the School for Thinking, recognizes the psychological priority of intelligence over learning.

Piaget's theory permits the school to separate conceptually what cannot be separated in practice: the learning aspect and the thinking aspect. One cannot have learning without (some) thinking, and neither can one have development of thinking without (some) learning. Children in a School for Thinking learn specific facts and skills as in any traditional school. But this learning aspect is subordinate in importance and emphasis to the thinking aspect, the primary reason for all activities.

## The source of development

A second unique principle in Piaget's theory centers around the word "interaction." This also has important educational implications. The word "interaction"—popular in the social sciences—usually refers to the existence of two of more given factors which together influence a third factor. In this sense heredity and maturation are said to interact with environment in the development of a child's native intelligence. If a child has learning or personality problems, one can always find proponents who put the major blame on heredity (IQ, constitution) or on the environment (disadvantaged milieu, family constellation). In any case, it is hardly possible for an educational institution to change either of these two forces substantially, and as long as theories focus only on these, the dilemma of heredity versus environment will constantly recur.

Piaget, too, has an interactionist theory, but in his case heredity, physiological maturation, and environment and their interaction in the development of intelligence are not the primary causes of this development: They are themselves subordinated to a regulatory mechanism of growth within the intelligence itself. Piaget calls it the "factor of equilibration," and it is fundamental to his entire theory.

An analogy will help. Sunlight, chemical elements, and water are necessary external factors for the growth of a plant. But these factors do not cause the growth of a specific plant: They contribute according to the mechanism of growth that is built into the plant. For example, the biological mechanism within the acorn is the principal cause in the growth of the oak tree to which the other contributions, such as sun and soil, are subordinated. At this point, however, the analogy stops because, distinct from physiological or instinctual functioning, human intelligence is not innately pre-formed in the infant but has its own active tendency of development. Two acorns will produce two oak trees with negligible differences whereas two infants will become two adults with unpredictable variations between them.

This perspective prevents teachers in the School for Thinking from going toward psychologically inappropriate extremes—expecting everything from heredity or from the environment. He can focus on what is strong and vital in any human child: the child's own mechanisms of intelligence. As the teacher expects the source of thinking to grow from within, he can have patience and be truly accepting of individual differences. And this message is not lost on the child. Equilibration as an internal regulation of development may be a difficult concept to grasp theoretically, but to the child it is as plain as life. Children may not know why they should learn this or that fact, but they understand readily that the only way to become intelligent is to act intelligently, and this is thinking. The School for Thinking attempts to provide an environmental setting that is favorable to active thinking in a direct and theoretically well-motivated fashion.

## High-level versus low-level thinking

A third point illustrating the uniqueness of Piaget's theory is its critical analysis of the conditions under which active experience becomes a source of intellectual development. To understand this position one has to realize that all human activity is permeated by thinking, but not at a fixed level. A two-year-old child thinks about many things that correctly apply to a car. For example, he knows that he goes out in it, that it moves and makes noise. This same object has increasingly more meaning as the child grows older. The formula, "if $a \times b = c$ then $c \div b = a$ and $c \div a = b$" can be used with equal facility by a fourth grader as well as a college student, but clearly they have different levels of understanding. Comprehension of words or phrases, such as "national election" encompasses a wide continuum of acceptable interpretations. According to Piaget's theory it is only through the application of thinking at a high level, that is, high relative to the child's own stage of development, that intellectual growth occurs.

The implications of this insight are opposed to the traditional emphasis on educational results. A certain "correct" behavior can be high level for one child and hence challenging, and at the same time low level for another child and hence routine or plain boring. What is worse, it can be "too high," that is, beyond a child's available mechanisms of comprehension. This results in the most harmful situation developmentally, the learning of facts by rote that should be learned with understanding. As an example, under pressure of showing results, a child may memorize the given formula relating division to multiplication without making an attempt to understand it for the simple and valid reason that he has not yet developed the requisite mental instruments for its comprehension.

Piaget's theory points out that high-level experience is the source of all intelligence. Abstraction, too, is a familiar term that can coincide with intellectual development, but only if it is understood as high-level abstraction that is relative to a child's present level of development. An infant "abstracts" coordination of his body movements in walking and at the same time acquires some practical knowledge of space. This is a high-level experience and abstraction for that infant; a similar behavior of purposeful walking would be routine and intellectually not challenging to a three-year-old child. A three year old in turn is beginning to abstract a "theoretical" spatial knowledge from this "practical" knowledge of moving around in space: He begins, for instance, to understand why things look differently from different perspectives. The typical five- to seven-year-old child is still very much involved in this same activity. We describe these body and sense thinking activities in detail in Part III.

High-level abstraction means abstraction from the child's own action upon objects in the environment. For instance, the concept of a logical class (more fully described in Chapter 12) is not something that can be found in the environment. The concept of class resides within the intelligence. One cannot point to a thing or a collection of things and say *"This* is a class." Rather, a particular collection of rocks belongs to a class, the concept of which is universal and, therefore, internal to the intelligence. This is, of course, the reason why it takes about six years of the child's life before he begins to have a mature class concept. It is abstracted from the child's actions toward objects, actions like comparing, contrasting, adding, taking away, sorting, observing similarities and differences, and evaluating what is an essential or an unessential attribute. What is abstracted here for intellectual growth is not from properties that are in the objects but from the general coordination of actions. These two types of abstractions—low-level abstraction from objects and high-level abstraction from actions—must be conceptually separated if the teacher wants to encourage high-level, intellectually challenging experiences.

During a child's early years there will be many different opportunities for high-level functioning, and from among these he will actually engage in high-level behavior a certain number of times. Nobody says that a child should always function at a high level, and all one can ask is that an environment be conducive to and encouraging with respect to high-level behavior. It is quite possible that the complexity and technology of modern life is a psychological milieu far from optimal for intellectual development. In any case, children construct life situations that are high level for them and thereby develop intellectually. They also find many situations to which they respond in low-level fashion. For example, a seven-year-old girl was asked to pull some green onions she had grown in the family garden, clean them, and prepare them for the dinner table. She proudly set a tray of green stalks on the table after having discarded the "dirty roots." Another example would be the conclusion reached by an eight year old who lived in Washington, D.C., whose mayor at that time actually was a Mr. Washington. He concluded that the mayor of Philadelphia is called Mr. Philadelphia. We call these situations low level, because we assume that the children would have been capable of thinking at a more mature level if they had been motivated to do so.

If under ordinary circumstances the level of a problem is too high, the child responds to it in a typically psychologically healthy fashion: He ignores it or turns the problem into a different problem which he then can tackle. Piaget's report that an eight-year-old child believed that the city of Geneva existed before the lake on which it borders illustrates several points about a child's psychology. First, an eight-year-old child does not spontaneously ask geographical questions relating natural terrain to human institutions; second, if this problem is posed, it is assimilated by the child in a distorted fashion. To the child who does not understand natural forces, the problem of the origin of the lake is falsely understood in terms of "who built it?" Since ordinarily the builder exists before the thing that is built, the people living near the lake would naturally be the people who built it. This exemplifies low-level reasoning in response to a question that was simply too high level for the child to comprehend. (See Situation 1 in Figure 1.)

We have illustrated a natural situation where the child is not obliged to give a correct answer under threat of failure. Now imagine a similar situation where a third grade child is supposed to learn certain geographical and geological facts. He may memorize quite well such verbal phrases as "natural forces," "water pressure," and "erosion of rocks," but he will assimilate these

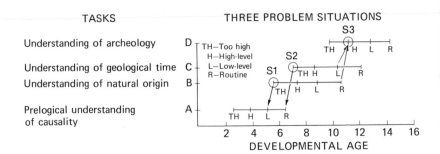

**Figure 1.**
**Three Situations of Task Difficulty**
Downward arrows indicate low-level solutions for situations 1 and 2;
upward arrows, a high-level solution for situation 3.

words to nothing higher than the making of artifacts—since this is the only level of comprehension of which he is capable. (See Situation 2 in Figure 1.) As a result of similar experiences, the child (a) adds more confusion to the already fuzzy notion of geological change, (b) carries the additional dead weight of meaningless words in his memory, (c) is robbed of the potentially exciting high-level abstraction of relating geography and geology, (d) acquires the habit of separating thinking and learning, or better said, learning in a low-level fashion, and (e) experiences himself as an intellectual cripple who cannot stand on his own feet.

Figure 1 illustrates how a given task changes drastically as the child develops with age: First, it is too high and cannot be properly handled; afterward it can become high level and intellectually challenging. Subsequently, as the child develops further, it may become low level and even routine. Task A represents prelogical thinking about causality that is low level and routine around age four. In contrast, Tasks B, C, and D represent the more difficult concepts of natural origin, geological time, and archeological findings.

What happens if Task B on the origin of the lake is given at a period that makes it too high? The child has no choice but to misunderstand the question and treat it as a low-level task as shown in Situation 1 by the downward arrow.

If another Task C, say, comprehension of geological time periods, is prematurely given to a child, he may learn it without understanding, as shown in Situation 2, as a routine of memorizing mere words of causality. Neither Task B nor C are therefore challenging the child's developing capacity of thinking. In particular, the regressive tendencies of Tasks B and C can be developmentally harmful if they reflect a habitual situation. In contrast, Task D (e.g., understanding archeological findings) is shown in Situation 3 (upward arrows) as being approached in a high-level manner: The child integrates already developed capacities of comprehension of natural origin (Task B) and comprehension of geological time (Task C) in the service of Task D. Consequently, Task D becomes a developmentally challenging, progressive experience.

What are the implications of high-level thinking as an action experience and not as an object experience? It means ultimately that truth is not given ready made in the world, nor is it an absolute norm that is imposed on the child from outside. The School for Thinking is founded on this theory of action intelligence—a theory of knowledge which engenders responsible, intelligent, and critically open behavior.

## Language and Thinking

A fourth point which is unique to Piaget's theory is the relation of thinking to language. Piaget's theory can give substance to thinking and its development without having recourse to a society's language, because thinking is a self-regulating activity that begins before language and goes far beyond language. All other current theories of development give language a prominent place.

Piaget's theory helps the teacher to recognize high-level thinking activities in any number of situations that are not tied to language. If language is used at all, it serves the purpose of communication and contributes to the thinking activity only in a most peripheral fashion. The majority of thinking games detailed in Part III fall into this category. Piaget's books abound with clever observations that illustrate how language, far from facilitating thinking, is frequently an obstacle to thinking. However, Piaget does not consider language a principal cause of childish thinking difficulties. If a child's thinking is "childish," his use of the language will also be childish.

Specifically, Piaget makes two things very clear: first, the difference between knowing a word (word knowledge) and comprehending a situation (intelligence), and, second, the need for "formal" mechanisms of thinking in order to master the difficulties of the linguistic medium. While the first point should be obvious, the whole weight of the scholastic tradition leads the teacher to oppose this conclusion. If it is true that a six-year-old child "knows more than he can verbalize," it follows that his thinking is ahead of his language, or more precisely, that his advanced thinking is not nurtured by language. Those children reared on the "Dick and Jane" series were given material which was beneath their level of comprehension. So they *learned* the words but the meaning of the sentences did not challenge their thinking. The books were primarily vehicles for learning, not thinking, except insofar as one had to think out the words. Word knowledge is no guarantee of a corresponding or even adequate intellectual comprehension. In fact, "verbal" thinking in a child who is not close to adolescence is usually low level. For that reason the School for Thinking does not base its activities principally on verbal language and especially not on reading and writing. High-level situations, that is, intellectually challenging opportunities for children of primary school invariably require action oriented activities in physical or concrete settings.

The second point puts the role of language in a developmental perspective and states that language can become a proper medium for challenging thinking and for further exploration. But language cannot play this role unless the child has "formal" mechanisms of thinking. By formal mechanisms Piaget means the advanced stage of development that characterizes adult thinking, principally the adult's capacity to theorize about possibilities and hypothetical situations and combine and keep in mind the meaning and interrelations of several hypotheses. In order to pay attention to these theoretical positions and communicate them to others some form of language is necessary. An artificial language (like mathematical notation) may be used for this purpose.

If an adult has considerable difficulties in assimilating the thinking which this chapter attempts to convey, this is in part because of the medium of verbal propositions in which the chapter is couched. The teachers in the School for Thinking—not unlike the children—comprehend more about Piaget's theory by means of their daily classroom activities than they could comprehend by means of reading or verbal discussion. This illustrates a fundamental order of priorities which other theories have failed to recognize: Verbal language is a most difficult medium for thinking and is quite unsuitable as the staple intellectual nourishment for children.

Children of primary school age are beginning to establish mechanisms that Piaget calls "concrete operations," where the word "concrete" refers to the particular objects to which such operations as classes, relations, numbers, spatial orientations refer. These are mental operations that classify, relate, number, and locate particular objects. In contrast, "formal operations" bear on the understanding of hypotheses and propositions, such as: "If a child's thinking is far ahead of his capacity to verbalize it follows that language cannot be a principal force in moving intelligence along."

The educational implication of Piaget's position on language is clear. In order to educate children so that they will one day be capable of using language in an intelligent manner, nothing is as important as developing the child's intelligence. To reach the intellectual stage where a person can function comfortably with verbal propositions, the medium of actions and physical encounters is appropriate; whereas a premature emphasis on language as a prime medium for thinking is bound to result in low-level activities that do not nourish intellectual development.

## Intrinsic versus extrinsic motivation

A fifth characteristic of Piaget's theory—the intrinsic, rather than extrinsic motivation for development—is perhaps not as unique as the previous points, but it is nonetheless an important antidote to the current faith in behavioral objectives and external rewards. His theory is not opposed to a moderate use of external controls or incentives; we acknowledge that in special cases these methods can be remarkably successful. The objection is to the wholesale importation of an educational model that considers every behavior an associated response to a positive external situation, one that confuses the intrinsic motivation of development with the extrinsic motivation of learning.

It is a fact that children—all children, both rich and poor, of low and high IQ, in developed and undeveloped societies—grow in intelligence, at least between birth and twelve years of age. This uniform growth cannot be attributed merely to external situations. It is intrinsic to the human person, as are other human characteristics. "Intrinsic" here means what biologists call "characteristic of a species." This biological perspective cuts across the heredity-environment controversy and places both terms within one biological life space. It follows that the human child most assuredly responds to situations around him, but these situations are not to be considered entirely external to the child; they are situations which correspond to the child's internal mechanisms, those mechanisms that develop with further living into adult intelligence. Far from saying that the child is under the control of external situations, it is more correct to say that the external situations are under the control of internal human mechanisms. The child has an internal "need to know" which causes him actively to seek out and select from the environment around him. The educator provides, the child decides.

Just as Piaget distinguishes the development aspect from the learning aspect in child behavior, he assigns different types of motivation to each aspect. And just as learning and development are mutually related and occur simultaneously, both types of motivations are present in any behavioral acquisition. We stress the difference between developmental and learning motivation, not to neglect the traditional learning motivation but to emphasize the developmental motivation for educators to use and build upon.

If a school emphasizes thinking, its structure must focus on the child's intrinsic motivation, as was done in the Tyler School. The children understood that what counted was their own activity and that high-level functioning was its own reward. We wanted the children to be pleased with their own accomplishments, not to do things in order to please the teacher. We wanted them to rely on their own internally controlled evidence, not vacuously look at the teacher's face for approval or disapproval. We wanted, above all, to leave the children free to move into those situations they found rewarding. In sum, our aim was to respect the children's individual capacities and differences and leave them in control of the situation.

In behavioral terms, the child provides his own schedule of intrinsic rewards and reinforcements. The teacher is an occasion of, not the implanter of knowledge. Whatever the terminology, the teacher must be firmly convinced that thinking cannot be taught as a subject matter and is not an object of knowledge that is remembered and can be forgotten. Piaget's theory provides the necessary framework that can give the teacher this reasonable assurance.

## The scope of intelligence

Two more characteristics of Piaget's theory deserve special mention, both of which rectify a psychologically impoverished stereotype of what intelligence is and how it functions and develops. We mentioned at the beginning of this chapter how poorly articulated our ideas on thinking are, apart from a few verbal clichés that carry little systematic meaning. Our ideas on intelligence are similarly impoverished except that here we have so-called intelligence tests which seem to free us from the necessity of thinking about intelligence. We hold that once the philosophy of a School for Thinking spreads in educational circles, the need for standardized tests will mercifully diminish. Teachers who continuously observe and evaluate children's activities of high-level thinking will know more about the children's developmental status than can be gleaned from a far from adequate standardized measure.

For us, thinking and intelligence are synonymous: Thinking stands for the active use of intelligence, intelligence for the instrument by means of which a person thinks. One point that Piaget's theory stresses, in sharp contrast to a view that limits intelligence into arbitrary confines (abstract, verbal, perceptual, performance, etc.), is the generality and all-pervasiveness of thinking. The intelligence that coordinates external action is the same as the intelligence that identifies and perceives an object; it is the same as the intelligence that forms symbols and images, that memorizes and uses language. The baneful split of these activities has been detrimental to the formulation of an adequate psychology of the human person and has slanted education in a one-sided direction. An educational theory that considers verbal intelligence to be superior to practical intelligence quite naturally leads to a devaluation of external actions and perceptual configurations. This in turn justifies the almost total absence of anything but book knowledge from the child's curriculum. Piaget, on the other hand, has consistently focused on the essential aspect of human intelligence. He looked for its source in the general coordinations of the child's external actions and carefully described the continuity of this basic intelligence.

Piaget holds that intelligence is always active and constructive—hence the word "operative"—and makes an active contribution toward any situation with which an individual is in contact. Input of an external stimulus is not conceived as an association of elements but as an assimilation of input in terms of the child's intelligence—intelligence being the totality of available thinking mechanisms.

In short, thinking (or intelligence) is present in actions, in perceptions, in images, in language, and it can be applied to any and all content areas of interest. This does not mean that all content areas of life are equally accessible to human intelligence at any age. Some tasks require a certain minimum level of development—as we discussed in connection with verbal propositions. What exactly is meant requires an explanation that will contrast Piaget's theory with more traditional positions.

Commonly, when one speaks of verbal, perceptual-motor, or

visual intelligence, one does more than classify certain behaviors according to modalities. One also ascribes to the modalities a certain controlling influence on the intelligence at work. Verbal, perceptual, motor, or visual intelligence are thought to define qualitatively different types of intelligence. In this view, there is an intrinsic relation between modality and intelligence. The danger in classifying an intelligence at an early age as being of one kind or another is that a child can be prematurely pigeonholed before he has had ample opportunity to explore the whole range of intelligent activities.

For Piaget, intelligence—at any level—is not modality tied and, consequently, a classification of types of intelligence based on modalities is arbitrary and peripheral at best and does not touch the common core of human intelligence. As a proof of this assertion consider that Piaget's is the only theory which can adequately explain the relatively normal intelligence of children born profoundly deaf or blind, or unable to move around. If language, visual images, or certain external actions really are essential ingredients of human intelligence, children affected with these sensory or motor deficiencies should be intellectually crippled in proportion to the severity of their bodily deficiency.[1]

These children are usually deficient in specific learning processes, which makes sense because learning is of course tied to specific content and frequently also to specific modalities. Additionally, learning often requires specific codes for symbolization and memorization. But intelligence is a *general* human capacity through which the person organizes his environment. This can take place as well in one modality as in another—provided of course an individual has at least a minimum amount of normal contact with the world through his sense and body activities.

Another arbitrary split that has hampered educational innovations has to do with creativity in relation to intelligence, as witnessed by separate standardized tests that are discovered to be not even closely related to each other. For Piaget, intelligence is constructive and creative; in fact, development of intelligence is but the gradual creation of new mechanisms of thinking. It is creation because it is not the discovery or the copy of anything that is physically present. Classes and probability cannot be found in the physical world. They are concepts constructed creatively by human intelligence and cannot be handed down by means of language or other symbols. A child has language for three to five years before he understands these concepts, and a deaf child—without knowing language—also comprehends these concepts at a corresponding age.

What is the origin of these new concepts? Piaget's answer points to the creative intelligence that feeds back from its own general mechanisms of actions. The general body and sense activities, emphasized in a School for Thinking, are considered to be the source of the developing intelligence and more vital and pressing than any specific academic skill or modality training for the child of primary school age.

## Developmental stages versus individual variability

A final point illustrates the uniqueness of Piaget's theory: its description of successive stages of development. For some people, stages imply inborn maturational processes that come about according to a rigid internal timetable regardless of life experiences. For others, stages are vaguely related to standard norms, such as is found on intelligence tests. For both interpretations, the existence of meaningful age norms that can be standardized is unquestionable.

Piaget rejects the idea of a fixed timetable for stages. Stage refers to differences in the structure of thinking, differences that are not merely due to an increase in knowledge. If a six-year-old child learns the telephone number of a friend, this information increases his store of knowledge, but is not likely to change the structure of his previous knowledge. If this same child is active in a permutation game and begins to discover a principle of sequential arrangements, this novel acquisition can lead to a new understanding of order, a new manner of structuring order; in short, there may come about a change in the structure of knowing and not merely in the content of knowing.

The reader will recognize in this example the difference

between learning (an increase of content) and development (a structural change) and relate it to the difference between low- and high-level activities. Whenever Piaget observed children's behavior, he looked for structural differences because he was primarily interested in the structure of thinking, not in the content of what a child remembered. Piaget then classified his behavioral observations into what he called stages or substages. For example, he observed that in the sorting of blocks and similar material he could differentiate a first stage when the child, quite oblivious to the task of sorting, formed pictures with the blocks— the graphic stage. Then came a stage where the child would attempt to make groups of classes according to some logical criteria, but these attempts fell short of a fully interrelated system of classification: A child would put all blue blocks in one heap, all big blocks of three other colors in a second heap and all small blocks of these same colors in a third heap. In other words, he classified blue blocks according to a different criterion (color) than the other blocks (size), and he entirely neglected classification by shape. This would be a second stage where the child makes "prelogical collections." Finally, there is the third stage when a child comprehends the system of classification and understands questions on quantification or class inclusion, such as, "Are there more dogs or more pets?" This is the stage where the child has established what Piaget calls the "concrete operations" of classification. Stage one or two is "preoperational" with stage two being the more interesting transitional stage because the child fluctuates between partial and complete comprehension.

Piaget described similar stages in connection with the many concepts he studied, such as time, physical causality, number, space, names, dreams, and morality. Gradually it became clear that the different stages found in studying one concept had parallel stages in other concepts insofar as similar qualitative differences characterized the different stages. Most important of all, Piaget developed the concept of "concrete operations," as a first framework of logical thinking that he observed across all concepts in children about six to eight years old. In this manner the notion of a child "being in the concrete operations stage" or "being in the preoperational stage" became popular, although Piaget always tied the stage concept to one particular task rather than to the child as a whole.

The teacher in the School for Thinking organizes a number of tasks for the children. All these tasks have a range of fairly obvious levels of difficulty or complexity. These levels of task performance are loosely patterned after Piaget's stage differences, that is, the differences between levels are not primarily due to different content but to a qualitatively different structuring of the task. It is of fundamental importance that the teachers do not label a child "preoperational" or "operational" but let the child be free to perform, so that, for instance, in parquetry block reversals he works at a transitional level, in mental map of fingers he is quite unsystematic or "preoperational," and in cross classification he is quite comfortably "operational." And moreover, it may well happen that a week later the same child becomes hesitant on cross classification and improves remarkably in mental map of fingers.

Some people accuse Piaget's theory of stages of being inconsistent since it does not fit into the model of a standard norm with a consistent cumulative increase. What if development is more closely modeled after the above example than the preconceived idea of a consistently increasing norm? We believe this to be the case. We therefore suggest Piaget's theory to the teachers in a school that emphasizes thinking, precisely because his theory recognizes lawful and meaningful stages in development and at the same time respects the tremendous range of normal variability.

This variability takes three forms, each of which is contrary to a normative ideal. First, different individuals differ on the same task and much more than an IQ mentality would have us believe. Remember that IQ tests eliminate tasks that do not conform to the rules for standardization, e.g., tasks with too large an age range of children who respond correctly. When one child acquires the basic concepts of chance and probability at seven years and another at ten years, it does not necessarily follow that one is a genius and the other is abnormally slow. This range of task variability between individuals (interindividual variability) makes the problem unsuitable for IQ purposes. Nonetheless, comprehension of probability is quite fundamental in intellectual development and the normal age range of acquisition simply is as large as illustrated above.

A second type of variability is found within a certain individual (intraindividual variability) as he performs on a variety of different tasks. Again, contrary to idealized norms, most children will be found to differ and at times quite substantially in terms of performance levels across tasks. Piaget's theory takes this variance for granted—he cites many examples of intraindividual differences. The reasons for this phenomenon are far from clear. Some of the possible reasons are: special facility tied to a modality (e.g., a good musical sense); special interest encouraged by the milieu (e.g., mechanical problems); special experience (e.g., card playing strategies).

A third type of variability is observed both within the same individual and on the same task. In other words, the performance of a child fluctuates from day to day—an entirely normal phenomenon that all of us experience. Everyone performs better after a restful sleep than at a time when he has had difficulty awakening in the morning. Recognition and acceptance of this variability is particularly important in the case of mechanisms of thinking which develop gradually and almost imperceptibly.

We have discussed seven points on which Piaget's theory differs uniquely from most other theories of child development. Piaget's theory was found to be goal setting and not merely method oriented; constructive and not just interacting; analytic and not vaguely based on experience; language transcending, not language controlled; with an internal, not an external motivation; coextensive with all areas of life, not restricted to arbitrary divisions; and finally, respectful of individual differences within a clear developmental perspective. These are some of the theoretical foundations on which the School for Thinking is based.

The following chapters describe the general structure of the school setting that incorporates these theoretical points and makes it possible for the teacher to translate theory into everyday practice. If a teacher's thinking is more articulate in practice than in theoretical discourse, that is precisely how it should be. Application of a theory must always run ahead of theory, and it is applied practice on which a School for Thinking is to be evaluated. Piaget's theory has its source in practice in terms of the real life observation of children. Like all theoretical thinking, the theory must be put into practice in order to be evaluated and to uncover new fields of theoretical investigation. A School for Thinking is therefore never merely the practical outcome of a complete theory; it must primarily see itself as an open-ended creative educational setting. This practical setting will eventually enrich the theory of thinking on which it was based in the first place and will contribute to the mainstream of future educational theory.

# II. A School for Thinking

# 2. The Project at Charleston

## How it began

In 1969 one of us was approached by the West Virginia State Department of Education to help with its programs in learning disabilities. At this time our interest had turned to the prevention rather than remediation of school failures, and this appealed to a federally supported project[1] of the Kanawha County public school system with headquarters in Charleston. The project had been established as a remedial resource for children with learning disabilities, specifically reading problems. We realized here an opportunity to put into practice a philosophy of education which one of us had just published in book form[2] and the other had worked out clinically in various children's programs—for mentally retarded, motorically impaired, and emotionally disturbed children as well as children of average intelligence with learning disabilities.

In the spring of 1970 we discussed our ideas with the staff of the project who were courageous enough to appreciate the advantages of prevention over remediation. Teachers and principals throughout the Charleston school district were invited to participate in the discussion. The superintendent and a majority of his staff encouraged these discussions.

## What we proposed

Our proposal was to establish an overall program starting with kindergarten and grade one the first year and eventually including grades two and three. The aim was to aid and nourish the normal developing process of thinking in the primary school age

33

child, subordinating all school activities to this first goal. One major outgrowth of this program would be prevention of many academic failures and learning disabilities—eliminating the tragic experience of failure for the young child and the excessive expenditures in remedial programs. Another aim was to prepare children for the task of further education. We proposed that a child who actively exercises thinking is in optimal condition to profit from all learning experiences, both in and out of school.

As a minimum goal, children in this program entering grade four should have mastered reading, writing, and other expected academic skills at grade level; however, in comparison with children from traditional programs they should be more motivated, better adjusted, and have a better foundation for further learning.

This program was limited to the primary grades because during this most critical period the child could form healthy habits of thinking as a foundation for intelligent reading and the successful acquisition of all other academic skills. This is also the time when the child is first exposed to a type of formal learning which holds him accountable for his performance. The program would prevent the child from forming faulty learning habits that ultimately lead to failure, frustration, and a general rejection of school.

Moreover, the program should be initiated with kindergarten or first grade children only. We wanted children to start their school experience in a Thinking School environment and not bring into our program children who may have already experienced failure in a school setting.

## How teachers were trained

Two first grade teachers from different elementary schools were enthusiastic about the program and agreed to start a School for Thinking in September 1970. They were motivated by their painful experiences at seeing a great many reading failures despite special efforts; they viewed our program as a possible answer to their needs for helping children.

During the summer of 1970 the two teachers and the reading clinicians from their schools attended a three-week inservice training session. Theoretical background was presented by us and practical applications of the thinking games were demonstrated. Children were brought in to play the games; and the teachers and clinicians also were made to experience them. Study material included *Piaget for teachers* and printed worksheets presently in use at the Pennsylvania Vision Institute. The teachers were shown how to make on-the-spot evaluations and how to adjust an activity to the developmental level of the child.

The second week of the school term was spent working with the teachers and the children in the classrooms. It soon became apparent that one school lacked the resources and the supervisory support necessary for initiating a change from the traditional academic setting. Consequently, we proceeded with the other school, Tyler Elementary School.

Both of us lived in different cities and a considerable distance from Charleston and we scheduled regular consultation visits. From September to December we spent two consecutive days about every two weeks working with the teachers in the classrooms as well as with administrative personnel and resource persons. From January 1971 till the end of the first school year the frequency of our visits diminished to approximately one day per month.

In the second year of the program one of us, together with the now experienced first year teacher, prepared the new teaching personnel who would be taking over second year instruction. During the summer this teacher gave a six-week inservice course on the School for Thinking which was also attended by other teachers from the county. As part of this inservice period one of us provided approximately ten days in specialized training of the new teacher and, with the beginning of the second year, visited the two classrooms of the School for Thinking about two days each month.

## Tyler Elementary School

The school is located in Mount Tyler, a rural suburb of Charleston. It is surrounded by steep hills and woods and bordered on one side by a creek running through a narrow valley. No other large buildings, business area, or industry are in the immediate vicinity. The relatively modern school is a one-story building containing nine classrooms. Every room is equipped with a sink and bathroom and has a direct exit to outdoors, which facilitates outside activities.

The school had no kindergarten when we started. The first year classroom, 25 by 30 feet large, originally contained traditional seats and desks, which on our initiative were replaced by tables and chairs. Additionally, for the purpose of our program, art easels and green chalk boards that could be tilted were brought in, the floor was carpeted, and two rope ladders were suspended from exposed steel girders on the ceiling. The second year classroom, similarly arranged, was adjacent to the first year classroom with a door in between.

## The teachers, the children, and the parents

Each classroom had a certified elementary school teacher and a teacher's aide. The full-time aide and a reading consultant, who devoted about eight hours a week to the program, were made available through federal support. The principal of Tyler School cooperated fully, particularly in the beginning of the project when support was so important. Several student teachers from local colleges choose internships in the Thinking School classrooms. During the second year some students from the local junior high school assisted as part of their academic program.

There always had been two first grades at Tyler, and the teacher who chose our program was usually assigned the slower children. In our original proposal we had requested to work with an unselected population of children. However, for reasons beyond our control, the first year classroom of the Thinking School was overloaded with academic high-risk children. According to a locally used cut-off point of a raw score of 17 corresponding to the 19th percentile on the American Guidance First Year Screening Test, 20 of 22 tested children in the Thinking School classroom were high-risk children in contrast to only 8 out of 20 children in the traditional first grade at the Tyler School. Of the 25 children in the Thinking School classroom 6 were repeaters. There were 16 boys and 9 girls.

The following year there were no repeaters in the first grade classrooms at Tyler. Five of the original children moved out of the school area, and 7 additional children were placed in the second year Thinking School classroom. These included 4 children from the traditional first grade classroom who failed to meet the standards necessary to pass into the traditional second grade, 2 second grade repeaters, and one transfer from another school. Seventeen children, 10 boys and 7 girls, were enrolled in the new first year classroom of the School for Thinking. Eleven were high-risk children in contrast to only 1 high-risk child of 14 children in the other first grade classroom at Tyler.

When in the summer of 1970 we discussed plans for involving parents to help establish the School for Thinking, school officials urged against any formal announcement prior to the start of the school year. It was suggested that an informal presentation be done at an early PTA meeting, and, if problems arose, the principal would handle them on a discrete individual basis. Not long after school started two parents demanded that their children be transferred to the other more traditional first grade where more time was being spent on reading. Naturally, their request was granted. Apart from these and other minor conflicts at the beginning, parents gradually became content and interested and several became quite enthusiastic about the effect of the Thinking School on their children. This situation of initial conflict and only gradual acceptance on the part of the parents repeated itself the second year. The increased acceptance was confirmed at the parent visitation day toward the end of the second school year when a greater than usual number of parents visited the Thinking School classroom and expressed favorable comments.

## The two years of the project

The project introduced an entirely new philosophy into a heretofore traditional setting. Time was required to assimilate the new ideas and to put them into practice. The teachers had to become accustomed to the freedom and noise of the classroom and the aide had to be trained. The acquisition of the furniture and equipment was delayed as is typical in large school systems. The concrete scheduling of appropriate activities and the different grouping of children were new tasks on which the teacher, the aide, and the reading consultant had to work and agree. The regular visits by both of us could do no more than encourage them since in the final analysis they had to do the job. Not until mid-January 1971 did the project become routinely organized.

The word routine does not imply that no further problems arose. However, the teachers felt that they had the project under control and were happy in being innovative and meeting new challenges. They did not resent giving of their own free time for discussion and weekly planning of new activities. To bring variety and innovative applications into the program we solicited the active collaboration of local resource people in science, music, art, and home economics, but since the time they could devote to the program was minimal, the teachers had to manage without this important ingredient most of the time.

Toward the end of the first school year increasing numbers of visitors came to observe the classroom. By this time the positive self-image of "thinking children" had permeated the classroom and neither the teachers nor the children were disturbed by the presence of visitors. In fact, an official visit by state inspectors found the children unafraid and eager to show off. From an initial attitude of caution and uncertainty there seemed to emerge a general acceptance and pride toward the project on the part of all involved. Typical was the remark of the teacher's aide: "When it started I wouldn't have given you two nickels for this school. I thought it was a school for dum-dums! Now I wish my son (now in third grade at Tyler) would have had this opportunity."

The somewhat abnormal situation of a single Thinking School classroom isolated within a traditional school changed as one second grade teacher at Tyler showed interest in being the second year teacher of the School for Thinking. Beginning in September 1971 the first and second year classrooms were working as independent units. A series of new problems arose. The teachers and the children were still working in isolation and did not cooperate and feel that they belonged to one project. With two separate entities it was difficult to coordinate the use of special materials and rooms, the grouping of children for activities, and the training of the new staff by the experienced staff. Much time and effort were wasted.

We quickly realized the necessity for an ungraded system and suggested that the classroom activities be combined, with some activities presented to the entire student body. This allayed the fear of the teachers that the second year students would resent working with first year students. A more appropriate grouping could now be effected for the benefit of the children. The teachers and aides were in a position to combine their efforts for the mutual benefit of themselves and the children. The children had no difficulties with this new plan and considered their respective rooms more as homerooms to report to rather than as designated grade rooms. Moreover, the teachers built into the schedule a short period for planning every day and a two-hour period once a week.

With second year children in the classroom, the pressure of accountability for reading made itself felt. With considerable diligence and prolonged planning the teachers evolved a plan that basically satisfied the exigencies of the Thinking School as well as the traditional reading requirement. In this manner, despite occasional difficulties, from November 1971 until June 1972 the two classes of the School for Thinking functioned as an exciting adventure for everyone concerned.

# 3. Guiding Principles of a Thinking School Classroom

A viable School for Thinking has to rest on a well-founded psychology of the child, especially with regard to the child's development of thinking. We subscribe to the assumption that the primary overall purpose of education is the acquisition of knowledge and hold that thinking is the chief source of all knowing. Since intelligence is nothing other than the capacity for thinking, the goal of our School for Thinking is "intellectual health."

To reach this goal requires more than good hunches, brilliant intuitions, or even an excellent theory. The most sublime ideas are of little value to education if they cannot be translated into the everyday language of classroom activities or if they require a teacher with an exceptional personality. The School for Thinking is geared for the average, intelligent teacher and provides him with a structured setting to realize the objectives of the Thinking School. We reject the notion that schools cannot be different from what they are because teachers cannot function differently from the way in which present schools are run. On the contrary, it seems to us that teachers by and large do what they do on account of the prevailing structure of the school system. Only the exceptionally creative person can work successfully apart from or against the structure. But if the teachers are given a different structure, a structure that encourages and guides them to be thinking and creative, we do not doubt, as our project in Charleston illustrated, that most teachers who now function reasonably well in existing schools would function better as teachers in Schools for Thinking.

## Long-range objectives

The long-range objectives of a primary School for Thinking can be stated in five points. Partially as a result of the experiences, a child at the end of grade three should have acquired (1) the habit of creative independent thinking, (2) a positively valued self-image, (3) attitudes of social cooperation and moral responsibility, (4) knowledge and appreciation about things, persons, and events in his environment, and (5) the basic academic skills of reading, writing, and arithmetic. Note that the first three objectives cover three inseparable aspects of the child's whole person, his intellect, his affect, and his social relations. No priority is implied in the proposed order except that the school can work on the child's developing intellect in a more direct way than it can on the child's affect or social relations. The fourth objective states the content toward which the young child's intellect, affect, and sociability has to be directed. This is the natural content with which the developing child is spontaneously concerned. The fifth objective is self-explanatory.

The first three objectives continue and reinforce the spontaneous development of general human capacities toward a healthy outcome; the fourth objective continues and reinforces a child's knowledge of self and his immediate environment that is continually being formed by his everyday experiences. It would not be necessary to plan a program explicitly for these four objectives if one could be sure that all children have sufficient experiences to develop these psychologically necessary capacities and contents of knowledge. Whatever may have been the case in earlier times when the present pattern of schooling was established, today it is patently clear that many, indeed most, children enter kindergarten with less than adequate all-round psychological development.

The causes of this state of affairs are too manifold to state in detail. Some are only too well known: poverty, discrimination, urban and rural blight, social unrest. Others are pervasive and cut across all strata of society: the technologically complex nature of our civilization which makes it difficult for the child simply to pick up meaningful knowledge about the environment, the rapid change of heretofore stable and basic values, the additional role of the employed mother. However, over and above these environmental conditions there are two more factors which educators in the past have not sufficiently taken into account.

First, children at birth are endowed with greatly differing dispositions. Barring undue mishap, they will develop and exercise those behaviors for which they have strong predispositions and neglect those in which they are less gifted. For instance, a visually observant child may have poorly developed musical skills at five years of age. The school is the natural place where these common situations of relative underdevelopment can be rectified before they cause significant problems. While the aim is not to do away with individualized patterns of skills, the school should provide occasions where even a musically less gifted youngster is exposed to the rudiments of rhythmic and musical situations.

The second point to consider is the most compelling and in practice, if not in theory, most frequently forgotten. When children enter school they are not little adults who lack a lot of skills and information that the school can provide; they are above all children who are right in the middle of a major developmental period. They are just beginning to know themselves and the world around them in terms that approximate those of adults. Between five and twelve years of age the child's mechanisms of thinking change drastically. The child, without a firm framework of judgment or reasoning, becomes a young person with powers of comprehension and reasoning quite similar to those of you and me. In other words, the second most dramatic expansion of intellectual powers occurs during the period of primary school, a period comparable only to the first two years of life during which the helpless newborn infant turns into an amazingly adept toddler with all his practical know-how of moving around and getting the affection and the food and the fun he needs.

The fifth point is the traditional objective of all primary education. Our school accepts this objective wholeheartedly. A right to intellectual health most certainly implies in our society a right to reading. The failures and frustration children and teachers have experienced in reading have become the challenge for exploring new avenues to education, just as they were the immediate occasion for our School for Thinking in Charleston. A school that realizes the preceding objectives will have little difficulty in achieving the goals of reading and arithmetic. A School for Thinking takes seriously the universally accepted notion that a child should have achieved readiness before he is taught reading. It accepts individual differences as a natural phenomenon in reading as in other forms of behavior. Moreover, many of the activities are familiar to teachers and will be recognized as pre-reading or remedial reading exercises. The main difference between a School for Thinking and a traditional school in the matter of reading is: Whereas in the traditional school the child and the teacher have imposed upon them an arbitrary norm of reading performance which they must reach on pain of failure, our school proposes reading as one of many other thinking activities in which a child is permitted to engage only if he has adequately developed the prerequisite skills; in the meantime the school provides the child with a rich variety of these prerequisite activities. In this way the school avoids unnecessary scholastic failure and its tragic consequences, and at the same time, as results at Tyler have already shown, no child is held back in reading relative to comparable children in other programs.

## General rationale of classroom activities

What type of classroom activities would be appropriate to reach the objectives outlined above? Before actually listing these activities we will discuss the general rationale to which the activities should ideally conform. As with the four basic long-range objectives, the sequence of six characteristics listed below does not imply an order of priority.

1. The activity of thinking is worthwhile in itself.

We like to call this the principle of *asset value*. This is not a difficult message to convey to young children because it conforms to their normal situation. Playing, running, singing, and exploring are four of many natural activities that carry their own reward. In general peer play no child is greatly disturbed that there are other children who run faster; he still enjoys running as fast as he can. Unfortunately this healthy asset attitude—running fast is fun —can easily be transformed into an unhealthy comparative attitude—fun is running faster than another. A school that stresses results and expects performance norms cannot but foster this comparative attitude, all the more so when the activity itself is not considered interesting by the child. In the traditional structure it is very hard to maintain and encourage the motivation of a child who is trying hard but nevertheless fails in performance. The results themselves tell the child that he is failing. In an overall comparative atmosphere even the best teacher's personal love and attention cannot easily overcome the objective experience of failure.

The activities of the School for Thinking are done by the child with no other end in mind except "to run as fast as he can." Every child is capable of this. The teacher is under no pressure to expect a given result and can wait patiently for the skills to develop while at the same time honestly reinforce the internal reward the child gets from his own best effort.

2. The structured activities are to enhance the child's developing intelligence, not to take away the individual freedom that is a condition of healthy psychological growth.

This principle of freedom within structure is perhaps the most characteristic of the School for Thinking. It puts the school midway between an open-ended school, where children are left to do as they want, and a highly structured program, where every response of the child is preprogrammed as true or false. The program definitely is structured. The teacher, as expert, prepares a variety of activities that represent so many occasions through which the child's thinking can be challenged. However, the child's responses to these occasions are as varied as there are individual differences and different styles. The equipment and the play items which the children used conformed to this prescription. We avoided items that are highly structured or allow only one type of performance so that the child has to work at the task until it comes out "right." No task is to be imposed on the child, much less any arbitrary level of performance. Each child must be granted the free choice not to participate in an activity.

This does not imply the license of avoidance. Each child must be left alone to work within the structure at his own level, at his own rate, and in his personal style. The teacher has reason to be confident that the children will freely participate according to their best abilities just as a mother is confident that children with a healthy appetite will gladly eat the food prepared and laid out for them on the table.

3. The activities are developmentally appropriate so as to challenge the child's thinking but not too difficult so as to invite failure.

This is the principle of "high-level" experience with the word "high" being relative to the developmental state of each child. A high-level experience is one in which a child's intelligence is active at its most comprehensive capacity, in other words, the child's thinking is being challenged. As was shown in Chapter 1, a high-level thinking experience is the needed occasion for intellectual growth and is the immediate forerunner of this growth because the challenge itself implies a direction of the child's thinking that leads to eventual success. If an activity level is too high, then it is too far removed from the child's available thinking mechanisms. In the normal run of things a child will not voluntarily tackle such a task. However, when the too-high task is imposed on him, this leads not only to failure but also to a psychologically unhealthy use of low-level thinking mechanisms. The final result of such a state of affairs is an habitual turning off of high-level thinking in favor of a low-level attitude of thinking-not-more-than-necessary-for-the-result, which plays havoc with intellectual growth and health.

The educator's task in this matter is to know the general type of activities that are potentially high level for the children in his classroom. He can never be sure whether a child will turn a given occasion into a high-level experience since there are many known and unknown psychological factors at work which in a given individual may favor or hinder this challenge. We concede that all classroom activities cannot be constantly at a high-level challenge. However, the concept of a School for Thinking requires nothing less than eliminating, if possible, all too-high-level activities and providing the opportunity for all children to have a maximum of high-level thinking experiences each day.

4. The child is involved in, and focuses his attention on, the activity and not on the teacher as if the teacher were the source of knowledge.

This principle of activity centeredness illustrates the new role which the teacher assumes in a School for Thinking. It frees the teacher from the impossible role of being the object of, the cause of, and the reason for all children's attention at the same time. The teacher in our school knows that he can do no more than provide the occasion and leave the child free to use it well. He can coach and facilitate and encourage; but in the final analysis it is the child himself who initiates intellectual growth.

5. Activities are performed by each individual child within a group of peers with whom he relates socially and cooperates.

This principle of small groups proved its effectiveness at the Tyler School, where the cooperative working in small groups contributed powerfully to a happy atmosphere of thinking. Each group was small enough that an individual was not lost in it, and there were different groupings for different occasions which avoided the forming of factions or cliques. These groups provided a psychologically natural environment in which a child could learn from imitation and be encouraged by the successful activity of another. In addition they became the informal occasions where social thinking was exercised and developed indirectly.

Since in the School for Thinking groups of children worked together the teacher did not find herself in the awkward position of having to correct a child as soon as a logical mistake was noticed. In this way she avoided the danger of suggesting to the child by her silence that a wrong choice was correct and at the same time encouraged the children to talk to each other about their performance.

6. The teacher provides the model of a thinking person for the children.

The activities must be challenging, not only to the children but also to the teacher. How is this possible? Of course, they are not challenging to the adult in the same ways they are challenging to the developing child. The individual teacher must be free from rigid regulations and take the initiative within the general structure provided by the School for Thinking, precisely because his task is to keep the activities challenging, if possible, for all the different children in his classroom.

The teacher, just as the child, is encouraged by the structure to use it as a thinking person, that is, the structure is in the service of thinking and not vice versa. Finally, a teacher can influence a child's developing intelligence in two ways only: by providing occasions and opportunities, and this is the teacher's foremost task; by presenting himself to the children as a model to imitate. In this second role he can and should have an additional positive influence that is consequently personally rewarding.

# 4. The Structure of the Classroom

## School activities program

The activities of the School for Thinking at Charleston can be grouped into nine categories:

1. Body and sense thinking games
2. Logical thinking games
3. Social thinking activities: drama, excursions, affect games
4. Reading and writing
5. Arithmetic
6. Science
7. Arts and crafts
8. Music
9. Physical education

The activities of categories 1 to 3 are games in the spirit of children's play for its own sake. But child's play is indeed thinking. Classroom thinking can do no better than build on and continue the developmental process of thinking in which play, with its spontaneous involvement and self-purpose, has a biologically important role.

Categories 4 to 9 are traditional academic subjects for the primary school. They can be taught within the framework of the philosophy of a School for Thinking. With respect to reading, the teachers at the Tyler School selected any reading program they felt most apropos. According to their judgment, they used different programs with different children. It is known that innovative programs in arithmetic and science stress the thinking aspect of the subject matter rather than memorization of rules and tables. These programs encourage the child to handle actively (or manipulate )physical objects. In this respect the activities of these programs are what we call thinking games. Art and Music can also be brought to the children in this spirit as witnessed by an increasing number of new creative art and music programs. Physical Education can be coordinated with body and sense thinking games. Developmentally, all children are not ready for all physical education games. At Charleston, relay games and other group games were played. To avoid failure children were not rated on an individual basis; instead there was competition between groups. Failure in physical competition can be as detrimental to the child's self-concept as failure in reading or other academic subjects.

In short, the School for Thinking provides a fertile setting for realization of the goals of innovative academic programs. Thinking permeates the child's total school day. He does not have one period for academic subject matter, another for art and music, another for physical activity, another for thinking.

We propose that all the primary school activities share the pervasive atmosphere of thinking. In this way the child can realize that the range of thinking is open and limitless as are all his real life experiences.

## Time Schedule of Activities

Table 1 illustrates a suggested proportionate scheduling of activities on an average school day as a function of developmental age.

The percentages in Table 1 are not to be taken literally or adhered to rigidly. They can, of course, change from day to day. An experience excursion for social thinking could well take up a

### Table 1 / **Percentage Distribution of Activities**

| Thinking Activities | K | Gr.1 | Gr. 2 | Gr. 3 |
|---|---|---|---|---|
| Body and sense | 45 | 45 | 25 | 5 |
| Logical | 5 | 15 | 20 | 20 |
| Social | 10 | 10 | 15 | 15 |
| Reading, Arithmetic, Science | — | 15 | 25 | 45 |
| Art, Music | 10 | 5 | 10 | 10 |
| Physical education | 30 | 10 | 5 | 5 |

substantial part of the day whereas on another day no formal social thinking activity is scheduled. Similarly a science, art, or music lesson or the visit of a resource person may extend beyond the allotted time for a particular activity. Moreover, rest periods, meal time, free play, opening activities, and administrative chores are not included in the table.

The reader will notice that in kindergarten and grade one most of the day is spent on body and sense thinking. At that age level children are in need of stabilizing their body and sense coordination and experiencing them as high-level activities. By second and third grade these activities should be fully known and readily available in any tasks where they may be put to use. For example, a child who knows the movements of his hands and arms and can coordinate them with his eyes for graphic thinking (as described in Chapter 11), will spontaneously transfer these skills to the task of formal writing. As a result a class in writing can be limited to the learning of the formation of the letters and need not become a laborious exercise in learning pencil or other stylus movements. Consequently, from grades one to three the amount of time for body and sense thinking drops from 45 per cent to 5 per cent.

In contrast, a constant increase in time for academic subjects is scheduled, from 0 per cent at kindergarten to 40 per cent in third grade. This is entirely reasonable when one realizes that many of the coding and decoding as well as communication exercises used in formal reading programs involve the games in body and sense thinking. Similarly some activities basic to arithmetic and science are also found in body and sense thinking games as well as in logical thinking games.

In kindergarten a good part of the day is spent in physical education activities. These should not be geared to the level of body thinking but rather should be used as occasions for developing social thinking. While the child freely improves physical skills he experiences the role of being a vital member in group activities. Our belief that the majority of kindergarten children are not ready for formalized academics is reflected by the lack of scheduled academic activities. Even if certain skills can be taught before the psychologically appropriate time, the knowledgeable teacher appreciates that this may occur at the cost of neglecting more appropriate developmental activities. Moreover, the kindergarten child at the School for Thinking is introduced to the thinking prerequisites for reading, mathematics, and science in the course of the activities throughout the school day.

This is the place to consider the case of a child who to an appreciable extent is accelerated or slowed in overall development. The general rule is that a child should be maintained and moved along a developmentally high level. With the slow child the teacher increases the time allotted to basic thinking activities, while the accelerated child is moved ahead. Where classes are ungraded, these placements pose no difficulties.

## General Plan of a First Year School Day

A typical day in the first year classroom of the School for Thinking could be:

| Time | Period | Activities |
|------|--------|------------|
| 8:45–8:55 | – | Opening |
| 8:55–9:45 | 1 | General movement (Reading 25 minutes) |
| 9:45–10:20 | 2 | Discriminative movement |
| 10:20–10:30 | – | Break for children and teacher |
| 10:30–11:00 | 3 | Mathematics, Logic |
| 11:00–11:30 | 4 | Physical education |
| 11:30–12:45 | – | Lunch, Recess |
| 12:45–1:00 | 5 | Story reading |
| 1:00–2:00 | 6 | Visual, Hand, Social |
| 2:00–2:30 | 7 | Auditory, Logic |
| 2:30–2:50 | 8 | Arts, Crafts, Music |
| 2:50–3:20 | 9 | Drama, Logic (Reading 10 minutes) |

This timetable covers about five hours of organized learning, broken down into nine periods of varying lengths. This time distribution of activities is, of course, not a rigid schedule. On the contrary, the Tyler teachers worked out a flexible scheduling that corresponded roughly to guidelines which we gave them at the beginning. We suggested that the activities listed above should, if possible, occur daily. Other activities, such as experience excursions, presentation by resource people, free time, student government, would be interspersed about once a week.

During the opening exercise the aide took over routine matters, freeing the teacher for making last minute modifications in the planned daily activities according to the children's day-by-day change of performance. The first period of 50 minutes was regularly devoted to activities involving much body movements as found in Chapter 6. During this time children judged ready for reading went into another room for reading instructions. Thus some children would spend the entire period in general movement activities while others spent 15 to 25 minutes of this period in reading. The teacher and the reading consultant gave the reading instructions while the aide supervised the movement activities, in which several groups of children were constantly in action. The children alternated from group to group. Those returning from reading instructions took the places of others leaving for reading. The second period was devoted to sitting down activities where the children could relax from the more strenuous exercises of the preceding period.

The rest of the day's activities was rather flexible except that physical education and story reading were regularly scheduled before and after lunch, respectively. During the last period of the day the children involved in reading were given ten minutes of reading review, home assignment, and preparation for the next day.

## A Week's Schedule of First Year Activities

An actual scheduling of particular activities is illustrated in Table 2 which assigns specific games and activities for the five days of the week. All the games on the schedule are described in detail in Part III.

This schedule for a week does not include the time for reading during the first and last periods for selected children. Generally the children are divided into at least as many groups as there are games listed within one period. The only exceptions are period 6 on Monday and Tuesday and period 9 on Thursday where the last activity of the period involves the entire class as a unit. Otherwise, as the table shows, as many as six or more games are played at the same time with groups of children moving from one game to another as the teacher would indicate. Heterogeneous grouping of children is the rule and each child within a group works at his own level.

Take period 6 on Wednesday as an example when six different games are planned. The period starts with the teacher assigning about four children of different developmental levels to each of the six games. After ten minutes she indicates to the children to move to another game, but she keeps back one child whom she knows to be quite poor on nonsense word discrimination so that he spends another ten minutes on this game. This child will thus only play on five games during the period. Similarly, another group that just played buzzer board moves to paper tearing. Knowing that one child in that group is quite excellent in this game, the teacher assigns him to parquetry communication where he is in need of further practice. In the course of this same period the teacher may notice that one child working in parquetry block communication is having more than expected difficulties. He may be upset for some known or unknown reason. The teacher does not wait for the end of the allotted time but moves this child to the comic faces game which is more appropriate for him at that particular time. But no child roams aimlessly or unassigned.

Moreover, a number of games could be played by more than one group. In period 8 on Thursday, for instance, where only three games are listed, each of these games could be presented as duplicates or on two different levels of difficulties, with two groups of children working on symbol picture logic, two groups on matrix problems, and two groups on permutation.

A few scheduled activities on Table 2 require explanations. The second half of period 6 on Tuesday was this week taken up by class discussion on a particular issue: noise in the lunch room. Such discussions were scheduled as the need arose and served as

Table 2 / A sample schedule of activities for a week. The games are described in Part III. Categories to which the games belong are in parentheses.

| Period | Monday | Tuesday | Wednesday | Thursday | Friday |
|---|---|---|---|---|---|
| 1.<br>(50 min.)<br>(General Movement) | Angels in the snow<br>Balance board<br>Bimanual circles on chalkboard<br>Body lifts<br>Trampoline<br>Walking rail | Body lifts<br>Body questions<br>Line walk<br>Rolling<br>Swimming in place | Angels in the snow<br>Body lifts<br>Body pinwheel<br>Push-me-over<br>Rolling | Bimanual circles on chalkboard<br>Crawling<br>Hopping<br>Rhythm walk<br>Trampoline | Body questions<br>Push-me-over<br>Swimming in place<br>Wheelbarrow<br>Where did I touch you? |
| 2.<br>(35 min.) | Construct-o-line<br>Perception bingo<br>(Visual 15)<br>Do-what-I-say<br>Rhythm<br>(Auditory 20) | Prewriting sequence<br>Tearing paper<br>Tongue movement<br>(Discriminative movement 35) | Conservation<br>Symbol Logic<br>(Logic 20)<br>Form board<br>What-am-I-where<br>(Hand 15) | Dots<br>Getman's SSTB<br>Graphic tracking<br>(Graphic 15)<br>Pegboards<br>(Visual 20) | Clap patterns<br>High-low<br>Loud-soft<br>(Auditory 20)<br>Familiar objects<br>Feel-find beads<br>(Hand 15) |
| 3.<br>(30 min.) | Cuisinaire rods<br>(Math 15)<br>Permutation<br>Probability<br>(Logic 15) | Cuisinaire rods<br>Graphs<br>(Math 15)<br>Circle classification<br>(Logic 15) | Arts and Crafts<br>(20)<br>Blocks of Clay<br>(Drama 10) | Arithmetic<br>Scales<br>(Math 10)<br>Probability<br>Seriation<br>(Logic 20) | Drama and discussion of experience excursion (30) |
| 4.<br>(30 min.) | | | PHYSICAL EDUCATION | | |
| 5.<br>(15 min.) | | | STORY READING | | |
| 6.<br>(60 min.) | Parquetry blocks<br>Pegboard<br>Tachistoscope | Templates<br>(Graphic 10)<br>Comparison | Parquetry communication<br>Parquetry match | Dominoes<br>Hidden-draw-me<br>(Hand 20) | |

| | | | | | | | | |
|---|---|---|---|---|---|---|---|---|
| …(Visual 20) | | …ration (Hand 10) | | …(Visual 20)<br>Buzzer board | | Loud…soft | | EXPERIENCE<br>EXCURSION |
| Dominoes<br>Familiar objects<br>(Hand 20)<br>Blindfold fellow<br>Touch fellow<br>(Drama 20) | Clap pattern<br>High-low<br>Sound patterns<br>(Auditory 15)<br>Symbol logic<br>(Logic 15) | Keep-looking-at-me<br>See-me-clear<br>(Discriminative<br>movement 20)<br>Discussion<br>(Social 30) | Mates<br>Story clap<br>(Drama 15)<br>Music (15) | Nonsense word<br>discrimination<br>(Auditory 20)<br>Comic faces<br>Paper tearing<br>(Discriminative<br>movement 20) | Free activity (30) | Number and<br>letter recall<br>(Auditory 20)<br>Button battle<br>Follow-the-bug<br>Flashlight fight<br>(Discriminative<br>movement 20) | Listening and<br>walking<br>(Drama 30) | |
| **7.**<br>(30 min.) | | | | | | | | |
| Art (20) | | Memory X's<br>Pegboard match<br>Tachistoscope<br>Tell-a-story-<br>about-picture<br>(Visual 20) | | Graphic puzzles<br>Getman SSTB<br>Hare and hound<br>Prewriting<br>sequence<br>(Graphic 20) | | Matrix<br>Permutation<br>Symbol logic<br>(Logic 20) | | |
| **8.**<br>(20 min.) | | | | | | | | |
| Talking body<br>(Drama 10)<br>Classification<br>Clay and scales<br>(Logic 20) | | Science<br>discussion (30) | | Familiar objects<br>Feel and find<br>(Hand 15)<br>Measurements<br>Time<br>(Math 15) | | Fit-a-space<br>Puzzle talk<br>(Visual 10)<br>Music (20) | | |
| **9.**<br>(30 min.) | | | | | | | | |

excellent occasions for social thinking. In the afternoon of that same day a resource science consultant gave a demonstration on purification of water. Wednesday a free activity was scheduled for period 7. One such period was planned on a weekly basis to give the children an opportunity for freely choosing an activity they thought best. It also provided an opportunity for self-government insofar as they could discuss rules which they considered appropriate for a free period. Self-government discussions took place on an irregular basis and contributed to social and moral development of the children.

This week Friday afternoon was scheduled for an experience excursion to the local police station and jail. The trip was preceded by one period of drama activities, discussion, and evaluation through which the children prepared their awareness and concern for the coming experience. This enabled them to ask intelligent questions and make relevant observations. In this way a frequently boring field trip was turned into a high-level experience of places and persons in their community.

During this particular week the overall distribution of time for type of activities varied somewhat from the average percentage distribution suggested on page 49. This flexibility is of course desirable. The main changes were due to the experience excursion which took up an entire afternoon and thereby increased the relative frequency for social thinking to 20 per cent and decreased logic thinking to 8 per cent. Another week the teacher may arrange the schedule in such a way as to make up for any significant discrepancies. Finally, as mentioned, those children who were instructed in reading, spent about 10 per cent additional time on academics. For these reading children the percentage of time spent on body and sense thinking was only 36 per cent that week in contrast to 45 per cent for the rest of the children.

## The Second Year Schedule

The second year program, as mentioned earlier, was combined for second and first grade students together and functioned as an ungraded class. As appropriate, children were assigned to different activities or different levels of an activity. The schedule finally arranged by the teachers for the children who were reading included on the average 37 per cent of the time on body and sense activities and 32 per cent on academics. These percentages were 55 per cent and 14 per cent, respectively, for the children not judged ready for reading. For both groups 8 per cent of the time was allotted to logic thinking, 11 per cent to social thinking, 7 per cent to arts, crafts, and music, and 5 per cent to physical education.

## Grouping of children

For most activities the children of the classroom were divided into several groups. As many different groups were formed as there were different activities. Grouping, based on performance level, was heterogeneous or homogeneous depending on whether the activity was a group task or an individual task. In group tasks such as tachistoscope and general movement, more than one child worked on the same program and here homogeneous grouping of children was attempted. In other games, such as pegboard and parquetry blocks, each child had his own material and his own problem and consequently homogeneous grouping was not required. In both types of grouping the social factor of how one particular child worked with another was taken into consideration. The heterogeneous groups especially afforded a good occasion for one child helping another child either on the task itself or on understanding the teacher's instructions.

At first this grouping according to different criteria and different tasks must appear rather formidable and indeed it cannot be accomplished without the teacher knowing each child as an individual. This of course takes time.[1] It took several months at the beginning of the first year when the project started but only several weeks at the beginning of the second year. The task of grouping was made easier by there being heterogeneous groups available for the placement of children who did not fit into a homogeneous group activity on some particular occasions.

It is important that the teacher feels secure and respected by the children and not threatened by letting the children work individually among themselves with the action and noise that freedom implies. For the teacher to develop this attitude it may take time, as it did for the teachers in Charleston. Eventually the teachers come to appreciate that the free acting of the children does not signify lack of respect or control and the noise of children's voices was welcomed as a natural by-product of children engaged in high-level activity. The structure itself of a School for Thinking classroom is a guard against the acting and the noise turning into pandemonium.

The grouping of children varied from activity to activity and in addition was not a permanent placement. As the performance of a child changed, he was transferred to another, more appropriate, group. The multitude of activities for which groups were established assured that no one child was or considered himself constantly in a slow or advanced group. This attenuated the risk of a child judging himself as being generally inferior.

Earlier in this chapter we illustrated the functioning and flexibility of the groups. The Tyler project proved that five or six groups, each engaged in differing activities, could successfully function in a normal size classroom or that the jumping on the trampoline in one group did not distract the children working on symbol picture logic in another group.

## Raising and lowering demands

A major role of the teacher in a School for Thinking is maintaining the activities on an appropriately high level. The rationale for this approach and how to deal with the problem of children who deviate substantially from the other children in the classroom was discussed in Chapter 3. Throughout this book the existence of individual variability is stressed and respect and acceptance of this fact is one of the tenets of a School for Thinking.

In this matter the teacher must become a capable diagnostician. He must know when and how to drop the demands of the task to a lower, more meaningful level if a child is having difficulty or raise them to a higher developmental level if the task becomes low level for a child. In other words, the teacher must always bring the task to the child's individual level rather than expect the child to "pull himself up by his bootstraps" and rise to the too-high level of the material being presented.

Consequently, all the thinking games that were used at Charleston followed a specific growth sequence. This avoided the danger of instructing the child on a specific task without regard to his development of thinking. The growth sequence was presented to the teachers as their tool to be used intelligently in a free and inventive manner. The sequence was not made into a rigid step-by-step curriculum as is done in some programmed instruction materials where apart from rate of proceeding through the materials all individual variability in developing thinking is disregarded.

All the tasks presented in Part III are sequentially organized. A detailed example of a sequential arrangement is found in Chapter 8 in connection with parquetry blocks. The teachers at Tyler considered the preparation of the appropriate activities and the continual monitoring during the ongoing activities their primary task, and they acquired facility in changing the level of a task as the situation required. It is here above all that the teachers emerged as thinking persons.

Consider the case of the child who succeeded on a task of matching an arrangement of four parquetry blocks to the point that he could transfer this success to the task of matching from a picture. He then tackled a third problem of matching from an outline design but failed rather miserably. The skillful teacher immediately knew to drop down and assigned the child the easier problem of matching an outline with internal demarcation. She gave the child the opportunity to work with it for some days before permitting him to attack again the problem on which he had failed.

What happened here is characteristic of all development. In contrast to cumulative learning by drill where constant repetition can be effective—with the usual risk of a low-thinking performance—the development of thinking proceeds in irregular steps where repetition alone is not only of no help but can be inhibiting. If the boy in the example had been required to repeat the more difficult task, this may have resulted in an imposed success where the task is learned but high-level thinking is effectively discouraged.

This day-to-day variability is therefore much more than a mere question of stable individual differences between one and another child. This is a within-the-child variability. It is the normal variability of a developing child who in the long run inexorably grows into a mature and thinking adult, but within short periods proceeds and recedes in almost imperceptible steps. By following each child's growth pattern the School for Thinking provides the psychologically healthy environment in which a child's particular thinking capacities are respected—and hence not deformed or inhibited—and at the same time the child is encouraged to engage in high-level activities which are the sources of all intellectual growth.

# 5. An Environment for Intellectual Health

Intellectual health is our school's primary goal. This includes the five basic objectives discussed in Chapter 3 on which a successful educational experience is founded. Piaget's revolutionary theory proposes that intelligence permeates all varieties of human behavior. It is theoretically futile and harmful for educational practice to isolate knowledge from physical actions, social attitudes, and emotional-motivational values. Action, motivation, and cooperation with others are inseparably intertwined and linked to thinking. The School for Thinking gave this vital message to the children in practical terms of challenging games, cooperation with others, and the encouragement of questions and a responsible attitude.

Consider the girl who had played the matrix game for several days and eventually came to understand the underlying principle of double classification. Here we observe the child in a high-level situation. But this intellectual aspect is embedded in three environments—a social atmosphere in which she cooperated with other children engaged in similar problems, a physical atmosphere where she handled materials and was free to move around and, finally, an emotional atmosphere in which she was permitted to experience her successful self. She expressed all this in response to being asked by the teacher how she arrived at the assurance of her performance: "I guess my lil' ole brain told me." In other words, she acted on the strength of an internal criterion that is hers and not something she had to accept from outside. And straightaway she proceeded in front of the other children in her group to show off her intellectual acquisition in a spirit of co-operative sharing and helping.

The many different occasions of this kind at the School for Thinking not merely furthered intellectual development but simultaneously afforded the child experiences of social-relating and self-achieving. Without the active physical environment, the social grouping, and the freedom to rely on self, the school never could achieve its goal of intellectual enhancement. At the same time, it would be hard to imagine a better way to foster social and emotional health than to let the child experience the sense of successfully acting on the strength of a criterion that he himself has constructed.

We hold that during the period of primary school a person's development is most conspicuous in the intellectual sphere; thus providing occasions for genuine intellectual achievement is a most opportune way of helping a child who may have some emotional or social difficulties. Intellectual health is therapeutic and contributes to general mental health just as intellectual underdevelopment and boredom can lead to alienation and emotional disturbance. While we certainly do not claim that the School for Thinking is a panacea against all social evils or emotional ills, we do hold that if the task of fostering and enriching knowledge in the child is started in a psychologically appropriate way, as in the School for Thinking, the school can at the same time take care of various degrees of personality disturbances. In other words, the School for Thinking by its structure not only prevents intellectual failure but also emotional and social maladjustment. The converse influence is only too well known: A school in which a child experiences himself as a failure and an intellectual drop-out is also the environment that contributes to this child's eventual behavior problems and emotional difficulties.

One boy who was apparently a slow learner had a past history of wetting his pants in reaction to stress. The teacher remarked that but for the Thinking School this would have brought forth teasing and taunting by other children. In her classroom, however, the children were sympathetic and at the first sign of this stress reaction reminded him quietly to go to the bathroom which he accepted as a friendly attempt to help him. This, coupled with the general no-stress environment of the Thinking School, resulted in his stopping the habit within a month.

Almost as a natural experiment his parents moved to another area for a short time during the school year. His new school placed him into a traditional classroom setting—his pants wetting started and continued until he returned to Tyler. Within two weeks his pants wetting stopped. This example vividly illustrates how the School's healthy intellectual atmosphere was conducive to overcoming uncontrolled emotional habits. We see here also how this environment brings out the best in children who, instead of vying for being the nastiest, mutually supported each other to help the child.

A description of what happened to a recently adopted boy who had lived before in various foster homes is another example of our school's healthy learning environment. Since he was not able to attend to a task or function in a group, one could not possibly envisage him in a regular classroom. He responded favorably to our teachers' use of the school's structure and toward the end of the first year was making marked progress. At this time he requested on several occasions to participate in formal reading activities. The teacher suggested to him that he was not ready for formal reading instruction but he persisted. Finally the teacher brought him over to observe the reading group and showed him how he would have to sit still at the table, listen quietly, and attend. The boy reflected for a while and said, "I guess you are right. I am not ready yet!" The chaos created by such a youngster would usually result in his being rejected by his peers. On the contrary, here he was generally liked. On one of our visits we observed children clapping their hands as he reached the top of the rope ladder. We were told that he had attempted this act on several previous occasions but had never before been able to reach the top.

Once, in an act of anger, this boy was found actually choking another youngster (the one and only episode of violence throughout the two years). After taking care of the other child the teacher gently took our boy to the principal, not as a punishment but as an opportunity for him to return to tranquility. The teacher then hastily returned to the classroom where she expected a general uproar about the incident and a request that the culprit be punished. Instead she found the children wondering and discussing excitedly how this could happen and what should be done with this boy. No one was angry. They all recognized he had a problem and unanimously wanted to help him. The teacher brought the boy into the room and in front of the class shared with him the conclusions of the class discussion. The boy was given to understand that he could not remain in this class if he could not control his angry outbursts. From that day on, when he felt he was losing his temper the boy could be observed muttering to himself, "I want to stay in this school." Obviously the success with the classroom activities and the acceptance on the part of his classmates was more gratifying to him than the acting out during his anger.

As in our previous episode with this boy too a natural experiment occurred, but this one had an unfortunate ending. The child's parents were anxious to have him in a more reading oriented program and at the beginning of the second year enrolled him in a nonpublic school. He stayed there less than six weeks in spite of special consideration and was expelled as being unmanageable. The parents moved in the meantime, and the child was then placed in and remained in a special education class of the local public school.

Here then was an apparently capable boy with a behavior problem who obviously needed help and responded well to the freedom within structure of the School for Thinking. We do not believe that this type of youngster belongs in a special education class, and we interpret the evidence of his first year's improvement as confirming the therapeutic effect of the Thinking School atmosphere.

One day a supervisory team from the state came to inspect the project. This forbidding group of adults soon found themselves involved with the children who had them playing various thinking games. Some adults were solving logic-picture problems, some were lying on the floor for general movement activities, some were placing pegs in pegboards. In the latter group one official praised a child who was successfully matching a complex pegboard pattern. This child's neighbor, a little girl, was working on a considerably simpler pattern and the official pointed this out to her. "It's just as hard as his is," the girl replied emphatically—and indeed it was, because she viewed the problem as a high-level activity, which is always relative to the child's developmental level.

The teacher noticed a tremendous difference in the behavior of these children during experience excursions in contrast to the children of previous years. The children were not shy in the presence of adults, they exhibited much curiosity, and knew how to ask relevant questions. At the grocery store, the police station, the post office, and on many other experience excursions adults were so delighted with the intelligent involvement of the children that they interrupted their own activities to engage in responsive conversation with them. This open attitude toward new experiences within their community expresses on the one hand a healthy social maturity; on the other hand it is a prerequisite for knowing how to get involved in one's community in a relevant intelligent manner.

A most gratifying effect of the School for Thinking was the transfer of socially responsible behavior from the school setting to the home and community. One boy—a repeater—was previously known to the teachers as withdrawn and unwilling to play with other children. He changed during this year to an involved, outgoing individual and articulated the reason for his positive attitude: his successes on the tasks, the absence of undue pressure to perform, and the teacher's focus on successes rather than failures. His mother and neighbors now considered him a responsible child who could be trusted with various chores.

The anecdotes in this chapter indicate that the children were helpful to each other. They were sensitive to other children's problems, as in the case of the hyperactive boy, and to the individual ability levels of different children. In many group activities children took turns as leaders and set the individual's task with a surprising sensitivity toward the various children's thinking level. On other occasions they would remark to the teacher that a certain task was perhaps too difficult or too easy for a given child.

The children liked the school. Absenteeism was very low. Some children who previously were chronic absentees came regularly to the School for Thinking. Apart from the one episode reported earlier there were no discipline problems. Obviously a positive self-image contributed to the social responsiveness of the children just as the spirit of helpful cooperation contributed to a child's positive self-image. When a child spends a major part of the day with activities through which he experiences challenge and success in developing his thinking capacities, he is less likely to engage in unkind and destructive behavior toward other children and adults. Often this type of unfavorable behavior is primarily a reaction to the frustration and boredom the child meets in the course of his long school day.

This entire chapter and episodes throughout the book testify to the soundness of the intellectual atmosphere and to the children's active involvement. They were involved in activities that challenged their intellectual capacities. Even the children understood that the principal purpose of the program's structure was to monitor the level at which a child worked at a given task, not too high and not too low. Recall the girl who so well knew that a simple pegboard task was equally as challenging to her as a complex pegboard task was to her neighbor.

When children are intellectually challenged they are not bored. The total absence of boredom in the classrooms of the School for Thinking was another observation providing evidence that the children were challenged. The teacher was constantly sensitive to the two chief sources of boredom in a classroom: a situation that is on a too high level on the one hand and a situation that is on a too low level on the other.

A further indication of intellectual involvement was the fact that the children were not easily distracted from their own activity. One visitor was amazed at the variety of simultaneously ongoing activities that included such things as trampoline jumping, rope climbing, sorting of blocks, and tachistoscopic flashing, all done in one small room. At the end of the period she expressed to the teacher her amazement: "How can the children concentrate? Don't they all want to jump on the trampoline?" To this the teacher simply remarked that the children liked what they were doing and knew that their turn would come.

On another occasion a visitor wondered whether the noise of the children's activities did not disrupt the teacher's attention. At the beginning this teacher was quite disturbed by the noise, an unavoidable by-product of children's activity. But by the time of this visit the question reminded her to what extent this was no longer a difficulty for her so that she was not even aware of the unobjectionable noise. Just as the children in the Thinking Classroom were not distracted by the noise produced in the course of their own activities, they were only minimally disturbed by the presence of visitors. Unless asked to interrupt, they simply continued being attentive to the task.

These three observable characteristics—individually challenging experiences, absence of boredom, and lack of distractibility—are strong indications of a psychologically healthy intellectual atmosphere. But the most compelling proof is probably found in the evaluation of the emotional and social behavior of the children. If there is evidence, as we attempted to show above, that the activities in the classroom contributed to a healthy emotional and social atmosphere, there is only one way in which this could have happened. That is, the activities must have been intellectually challenging and rewarding to the children. In this manner intellectual health includes as a natural consequence the main ingredients of what makes a happy, healthy, developing child.

# III. Thinking Games

# 6. General Movement Thinking

Piaget's theory erases the traditional distinction between activities of the mind and activities of the body. Movement and thinking are interdependent. Many children perform academic tasks inadequately because they have not mastered the movement control on which these tasks depend. In this chapter we describe twenty-four movement thinking games designed to engage the child in meaningful and structured play which should enable him to gain increased mastery over his body movements. To the extent that the child is able to control his movements with ease, he will be free to focus on the more abstract aspects of problems. The plan used at the Tyler Thinking School is designed to allow children to move through a series of "exercises" that should prepare them to perform increasingly difficult tasks successfully.

We use the term "exercises" advisedly because when speaking of movement we do not refer to purely physical exercises. We are interested in the thinking implied in body actions. Actions are directed toward goals and should be performed intelligently, efficiently, and in a manner that minimizes stress. Actions always imply thinking—the knowing of "How?" "When?" "Where?" "How much?" "In what direction?" "In what sequence?" As adults we may forget the complexity of what appear to be, on the surface, simple movements, yet the majority of us do tend to be somewhat clumsy when mastering a new physical task. Our performance may fall short of our expectations when we are beginners. For example, merely memorizing the keyboard of a typewriter will not lead to fluent typing. The typist must also learn the finger movements. Until he does, his movements will be slow, planned, and deliberate. His attention will be divided between what he is doing and how he is doing it. After he has mastered the movement thinking control, he is free to concentrate exclusively on the material being typed. Similar problems are faced by the child when he is first given a pencil and asked to write.

When a child is unable to perform a task, he is often given specific training on that task, for many educational assumptions are made on chronological age rather than developmental age. The clumsy child, the uncoordinated child, the physical education incompetent child is easily singled out in the group. He is often "taught" how to master the deficient skill with little or no thought being given to his level of movement thinking development. If he mastered skipping, or hopping, or walking to rhythm, the program was considered successful.

In a Thinking School environment the teacher is not so concerned with the child's observable performance as with his use of movement to solve various nonrelated tasks. Skipping, for example, is more than the learned combination of step-hop actions, which a child may have been taught to perform, first on one foot, then on the other. This *performance* does not imply necessarily that he has a grasp of the principles of general movement thinking involved in skipping. Similarly, a child may be taught to *say* that the same quantity of water will fill either a short, wide glass or a tall, narrow glass. It does not follow that he has an intelligent grasp of the principle of conservation of liquids. A child may be taught to write with the required coordinated action of thumb, index finger, hand, and arm. But if he learns this as a specific skill rather than as an application of a repertory of well-developed discriminative movements, he may not be able to shift these skills to the function of carving in wood, leather, or clay. On the other hand, the child who truly knows fingers-hand-arm discriminative movements should be able to apply this knowledge as the situation demands. His learning to write or carve will be an application of internalized knowledge of appropriate movement rather than rote learning of a specific skill.

The first thing to evaluate then is how a child performs general movements. The degree of coordination in his action determines whether the child is ready for the advanced phases of general movements. To impose higher levels of movement thinking on a child who functions at a lower movement thinking level is similar to imposing structured academics too soon. This psychologically unhealthy situation of a too-high task (discussed in Chapter 1) could result in the experience of failure for the developing child. The teachers in the Tyler Thinking School were encouraged to be effective observers of purposeful, knowing movement as opposed to rote movement or random activity. If the child was unable to perform on the task, the teacher was shown how to drop to a more basic level of success in the sequence of movement development.

A general discussion of body movement thinking should make the philosophy of the movement thinking games clearer to the teachers and parents. Although all body movements are interrelated, a convenient distinction can be made between those activities which involve "large" muscles and those which involve "small" muscles. Those activities which involve large muscles are referred to as *general movements*. These movements utilize large muscle groups such as those of the trunk, arms, legs, or neck. Examples are balancing, walking, running, jumping, throwing, wrestling, swimming, and kicking. Some of these activities have been incorporated into the thinking games for the classroom described in this chapter.

Those activities which involve small muscles are referred to as *discriminative movements*. These movements are minute and contained; they utilize the muscles which manipulate the eyes, fingers, and tongue. Examples are handling tools, sewing, buttoning, tying shoelaces, speaking, reading, and writing. Thinking games that develop discriminative skill movement will be discussed in Chapter 7.

General and discriminative movements are closely related: The body parts for discriminative movements are transported through space by general movement activity to a position appropriate to their functioning. These specific body positions are often referred to as *postural set* and always imply *spatial coordination,* the child's understanding of the space which surrounds him at any given time.

Movement thinking includes the coordination of two body senses: *kinesthesis* and *proprioception*. These sense systems are interdependent. Kinesthesis results in awareness of overt movements of bones and joints and overt or covert movements of muscles and tendons. Proprioception is the intuition or internal awareness not only of the body's location in the present but also in the past or future. It is the sense of where we are, where we have been, and where we are going. It involves an awareness of the various parts of the body in relation to any ongoing activity. For example, in a game of catch the child would be aware of the position of his arm in relation to the rest of his body and of where his arm should be positioned the next time a ball would be thrown to him.

In a sighted individual, vision plays a concomitant role to kinesthesis and proprioception; the connection among them is so close as to be inseparable. Vision, in this sense, includes depth perception, spatial positioning, and all judgments which must be made on the basis of information received through the sense of sight. Efficient movement thinking depends to a large degree on how well the visual process is integrated with movement. The interaction of vision and movement will be discussed in more detail later in this chapter.

The importance of movement thinking should not be underestimated. If the six-year-old child does not have fundamental control over both general and discriminative movements, he will find it difficult, if not impossible, to move his eyes across the page, look up and down from the chalkboard to his paper, hold a pencil, or compete in play with his peers. The Thinking School program develops thinking activities on the foundation of adequate body coordination. If bodily movement is well under control, children can expend minimum energy on the physical mechanics of the task and maximum energy on the thinking related to the task's solution.

Consider, for example, the classroom task of tracing a complicated design of curves, angles, and intersecting lines. If the child in solving the tracing task knows how to move his eyes, his hands and his fingers, he is free to observe the total design and to prepare the movement of his hand: "Where should I begin? Where should I end? Where do the lines continue after the intersection? What path should I follow?" If the child has not yet developed the thinking pattern of sequential finger control and coordinated action of finger, arm, and eye movement, some of his mental activity will be diverted: "How should I hold the pencil? How should I move my hand? Where should I look?" This preoccupation with movement control may detract from high-level thinking that should go into the solution of the task.

As the child matures, his movement thinking develops; he is able to cope with the input from the environment in increasingly sophisticated ways. To provide guideposts for the teacher who observes and directs the developing child, we have classified five major components of general movement thinking:

1. Reflexive control
2. Mental map of body
3. Coordination of the body's axes
4. Body balance
5. Coordinated action

This is neither a developmental nor a physiological-anatomical classification; rather, it is a pragmatic division of general movements. As the child develops, stages of this development can be observed within each component.

The children were given many opportunities to develop basic general movements as a foundation for discriminative movements of hands, eyes, and tongue. This was done right in the classroom as part of the children's everyday activities and permeated the general plan of the entire school year. *Movement and thinking became synonymous.* We called these activities "movement thinking games"—and the children loved them! In the following pages, we describe some of these games according to our classification of general movements.

## THINKING GAMES OF REFLEXIVE CONTROL

Reflexive movements in the form of involuntary or instinctual responses are most easily observed in the new-born child. Reflexive control refers to the transition from uncontrolled random movement to controlled activity. Even as an adult learns a new activity, coordination and integration of reflexive movement are still part of the total learning process. In fact, elimination of redundant random movements often makes the difference between master and beginner, whether the task is playing tennis, riding a bicycle, or playing a piano.

If older children do not grow out of interfering uncontrolled movement, it may be necessary to make them aware of this interference in order that they may develop the necessary controls. Children suffering from cerebral palsy typically have difficulty functioning at the level of reflexive control and require specialized activities. None of our children at Tyler were physically impaired, and they did not require any games at the level of reflexive development. For purposes of illustration, however, we have included two thinking games that are suitable for classroom activity. These games are designed for children who are deficient in the basic activities of purposeful grasping and pushing.

### Grasping / Game 1

The first game is borrowed from E. C. Seguin.[1] A ladder is placed on the floor. The child lies prone (face down) on the ladder. One teacher takes the child's hands and places them firmly but kindly around a rung of the ladder. Another teacher raises the ladder at a slant. The first teacher attempts to release his hold of the child's hands. The child should continue grasping the ladder to keep himself from sliding to the floor. Other similar procedures may be used to aid the child in the development of grasp.

### Pushing / Game 2

The second game is designed to develop purposeful pushing. The child is expected to resist enforced *flexion*, the bending of an arm or leg, by *extension*, straightening of that arm or leg. The child lies on the floor in a supine (face up) position. The teacher pushes against one or both of the child's feet, bending the child's knees until they rest against his chest. At this moment, the child's feet should be pushing against the teacher's hands. Although the child is held in this position, he is encouraged to resist by straightening his legs. The procedure is continued until the child is able to exert the proper force and movement control to propel his body away from the teacher. The teacher's function could be replaced by a wall or a board, and the technique can lead into more involved activities. In time, the child should be able to propel his body in space by using his hands or feet—for example, on a scooter board or swing. This game makes the child aware that he can control a particular body joint and make it work for him at his own request.

## THINKING GAMES OF MENTAL MAP OF BODY

One should not assume that every healthy, active six year old has adequate knowledge and mastery of his body. Many children entering the first grade (even those with nursery or kindergarten experience) are not able to initiate the appropriate body movements when they are asked to solve problems. They may not be able to follow verbal commands to move in a certain manner. The child may not be aware of his *body map* or the way in which the parts of his body relate and work together. Such a child, when placed in a problem-solving situation, is preoccupied with thinking about where a particular body part fits into the general scheme of the task rather than about the task's solution. In other words, he is uncomfortable in assuming the prerequisite postural set for a task and lacks the appropriate spatial coordination.

Many normal six-year-old children are still developing a mental map of body. In a traditional classroom they often fidget and squirm in the confined space behind their desks. They cannot cope with the situation because they are not ready. They are in a stage of development where they are still exploring their body inventory. Containing them behind a desk cannot possibly facilitate this needed growth, and can actually thwart movement thinking development.

Before a child is ready to use specific body actions to accomplish a defined goal, he must have developed an adequate knowledge not only of the location of his body parts but also of the relation of these parts to each other and to the total body. He must know how the activity of each part is limited, and he must know how to select the body part best suited to the task at hand. Even blind or partially sighted children develop a map of their spatial world; without it, movement would be a series of clumsy, stumbling, trial and error motor acts.

The games described in this section are designed to help the child form a mental map of his body. No attempt is made to list all possible games. When the creative educator understands the underlying philosophy, he will be able to add or substitute other games.

### Cross-Legged Walk / Game 3

An area of floor marked with a straight line is all the "equipment" necessary for this game. The teacher should have the child straddle the line with his right foot on the left side and his left foot on the right. He should then be encouraged to walk the length of the line alternating his feet in this manner. When he has accomplished the task, he may attempt to walk the line in the same manner—only backward. Most children can walk cross-legged by the age of five, but many children, even at the age of eight or nine, have difficulty walking cross-legged backward. These children may have difficulty controlling their feet or operating in the space behind themselves. When doing the cross-legged walk backward, these children often cross their feet in front and then attempt to push one foot through the other. They must be encouraged, but not taught, to swing the foot around and behind.

Depending on the length of the line, this game can be played by groups of six or more. The speed with which the game is played is not important. Acting as observer, the teacher can isolate and help provide insight to any child having difficulty.

## Wheelbarrow / Game 4

The goal of this game is knowledge of the arms and hands: knowledge of their placement with respect to body, knowledge of their relation to each other, and knowledge of the extent of their reach.

This is a two person game which can be played by a teacher and child or by two children. The child places his hands on the floor and the other person raises the child's torso by lifting his legs. The child then walks on his hands. There are many variations to this game ranging from the simple to the complex. For example, the child can walk freely about the room moving forward, backward, or sideways. Or he can walk a straight line. Or he can walk cross-handed following the principle of the cross-legged walk. In this variation, he can move forward, backward, or sideways. In another variation, the child can walk through a maze or a puzzle track of intersecting paths. (Both the maze and the puzzle track can be made by interlacing strips of masking tape on the floor in curves, angles, and straight lines.) Still another variation is for the child to pick up and drop objects in containers while hand walking across the floor. A complex modification of this game requires the child to draw simple figures with chalk or crayons at designated spots on the floor.

## Where Did I Touch You? / Game 5

This game requires two participants. The first child stands facing a lined drawing on the chalkboard in front of him. The drawing represents his head, neck, and shoulders, and trunk. The teacher or a second child stands behind him and with the forefinger touches or "draws" a design on the first child's back. The first child is to reproduce the picture he "felt" on his back. There are three phases of this game.

1. The second child or teacher touches the first child anywhere on the back of head, neck, shoulders, or trunk. The first child draws an "X" on the picture in the spot where he thinks he was touched. For verification, a bit of masking tape can be pressed onto the child's back to designate "the spot" for later comparison.

2. The first child is shown simple line designs which have been sketched on cards. (These same cards are used in Chapter 8, Game 89 where they are described in detail.) While he views them, the teacher or another child draws one of the designs on the first child's back. The first child points to the card representing what he felt was drawn on his back. The complexity of the drawings on the cards should depend on the first child's level of success on the task. (This illustrates an important aspect of most of the Tyler Thinking School games. One technique can span a wide spectrum—for example, in this case, from simple line drawings to complex overlapping curves and angles.)

3. At this level, the child draws on the chalkboard diagram of his body the design that he feels has been drawn on his back. No cards are used. In his drawing, size, accuracy of placement, and accuracy of design are all significant. Again, the complexity of the design is dependent on the first child's level. Both the first child (the receptor) and the second child (the expressor) are developing body knowledge from this thinking game.

## Broomstick Straddle / Game 6

This thinking game requires two broomsticks without the brooms. In the first variation, the child straddles one broomstick, grasping it with one hand in front and one hand behind. The goal is to get the broomstick out from between his legs without letting go with either hand. The reader may be surprised at the number of five to seven year olds who will have difficulty thinking through this task.

In the second variation, two children stand face to face and encase themselves in a trap by holding broomsticks behind each other with their arms intertwined. One child has his right arm between the other child's left arm and body; his left arm, however, is outside the other child's right arm. The other child's position would be the reverse of this one. Can they escape without letting go of the broomsticks? The answer is no, but unless the child has a good mental map of his body and can cooperate with his partner he will not understand why this is so.

## Body Lifts / Game 7

As we explained in Chapter 4, the teachers were taught how to adjust the level of difficulty of a task. Rather than always starting at the most basic level, they started at a high level and proceeded upward or downward according to the child's level of success. As an illustration our description of body lifts moves from a complex level to a less complex level and on to a simpler level.

Successful accomplishment of moving isolated body parts such as arms, legs, or upper trunk in response to the slightest touch indicates a child's increasing awareness of how he is put together. The purpose of this game is to lead the child to construct an improved mental map of body through which he can control movement of specific body parts.

This body map thinking game requires no equipment and can be played with teacher and child or with two children. The child lies prone on the floor. The teacher first touches the child's right elbow and left knee, then his head, then his left leg, and finally both legs. The child is to respond in the same sequence by raising and lowering each specified part. This involves *recall in sequence*. If the child is not able to respond at this level, the teacher touches two body parts simultaneously and the child is to give an *immediate response*. The task is more difficult when *opposite sides* (left arm–right leg) are touched than when the *same side* (left arm-left leg) is touched. If only one body part is touched, the task is even easier and more basic. Should the child have difficulty responding to even a single stimulus, he is asked to lie on the floor in a supine position. When responding to touch children generally have less difficulty with raising a foot or an arm forward than backward because internal knowledge of front space is usually better developed than internal knowledge of back space.

## Body Questions / Game 8

The child's mental map of body can be further developed to include an awareness of the extent of his reach and the bulk of his body. The Tyler teachers gathered a group of six to eight children and asked each child questions such as: "How high can you reach?" "How close must you come to the wall before you can touch it with your arm outstretched?" "Sitting there, could you reach that object with your foot?" "Lying on your back, can you touch your right shoulder with your left hand in three different ways while keeping this hand in contact with the floor at all times?" "What position should you be in to be able to crawl under that chair?" There are many possible variations. The children at Tyler were encouraged to think of other games by themselves.

### Swimming in Place / Game 9

This individual or group game requires no equipment. The child lies prone on the floor with his right arm and right leg moved forward; his head should be turned toward his right arm. His left arm should be bent across his back and his left leg should be extended behind him. After holding this position for a second, he switches and simultaneously points his left arm and leg forward with his head turned to the left (Figure 2).

This "swimming" activity should be continued until the child's movement is well coordinated and he moves in a specific rhythm pattern without becoming confused. (The rhythm pattern can be supplied by a metronome.) This is a discovery activity, not a drill; the child should discover that he is moving the arm and leg on the same side of his body to a certain rhythm.

An additional discovery comes when the child "swims" by moving arms and legs on opposite sides of his body (right arm— left leg) and discovers they are "not same." The awareness that a bodily side can be same or not same is not only a basic prerequisite for an adequate understanding of laterality but also of the general concept of sameness. The teachers used this game to develop the children's awareness of same and not same.[2] The children discovered these concepts by moving their own bodies rather than by rote learning of the words "left" and "right" or "same" and "different."

**Figure 2.**
**Swimming in Place**
The girl in the upper right has her arms and legs placed in "same" or homolateral position. However, for maximum results, her right arm should be placed across her back rather than beside her on the floor.
The arms and legs of the boy in the center left are in "not-same" or contralateral position, but for all body parts to be correctly placed his head should be turned toward his outstretched left hand.

## THINKING GAMES OF COORDINATION OF THE BODY'S AXES

The development of coordination, the harmonious adjustment and interaction of body parts, is a major goal of the movement thinking program. In this section, we consider the coordination of the body's axes and its relation to vision. Seven games are described. Before presenting the games it may be helpful to show briefly how our philosophy relates to physiological concepts underlying the activities.

In order to deal efficiently with his environment, the child must know how to coordinate (1) not only the two sides of his body, but also (2) the upper and lower parts of his body. In addition, (3) he must know how to perform general movements which involve pivoting and twisting.

The human body is a bilateral (two-sided) organism which may be further divided into quadrants (upper right, lower right, lower left, upper left). When the quadrants of the body function with appropriate movements at appropriate times, we say the body is coordinated. Each action of one quadrant of the body then has a harmonious counteraction with the other. It is the intellectual integration of all these quadrants that gives us the knowledge of an internal spatial body scheme.

There is a sort of reciprocity of action-counteraction among body parts. D. B. Harmon[3] refers to this interaction as the *reciprocal interweaving* of the three main internal body axes: vertical, horizontal, and transverse. These axes control different body movements: side-to-side, toward-away, clockwise-counterclockwise (See Figure 3).

Only after the child has become intuitively aware of these body axes can he use them as references for all spatial coordinates. If the child lacks this internalized knowledge of his body axes, he may have difficulty understanding and applying basic concepts relating to spatial coordinates. To work efficiently with three-dimensional concepts and spatial transformations depends on the internalization of the body's own spatial scheme. These concepts are of fundamental importance in such varied subjects as art, math, science, geography, and industrial arts.

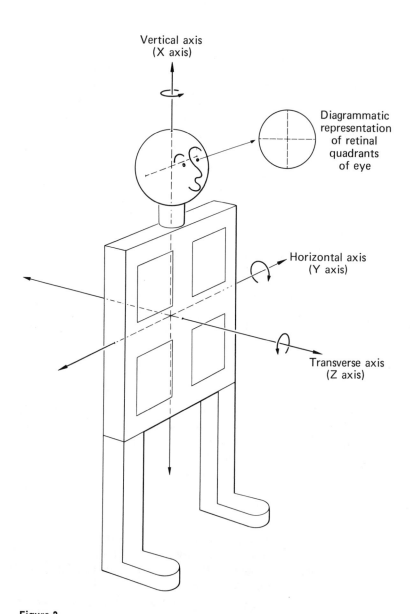

Vertical axis
(X axis)

Diagrammatic
representation
of retinal
quadrants
of eye

Horizontal axis
(Y axis)

Transverse axis
(Z axis)

**Figure 3.**
**Diagramatic Representation of Body Axes**
This is a graphic illustration of how the head, trunk,
and eye can be anatomically subdivided into four
quadrants: upper and lower right, and upper and lower left.

When a person is working on a horizontal surface, the vertical body axis of the natural upright position becomes related to the flat surface and the transverse axis to the vertical walls. To illustrate this relation hold the book upright. The body axes are represented in Figure 3. To relate them to a horizontal working surface, change the position of the book from upright to lying flat on a table top. Now the vertical axis of the sketch is seen as parallel to the flat surface (floor or ceiling), the horizontal axis as extending right and left, and the transverse as extending up toward the ceiling and down toward the floor. The book then can be rotated around each axis as an automobile wheel rotates around its axle. The vertical axis provides a side to side rotation; the horizontal axis, a toward and away rotation; and the transverse, a clockwise and counterclockwise rotation. A reversal problem in reading, writing, or drawing can thus be related to inadequate general movement around a specific body axis. Aided by this diagnosis, the teacher then may be of help and provide occasions in classroom activities for proper development of general movement thinking around that particular body axis.

Knowledge of the body's axes and visual thinking are mutually related. The neurological arrangement of the retina of the eye plays a fundamental role in the child's orientation in space and thus in his controlled movement. Like the body, the retina may be divided into quadrants: upper right, lower right, lower left, upper left. See Figure 3. These quadrants are neurologically organized to match spatial projections similar to those on a radar screen. This organization informs the sighted individual of the location of objects in the world around him.

To move toward objects in space requires an intelligent matching of the retinal quadrants with the body quadrants. Objects in the individual's right visual field stimulate the left half of each retina, and objects in the left visual field stimulate the right half of each retina. Similarly, objects in the lower visual field stimulate the upper half of each retina, and objects in the upper field stimulate the lower half.[4]

Thus through the structure in the retina of each eye the person computes the spatial coordinates of the world around him. About 80 per cent of the optic nerve fibers send "picture messages" to the brain. Another 20 per cent of the nerve fibers send "direction messages" to those motor nerves that are involved with the movement of large and small muscles. Here the anatomical-directional maps of both the eye and the body integrate and function as two coordinated members of the same team: "Something in my field of vision stimulated my eye, sending a message to my brain that this object is up and to my left, and my hand reaches out to grasp it." The important concept here is that the retina has a directional neural network which both sends and receives messages that lead to directed body movement. The match between the eye's "map" and the body's "map" determines how each of us moves in our space world. Visual thinking locates an object, and movement thinking enables us to deal with this object.

The movement thinking games described in this section develop knowledge of the relation of the body's vertical, lateral, and transverse axes to each other and to the total body scheme. In particular, *laterality* (the relation of the two sides of the body to each other and to the total body) is vital to appreciate the relation of the body to other objects in space. It is also the foundation for learning *directionality* of letters, numerals, and words involving patterns like "b" vs "d"; "13" vs "31"; and "saw" vs "was." Through visual thinking, integration of laterality and directionality provides a relative constancy of positions of objects in space.

At primary school age, children begin to show preference for the part which will lead in the thinking action of any movement thinking task—referred to as "right-handedness" or "left-handedness." This results from a spontaneous inclination toward a lateral preference not only of hand but also of foot, eye, and ear.

Three points can be made regarding lateral preference. First, if the child has not yet established consistency, do not impose a permature decision on him. Second, do not change an already established hand preference. Third, arrange proper seating and working conditions in accordance with this preference to prevent postural warps.[5] According to these points, activities in the Tyler Thinking School program were designed to encourage the emergence of a consistent preference for one arm, hand, foot, eye, and ear.

**Figure 4.**
**Angels in the Snow**
Only the boy in the center has achieved the desired position.
The other children have not brought their hands together over their heads.

### Angels in the Snow / Game 10

This is a popular movement thinking game, played in many developmental programs. The child lies supine on the floor. He then slides his fully extended arms along the floor until his hands meet on the floor beyond his head. In the same manner, he slides his fully extended legs along the floor until he achieves maximum separation. He will then be in the position illustrated in Figure 4.

Occasionally the child will not know how to begin. When this happens, the teacher or another child can help move the child's arms or legs. Sometimes it is necessary to restrict the passive movement to only arms or only legs until the child discovers the rules of the game. The child can then move his own legs and arms apart and together in various sequences and rhythms.

To develop *immediate response*, the child is verbally instructed to stop or to start moving a specific leg or an arm. If necessary, the teacher can also point to, touch, or label the designated limb. The goal is for the child to respond as quickly as possible—first to a single limb command, then to a two limb command, then to a three or four limb command. The instructions may include directions for stopping, starting, or stopping and starting simultaneously. At a later stage the instructions can be printed on cards which are then held up for the child to read. These cards can be preprinted or written on a portable, hand-held chalkboard by a child-leader in the group.

The basic technique used to develop *delayed recall* is the same as that for immediate response, but the command to start or stop movement is delayed until after the proposed commands have been given. The goal is to stop or start movement in all limbs as rapidly as possible upon the command "Now!" Children usually have more difficulty simultaneously stopping or starting movement of an arm and leg on opposite sides of the body.

At the level of *sequence*, the child responds in a sequential rather than a simultaneous action. He is told, for example, "First that arm, then this leg, next move this arm," and so on. Both immediate response and delayed recall are utilized at this level.

### Crawling / Game 11

At the Tyler Thinking School, crawling was used to develop synchrony between the right and left side of the body. In this situation where the effect of gravity is minimized, the child can concentrate on the body movements of crawling while giving minimum thought to activities such as balance. In *homolateral* (same side) crawling, the child lies face down, stomach on the floor; he then reaches out with his right arm while bending his right leg. His head is turned toward his right hand. The left arm and leg remain extended downward at his side. The child pulls himself forward as far as possible with his right arm and leg and comes to a complete stop. The child then reverses the procedure and brings the left arm and leg forward while turning his head toward his extended left hand. He pulls with his left hand and pushes with his left foot to propel himself forward. The movement is continued—alternating between right and left sides—for a short, predetermined distance. If he moves the other side of his body too soon, it will result in a "swimming" action which is to be avoided.

In *contralateral* (not the same side) crawling, the procedure is the same except that the left arm is moved forward with the right leg, and the right arm is moved forward with the left leg. The head is always turned toward the forward arm. Eventually the child should be able to adapt to commands of "same" or "not same" and alter his movements accordingly as he crawls across the floor.

### Creeping / Game 12

In this activity, the child should be on his hands and knees. Initially, he moves the opposite hand and knee forward, balancing on the other hand and knee. His head should always be turned toward his forward arm. He should try to lift the arm and knee simultaneously, and to place them forward on the floor simultaneously. He repeats this procedure with his other hand and knee as he creeps across the floor. Harmony and synchrony are the goals. Later the child can vary both the pattern and the timing. He may also creep to the fast or slow beats of a metronome or a flashing light.

Another variation is placing markers with "R" or "L" printed on them in a stepping stone pattern along the floor. The child is to place his right hand on the "R" markers and his left hand on the "L" markers. If he has not learned the labels "right" and "left," he can be told to touch the markers with "this" hand or "the other" hand as he comes to them. Combining rhythm and markers is an even more advanced variation of the creeping game.

### Rhythm Walk / Game 13

Man walks in a contralateral pattern: He swings his left arm toward his right foot and vice versa. We emphasized this contralateral movement by having the children walk to a fast or slow beat of a metronome and point exaggeratedly: right hand to left foot, left hand to right foot, and so on. In addition to rhythm walking forward, the children walked sideways in an apart-together step while they pointed right hand to left foot and vice versa.

### Rolling / Game 14

To roll, the child must develop the ability to thrust one entire side of his body across the other so that he transfers from a prone to a supine position, and vice versa. Movement is rotary around the head-to-feet axis. The arms and feet should not be held rigid; they should be flexible and help in the act of rolling.

The child should roll along a carpet or some other designated path. The goal is to roll within a specified track for eight to ten feet. Once this goal is accomplished, the child is requested to make a ninety degree turn (first right, then left) onto another track. This is done in both directions so that at one time his head is the pivot point and at another time his feet. Staying within the track requires knowledge of body position, interrelated movements of body parts, and limits of the activities field.

The child should be aware that his neck and feet are functioning as pivot points; he should also be aware of the relation between his upper and lower body parts. This is particularly important when rolling around the ninety degree corner. Should a child have difficulty with this, he should be encouraged to play the following game of pinwheel.

## Body Pinwheel / Game 15

This is a good game for the child who has difficulty rolling around corners. A square or circle about one foot in diameter is drawn or marked by tape on the floor. The child lies supine on the floor with his head within the designated area. The goal is to move the body in a large circle, first clockwise, then counterclockwise, with the head as pivot point. The child's head should not move out of the designated area.

This game affords the child an opportunity to coordinate and learn control of the upper and lower body, at the same time as he uses the sides of his body. That is—his feet and legs must move sideways while his head remains in one small area. In order to accomplish this, the child must understand the reciprocity of movement of body sections—right side, left side, upper body, lower body.

## Bat the Ball[6] / Game 16

The child holds a long rounded stick (a broomstick will do) with one hand on each end. He then bats a ball suspended from the ceiling. Initially, this game is played to develop bimanual control. Then directionality is incorporated when colored tape is used to mark a specific point on the bat, and the child tries to make the ball move in a particular direction by hitting it with the taped section of the bat only. At this point the game may be played by two children who bat the ball back and forth.

This game requires timing and a knowledge of the relative thrust of both arms. The child acquires an awareness of his body sides and learns how they relate to each other and to objects in his visual world.

**Figure 5.**
**Bimanual Circles on the Chalkboard**
The bottom of the board is tilted to an angular position
to match the child's skeletal structure and arm-shoulder
forward swing (see Note 7, p. 284). Child stands on a
small platform modeled after Harmon's walking rail
(Game 18). Note parquetry blocks on child's hands.

## Bimanual Circles on Chalkboard[7] / Game 17

The child stands facing a chalkboard and holds a large piece of chalk in each fist. He places the chalk against the board and simultaneously moves both arms in rhythmic circular movements. In this manner circles are drawn on the chalkboard. See Figure 5.

The goal of this game is to move both arms upon command in a synchronized, purposeful direction. Many first and second graders have difficulty controlling and directing the circular movements of both arms simultaneously. The child with adequate bilateral coordination will be able to change direction or interrupt movement of one arm or drop one arm to the side continuing the same circular movement off the board while circling on the board with the other hand. In all of these movements, rhythm should be maintained.

As a variation of this technique, the child holds two erasers or two synthetic brick-shaped sponges against a chalkboard. He is directed to rotate his arms while keeping his fingers pointed toward the ceiling. Placing a parquetry block on top of the eraser teaches the child to move from the shoulder (using the whole arm) and not from the wrist. If the child has inadequate control of his hand or arm position, the eraser will tilt and the block will fall. This prevents low-level thinking and promotes high-level thinking of shoulder, arm, wrist, and hand movement.

Bimanual circles is played individually, but several children can be playing at any given time. In the last variation, competition can be encouraged: How long can the child continue making the bimanual circles without the parquetry block falling off the eraser?

## THINKING GAMES OF BODY BALANCE

In a classroom the child with poor balance presents a problem to himself and others. The four thinking games described in this section help the child to develop a sense of body balance: He becomes sensitive to the force of gravity and avoids situations where he can no longer compensate for it; in short, he intelligently makes use of gravity to stabilize and increase efficiency of his body movements.

The child, while sitting or standing, should know how to balance in four directions: forward-backward, side-to-side, rotational or spinning, and diagonal. In order to move with a minimum of stress, he must know how to switch from a static state (stationary position) to a dynamic state (moving position). The more efficiently a child can stop and start, the less stress he experiences in any movement activity. In addition, he must know how to change direction and speed of body movement when he is in a dynamic state. For example, a well-developed child walks or runs effortlessly not only in a straight line but also around a corner.

Research has shown that the entire body is affected by the interrelation of body parts and of information received by the senses. Posture and vision are interrelated; if a child shows stress when performing a near-point vision activity such as reading, this stress may be alleviated by wearing of simple "plus lenses."[8]

The major general movements in balance activities involve the coordination of the movement of the head with the rest of the body. To achieve this coordination, the neck acts as a message center which correlates and integrates messages coming from the head, predominantly the eyes and the ears, with the rest of the body and vice versa. When one is standing or sitting, inputs are sent upward from the feet or the buttocks to the muscles of the neck and downward from the labyrinth (inner ear) and the eyes to the neck muscles. The neck muscles collect and collate these inputs to allow the body to achieve proper gravitational compensation or balance.

If the child has not achieved balance, he may have difficulty orienting himself in space and may continually need to readjust his postural set. This constant readjustment is stressful and lowers his efficiency in the classroom situation. In addition, a child with a balance malfunction tends to develop functional and structural warps such as vision problems, skeletal malformations, behavioral maladaptions, and even dental malfunctions.[9]

In short, the better a child reacts and counterreacts to gravity, the better is his balance. The better he balances, the more efficient is his movement. Good balance provides the foundation for efficient movement with a minimum of stress to the child.

## Walking Rail / Game 18

Extensive discussion of the walking rail in the literature has made it a symbol of the movement thinking game concept. Actually there are two different types of walking rails. One rail, a two-by-four is designed for use on either the four-inch side or the two-inch side (Figure 6). The other, the Harmon slanted walking

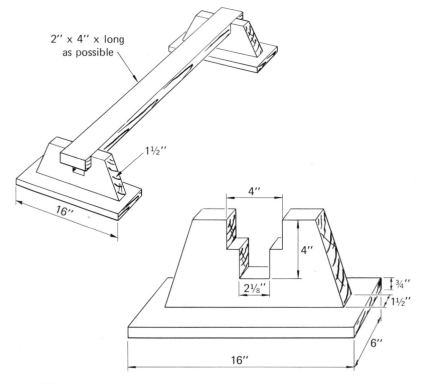

**Figure 6.**
**The Two-by-Four Walking Rail**

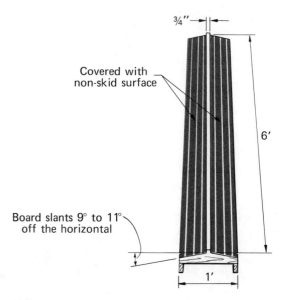

3/4"

Covered with
non-skid surface

6'

Board slants 9° to 11°
off the horizontal

1'

**Figure 7.**
**The Harmon Walking Rail**

rail,[10] slants like an inverted "V" with the apex at the center of the board (Figure 7). As the child walks on the sloped sides, the slight angle shifts the weight of the body to the outer edge of the soles of the feet. This brings the body into alignment. Walking back and forth on the Harmon slant rail with the child's central vision directed toward a specific target and his peripheral vision made aware of the surroundings, develops the child's control of his posture. A child with efficient postural control is in a favorable position to manage the stress of any contained activity such as reading. The clinical differences between the two walking rails are these: The two-by-four develops integration of vision input with knowledge of how to control placement of the feet to maintain vertical balance in a spatially limited off-the-floor activity. The Harmon slant rail does not specifically present an antigravity problem; its value is to promote integration of visual input with

**Figure 8.**
**Two-by-Four and Harmon Walking Rails**
The boy walking the two-by-four rail on the left is balancing a bean bag on the back of each hand to provide an occasion for high-level general movement thinking. Note his visual concentration on a straight-ahead target. The two girls on the right are walking on the Harmon slant rail. They are balancing objects on their heads to raise the task to a higher level of general movement thinking.

**Figure 9.**
**A Sequence Task with Walking Rails**
The boy in the center is walking on the Harmon slant rail. The boy
on the left is walking sideways along the two-by-four; the girl
is about to navigate a right-angle turn; the boy
on the right is walking forward along the two-by-four.

general movement thinking by forcing (through its slanted surfaces) proper skeletal alignment in any visually directed bilateral activity.

One suggested activity is for the child to balance on the two-by-four rail and choose a fixation point in front of him. Then with arms stretched out sideways, he proceeds to walk slowly and deliberately along the length of the rail—forward, backward, sideways, first on the four-inch side, then on the two-inch side. Sometimes a yardstick held in both hands provides a good visual reference for the horizontal plane. See Figure 8.

Another activity is for the children to move from rail to rail in a prescribed sequence (Figure 9). From the Harmon slant rail, the boy will next move to the two-by-four now on his left (upper right in the picture). The boy on the far left will proceed to the Harmon rail. The girl will walk sideways as she steps onto the rail at the far left in the picture, and the boy on the right will proceed forward to the corner and then duplicate her action. This playing in a sequence is helpful for social thinking as well as concentration: The leader (sometimes a teacher, sometimes a child) will occasionally give the command for the children to reverse their direction. This then becomes a transformation task of general movement thinking. Note the straight-ahead visual concentration of each child.

More complicated procedures may be introduced: stepping over obstacles; balancing things on head or hands; bouncing, throwing, or catching balls. In these, like in all spatial positioning activities, peripheral visual awareness plays a major role. In order to increase peripheral awareness walking rail games and the following balance board games can be played while wearing semi-blacked-out eyeglasses. See Figure 10. Wearing these glasses while traversing the two-by-four sets the occasion for high-level thinking to match an awareness of body balance and movement with peripheral vision. This opens up the child's visual awareness of the world around him and develops efficiency of movement within his expanded visual space world. He develops more knowledge of where he is and how to get where he wants to go with minimum stress and maximum efficiency.

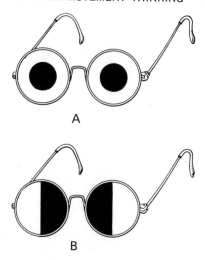

**Figure 10.**
**Semi-Blacked Out Eyeglasses**
The upper figure (A) has the centers of the glasses
blacked out with an opaque material. The child looks
straight ahead, but can see only his peripheral field
above, below, nasal, and temporal. His forward field is
blocked from view. In the lower figure (B) the entire
nasal section of each glass is covered and the child can
see only the temporal field on each side, while his forward field is half-covered, half-exposed.

## Balance Board / Game 19

This game requires a balance board. There are several varieties.
The model illustrated in Figure 11 is easy for the child to control,
and it makes the teacher's analysis of the child's actions easy.

This game can also be used as a lateral coordination thinking game. If the child has difficulty, the teacher should keep in
mind that both balance and laterality are here involved. (See the
following section on coordination of the body's axes.) In fact,
as movement thinking activities grow in complexity, the components of general movements become increasingly difficult to
isolate.

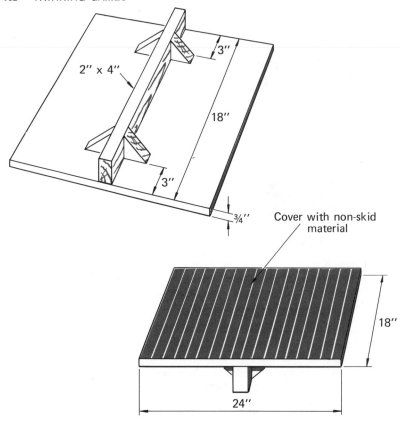

**Figure 11.**
**Diagram of a Balance Board**

Movement thinking activities on the balance board can be described in three stages. (1) The child stands with both feet near the edge of one side of the board and parallel to the fulcrum. The teacher should instruct the child to look at a fixed point in space; the child's arms should be held out at shoulder level. When the teacher exerts pressure on the other side of the board, the child is set off balance and must sustain an upright position by shifting his weight. Thus he develops *side balance* (Figure 12).

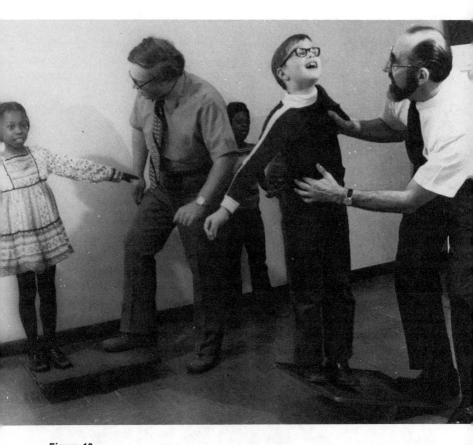

**Figure 12.**
**Side Balance**
Note that the child leads away from the fulcrum to maintain balance.
The boy on the right also maintains visual concentration
on a straight-ahead fixation target.

Figure 13.
Front-Back Balance on Balance Board

**Figure 14.**
**Bilateral Balance on Balance Board**
The girl on the left is balancing a brick-shaped sponge
on the back of each hand, and the boy on the right is playing catch-ball,
while each attempts to balance his board.

(2) The child stands near the edge of one side of the board with both feet perpendicular to the fulcrum. Pressure on the other edge of the board now sets the child off balance in a front to back direction, and he must compensate by shifting his weight either forward or backward. Thus he develops *front-back balance* (Figure 13).

(3) Once the child knows side balance and front-back balance, he is ready to master *bilateral balance.* The child straddles the center support of the balance board by placing one foot on the right half of the board and the other foot on the left half; thus he assumes a seesaw position with the center support acting as the fulcrum of the seesaw. It is important that the teacher instruct the child to look at a point in space ten to twelve feet in front of himself; there should be natural vertical and horizontal lines which the child can use as reference points. In his first effort, the child usually tips the board to one side or the other. He must counteract this tip by pushing downward on the other side of the balance board. He rocks from side to side until he successfully matches gravitational pull with an equal distribution of his body weight; the board should stabilize in a level and balanced position (Figure 14).

After the child knows how to maintain the board in a stable, balanced position, he may develop higher-level control by throwing or catching balls or bean bags while maintaining his balance. Other advanced activities which can be performed while balancing include winding a windlass, placing the feet in various positions on the board, and balancing objects on head or hands. A resourceful teacher will think of many more activities.

### Trampoline / Game 20

A child-sized trampoline was used to help the children develop an awareness of balance. In this activity, the teacher was always with the child. The goals were to stand, walk, jump up and down on both feet, fall into a sitting position and jump back onto the feet, and finally play jumping-jacks on the trampoline surface. All the children enjoyed the game, and it was especially useful for those with disorganized movement thinking.

## Push Me Over / Game 21

This game must be played on a carpeted floor. One child lies on his side while another child pushes against him trying to roll him over. The first child, without using his hands, attempts to resist. After showing that he can keep his balance in this manner, the child sits tailor-fashion while others attempt to push him over. In another form of the game, the child kneels, then assumes a creeping position on all fours, then balances on his hands and feet with his knees lifted; all the while others try to push him over. The final refinement is the game of chicken-fight, played by two or more children holding their arms crossed in front of them while they hop back and forth, each attempting to upset the other or to push the other beyond a certain barrier. All push me over games may be played by two or more children.

## THINKING GAMES OF COORDINATED ACTION

The coordinated action component of movement development is a rather early development in the child but it never reaches completion—even in adult life. We are constantly striving to perfect agility in activities such as golf, swimming, skiing, tennis, bowling, knitting, and playing musical instruments.

In this phase of coordinated body movement, the child incorporates all components of general movement thinking. He develops knowledge of how to sequence his movements, how to classify his movements, and how to judge space and its relation to him through vision and sound matching. At the level of coordinated action, the various components described in this chapter are combined. The child eventually moves freely, with minimum thought to the choice of body part and its movement. He concentrates instead on the sequence and direction of movements and the amount of effort to exert. Classroom activities of coordinated action include creeping, rhythm walking, hopping, skipping, jumping rope, throwing, catching, and kicking, some of which have already been described.

A few of the coordinated activities that incorporate these movements in a variety of ways and at complex levels include dodgeball, relay races, and running obstacle courses. All coordinated activity games have a common goal of varying the child's movement thinking and helping him to acquire the knowledge that there are several ways to solve a movement problem. The child should be able to modify his performance according to new demands and apply what he has acquired in one area to another.

## Hopping / Game 22

Hopping may be either an individual or a group game. When played in groups, the teacher or group leader issues position commands, "Right foot," "Left foot," "Both feet," and so on. The children hop on command. The directional commands "Forward," "Backward," "Sideways" are also used. "Freeze," meaning that the children should stop, listen, and not move, talk or fidget, is a command issued throughout these activities.

Acquiring good balance on each foot should precede hopping games, but if a child is able to hop before he can balance well, he should not be excluded from hopping games. Each activity will help in the acquisition of the other.

For good one-foot hopping the child is encouraged to position his raised foot behind, not in front of, himself. He should bend his arms at the elbow and clench his fists. Short hops, not long awkward jumps, are encouraged. The child is told to swing his arms forward and use the upper part of his body to assist him in his thrust for locomotion. When hopping on both feet, the children are told to try to raise both feet at the same time and have both feet land on the floor at the same time in short hops, not long jumps. The goal is smooth, consistent movement with rapid response to a change in hopping position or hopping direction or both. Both one foot and two feet hopping can be in place as well as moving forward, backward, and sideways. Gaining control of the self in a dynamic activity such as this will promote self-control in a contained classroom learning activity.

### Skipping / Game 23

The development of good general movement thinking enabled the children to learn readily to skip in the hop-*slide* fashion. Teaching a child to skip by the hop-*step* approach is to be avoided. Skipping is not a hop-step action; it is rather a forward locomotion of consistent alternating hop-slide movements. There should be no stop or hesitation. The arms should be thrust forward across the chest, and the knees should be raised forward as high as possible, with the upper trunk bent slightly forward. Speed and smoothness of motion is the goal. Skipping lends itself well to relay races, action games, and musical games. Like hopping, skipping develops control of dynamic movement and promotes self-control in contained minimum movement classroom activities.

### Jump Rope / Game 24

Commercial jump ropes are available with wooden handles attached in such a way as to permit the rope to swing freely and not twist. This coordinated action game can be divided into gradual steps.

For the beginner, the rope is dragged across the floor toward the child, who must think through the concept of jumping at the proper moment—the moment when the rope approaches his feet. In the second phase, the rope is slowly arched in movement over the child's head and then dragged across the floor. Timing and peripheral vision are thus added to his movement thinking. Gradually the tempo of the rope swing is increased until the child can match his jumping movement to the rhythmic movement of the rope. At this point, the child is ready to hold the rope himself and match his arm and leg movements in an increasingly faster rhythmic pattern—first forward, later backward.

This is an individual or group activity which may be incorporated into relay races.

At the Tyler Thinking School at least one specific period each day was devoted to general movement thinking games; in addition, many movement thinking activities were interspersed throughout the daily activities. For most observers it would seem an unusual situation to see a child jumping on a trampoline in the middle of a classroom without distracting other students engaged in sit-down activities. However, the children's involvement with high-level thinking activities provided enough interest and fun for them that they paid little heed to other children engaged in more physical activities.

The thinking games were all sequenced activities. The teacher was skilled in presenting the game to the group and in adapting the level of successful accomplishment to each child and his needs. This is the key to all thinking games: The teacher should present the material just a little above the child's level of accomplishment but still within his level of success; the teacher should challenge the child's creative thought without stifling his desire to succeed. Constructive suggestions should be made; the child should never be downgraded. Honest praise of his efforts encourages the child to realize that movement, thinking, and learning are all related. As Newell Kephart[11] said, "The child must learn to move, before he can move to learn!"

# 7. Discriminative Movement Thinking

While general movements are concerned with activities of transportation and body position, discriminative movements are particular manipulatory skills—skills necessary for success in academic and vocational situations. The subsystems of eye movement, lip-tongue movement, and finger movement are discussed in this chapter as discriminative skill movements. As in Chapter 6, we focus on these movements not as physical exercises but as integral to the growth and development of the thinking child.

Discriminative movement thinking always involves multiple inputs, and unless these inputs are properly integrated, the child will experience stress from what is referred to as "noise on the circuit." It is easy to understand that if a person has a vision control problem, it would be difficult for him to follow a line of print or to change his eye fixation from far to near. Similarly, improper pencil gripping can cause stress and fatigue when writing or lack of control when attempting to reproduce a visual design. Lack of tongue control can cause an articulation problem. While each of these problems does not in itself cause an academic problem, inadequate discriminative movement control will render the child less efficient; he will expend excessive energy on the "how" of the task at the expense of the solution of the task. The thirty-six discriminative movement games described in this chapter should improve the efficiency of the subsystems of eye, lip-tongue, and fingers so that these subsystems will enhance rather than interfere with the child's performance. The components of reflexive control, mental map, coordination of the body's axes, and coordinated action which were previously described in Chapter 6 apply to discriminative movement thinking as well.

Certain discriminative movement patterns are common to all three subsystems of eye, tongue, and finger. One can track an object with the eye as the object moves across the visual field; one can track with the tongue along the teeth or lips; one can track with the finger. An object is "picked up" with the eyes in order to see it and with the fingers in order to manipulate it; the infant picks up an object with the mouth in order to study it with lips and tongue. These common movement patterns of tracking and picking up serve different functions depending on the subsystem used: eyes for guiding or locating, tongue for speaking or for controlling of breath, hands for grasping or writing. Discriminative movements are initiated by interdependent subsystems of a single organism, the human being. It is conceivable that improvement of movement control in one area could contribute to improvement of movement control in another area.

A cycle common to all three subsystems is that of "reach-grasp-hold-release." The teacher must be aware of the child's control of this cycle, for proper control allows the child to let go when a task is too demanding and move to the next task with ease. In *reach*, the child establishes where an object is and moves in space toward it. In *grasp*, the child encircles and grasps that object. In *hold*, the child sustains his grasp of the object. In *release*, the child deliberately lets go of the object; he is thus able to start the cycle once again. If the child is unable to perform the cycle, stress may develop.

The subsystems of general or discriminative movement do not operate as a machine, in which each subsystem has its own individual motor. There is really only one "motor" and this is the thinking person. We can concentrate on a single subsystem, but the goal, as with all thinking games, must be the development of the total functioning person who uses all subsystems. The purpose of all the games is not to train one subsystem, but to develop the thinking person.

## EYE MOVEMENT-THINKING GAMES

Each child in the Tyler Thinking School was screened for possible vision defects by a method which picks up defects not ordinarily found when the standard school-screening eye tests are used. This inexpensive and easy to administer test was designed by one of the authors (see Chapter 8, note 1 where the test is described). Several children were discovered to have vision problems, and we referred them for more comprehensive vision care.

Visual thinking plays a prominent role in the thinking of sighted children; its successful accomplishment depends in part on the child's control of his discriminative eye movements. Merely fixating on an object as it crosses the visual field does not necessarily imply efficient and purposeful control of all eye movement. The following twenty-two games have been devised to maximize this control. The games have been divided into five categories according to types of eye movement: focus, mental map, tracking, jump fixation, convergence. The games can be further subdivided into (1) those games where the child's hand is passively moved and his eyes follow his hand movements; (2) those games where the object moves and the child's eyes tell his hand where to move to track the object; and (3) those games where the object moves and the child fixates on it without the use of his hands.

## FOCUS MOVEMENT GAMES

Man is not naturally a near-point animal; for many centuries, his sight was directed toward the distant rather than the near. Modern man does, however, do a disproportionate amount of near-point work; he is increasingly plagued with vision problems resulting from eye strain. A recent study of a group of Eskimo children is typical and enlightening.[1] When entering the first grade of a recently built, traditional school, these children had no myopic vision problems, and there were no myopic vision problems in their family histories for several generations. By the end of their first year in school, 20 per cent of the children had developed problems with nearsightedness; by the end of the sixth year, the percentage had increased to 60. This illustrates the impact of the many demands placed on a child's vision when he is in an academic situation. The two games described in this chapter should increase the child's ability to focus from a near point to a far and from a far point to a near with a minimum of strain. The child is thus enabled, for example, to look from the chalkboard to the paper on his desk and back again without straining.

## See Me Clear / Game 25

The child should be encouraged to focus alternately on a target held close to his eyes and then on a target across the room from him. The target can be letters, numbers, geometric shapes, or a group of dots.

There are many possible variations; in all of them, the child follows the same procedure, rapidly shifting focus from a near target to a far and vice versa. He may focus with either eye covered or with both eyes viewing the target in binocular fashion. In another variation, a piece of paper partitioning the two fields (a *septum*) is taped from the child's forehead to the center of his nose. He is then asked to look at an object slightly to the side. The teacher asks the child, "How many eyes are you seeing it with?" The child often imagines that he is seeing with two eyes but by having him close alternate eyes the teacher enables him to discover that he is seeing only with the eye on the side where the object is located.

## Trombone / Game 26

In this game, a *septum* is taped from the child's forehead to the center of his nose. Using only one of his eyes, but with both eyes open, the child is asked to focus on a piece of paper covered with small print which he moves toward and away from his eye in "trombone" fashion. The object is for the child to attempt to see the letters clearly as he moves the paper back and forth. The child should attempt to keep the printed letters in focus at a point nearer and nearer to his eye.

### MENTAL MAP OF EYE MOVEMENT GAMES

The four games in this category are fundamental in that they develop knowledge of "Where are my eyes?" and "Can I make them move where I want them to move?" The child directs his eyes to move toward each of nine spatial areas, and he does this without accompanying movements of head or body:

| | | |
|---|---|---|
| Up and left | Up | Up and right |
| Left | Straight | Right |
| Down and left | Down | Down and right |

## Open Eye Stretch / Game 27

The children may either stand or sit in a circle; they should be relaxed but erect, looking straight ahead with their eyes open. They are instructed to move their eyes, not their heads, to the extreme right and to hold them there for a count of ten. They are to be careful to keep their heads from turning—even slightly. Then they are to move their eyes to the left, up, down, and so on. "Move your eyes to this side. Try to stretch your eyes over there. Pull them hard." (Young children initially confuse the verbal labels "right" and "left.")

## Closed Eye Movements / Game 28

In this variation of open eye stretch (Game 27) the child performs the same eye movements but with his eyes closed. (Performing these movements in a dark room with the eyes open is not the same.) After having the child do "right, left, up, down, and diagonal," the teacher should add clockwise and counterclockwise movement.

## Crossing the Eyes / Game 29

Control in crossing one's eyes is beneficial, not detrimental, to the eye movement. The child should acquire the ability how to cross and uncross his eyes when they are both open and closed.

## Head Swing / Game 30

In the previously described games, the child moved his eyes as he held his head still. Now he attempts to hold his eyes still as he moves his head. While he sits or stands, erect but relaxed, his eyes remain fixed on an object somewhere in the room. He moves his head from side to side as though gesturing "No"; then he moves his head up and down as though gesturing "Yes"; then he moves his head diagonally; and finally in clockwise and counterclockwise rotations. While the head is moving, the eyes should remain fixed on the specified object.

## OCULAR TRACKING GAMES

In *ocular tracking*, the eyes are fixed on an object which moves. We describe nine of the many possible games that develop ocular movement tracking. We hope to give the teacher an idea of what he might do to help the child develop ocular fixation control. In reviewing each of the games, the reader will realize that some games employ "targets" to show the child where to move his eyes while in others such as flashlight fight (Game 35) and follow the bug (Game 38), the child creates his own targets. These games develop the purposeful eye movement control which is necessary to reduce stress and improve the child's visual efficiency.

## Keep Looking at Me / Game 31

This reflexive activity is suitable for the child who lacks adequate control of his eye movements. In this game, the hand leads the eyes. The teacher holds the child's hand, his index finger against the child's index finger. While the teacher moves the child's hand, the child fixes his gaze on his own finger. (If a finger puppet is used or a face is drawn on the child's fingernail, his interest in the game may be increased.)

When the child has mastered this technique, he is ready for a more complex variation played between two children. One child moves an object which he holds in his hand; the second child tries to put his finger on the object or through a hole in it.[2] Here the eyes lead and the hand follows.

## Swinging Ball / Game 32

A solid rubber ball, about four inches in diameter, with various shapes or letters printed on it,[3] is suspended from the ceiling.

Maintaining equilibrium, the child stands, sits, or lies on the floor and watches the ball as it swings. He may "track" it with the eyes only, with the eyes and hands, or by any other technique which he or the teacher may devise. He can "center" the ball by looking through a wire loop held in front of himself. He can follow its swings with his hands or a flashlight. He can allow it to swing above his head as his eyes follow its movement. As the letters on the ball appear in his view, he can search for and identify the letters spelling his name. He may also lie on his back under the ball and follow it as it swings above him.

In another variation[4] the child dangles the ball by holding one end of a string attached to the ball in his teeth; he makes the ball swing freely by moving his head not his hands. He then observes the ball and—while swinging it—tries to avoid objects, or strike them, with the ball.

### Follow the Wheel / Game 33

A geared-down turntable is necessary for this game. Various small objects are placed on it. Using only his eyes, the child follows one target which is moving on the turntable disk. In another variation, containers are attached to the disk; the child is instructed to drop specified objects into them.

Still another variation pictured in Figure 15 is used to train the eyes to converge. The turntable disk is slanted sideways and an object is attached to the outer edge. When the disk rotates, the child observes the object as it moves toward and away from him.

### Moving Movies / Game 34

In this game[5] slides, movies, or film strips are projected, not onto a stationary screen, but onto a revolving mirror which reflects the image around the room. Many types of images may be projected—for example, movies, or a simple maze which the children must solve, or a picture puzzle in which the children must find hidden objects.

**Figure 15.**
**Convergence Rotations with Rotor**
The child is fixating the small ball
as the wheel rotates (Game 33).

Motivation may be increased by dividing the children into teams and giving points to each team for its proper answers. We encouraged group rather than individual competition. Thus the child identified with his group, and even if his team lost, he did not consider himself a personal failure.

The teacher should be able to spot those children having trouble with "tracking" and work with them individually at a later time.

### Flashlight Fight / Game 35

The children are divided into teams; one team is given a red flashlight, the other a green. They "duel" by flashing the light beams on the wall—one attempting to "catch" the other.

In a variation, a circle can be drawn on the chalkboard. The children shine their flashlight beams within it. One player can try to sneak his flashlight beam out of the circle while another tries to "trap" him by superimposing his own flashlight beam on the other child's before it crosses the boundary of the circle. The child who manages to get out of the circle without his light being touched by another light is the one who scores.

### Cookie Sheet Eye Tracking / Game 36

For this game a handle should be attached to one of the long sides of a shiny cookie sheet. Some sort of revolving disk—such as a turntable—should be attached to the wall at the child's eye level. The child holds the cookie sheet in front of him so that one short end bisects his face and the other short end bisects his view of the slowly revolving disk. Thus, as is shown in Figure 16, he can see one half of the revolving disk with his right eye and the other half with his left.

In the simplest variation, the child's eyes track a target on the disk as it revolves from his right field of vision to his left and vice versa. A more advanced technique is for the child to track the reflection of the moving target on the cookie sheet. Whichever technique is used, the child should be constantly and simultaneously aware of both the real and the reflected images.

**Figure 16.**
**Eyetracking with Cookie Sheet and Rotor**
The child is fixating the series of small circles at the edge of
the rotor target as the target rotates clockwise or counterclockwise.

## Marble Tracking / Game 37

The child follows a marble with his eyes as it rolls around in a shallow pan held horizontally at eye level. The game can be played by one or two children. When two children are playing, one child manipulates the pan and both children observe the rotating marble.

## Follow the Bug / Game 38

It is possible to track a stationary object by having the eyes trace around its edge. In this game, the child tracks an imaginary bug along the ceiling-wall border, down the corner, across the floor-wall border, and so on. When the teacher commands, the "bug" stops, rests, reverses its path, or changes direction.

## String Tracking / Game 39

All one needs for this game is a white shoelace. The child holds one end in one hand and the other end in the other hand. He positions one hand at the tip of his nose and the other hand directly in front of his nose with the shoelace fully extended. The child should fix both eyes on the far end of the shoelace. He should see a "V" coming to a point at the far end of the shoelace. The "line" he sees on the left will come from his right eye, the "line" on the right from his left eye. This double image is caused by a rather complicated process called *physiological diplopia*.

The child should move the shoelace slowly from right to left, up and down, diagonally, clockwise, and counterclockwise. Proper results are obtained when the shoelace can be moved smoothly and at moderate speed with no part of the shoelace disappearing and the point of the "V" remaining at the end of the shoelace.

Should one of the sides of the "V" disappear, it will mean that the respective eye is not functioning as it should; for example, if all or part of the left side of the "V" disappears, the right eye is not functioning all of the time. Conversely, if all or part of the right side of the "V" disappears, the left eye is not functioning at all times. Intersection of the lines before the hand furthest from the nose or no intersection at all would indicate inadequate eye movement control. A word of caution is in order: If the shoe-lace is held too far to one side, one of the sides of the "V" may be totally or partially obscured by the nose.

## OCULAR JUMP FIXATION GAMES

In ocular jump fixation or *saccadics*, the eyes jump from stationary object to stationary object. Saccadics is the ability of the individual to direct his eyes so that they can jump from point to point smoothly and efficiently with stops at the proper times and without overshooting or undershooting a specific point in space. In saccadics the observed objects are always stationary, whereas, in ocular tracking, the objects are generally moving. The sequential development in saccadics games is much the same as in games of ocular tracking. We have selected five to be described in this section from the large number of saccadics games available.

## Hands Leading Eyes / Game 40

Often the child's own hands are used to help him know where and how far to move his eyes. To have a *saccadic situation* where the hand is "pulling" the eye, the child puts his hands on separate objects, each of which lights up, buzzes, vibrates, or in some manner stimulates the hand so that the hand can "tell" the eye where to look.

In one variation, the clue that tells the child where to look is the wiggling of one of his fingers by the teacher. The child is to fix his eyes on the finger being wiggled. The teacher may wiggle fingers on either hand or hold the hands in different positions in space. Rhythmic tongue clicking by the teacher synchronized with the wiggling of the finger will help the child to begin to integrate hearing with seeing.

## Eyes Leading Hands Games

In these games, the child fixes his eyes on a series of objects while directing his hands toward them. This matching of eye and hand movement provides maximum feedback to develop fixation accuracy.

## Chalkboard Fixation / Game 41

In chalkboard fixation, numbers are written on the chalkboard in random or sequential order. If the child is too young to understand numbers, pictures may be used instead. The child is directed to fixate his eyes on a figure on the board; he then points to it. For example, the teacher could initiate a search process by saying, "Find number two, point to number two; find number six, point to number six; find number ten. . . ." Various rhythm patterns can be introduced by having the child synchronize his pointing to the beat of a metronome.

## Flashlight Tag / Game 42

In this game the teacher indicates or places various targets around the room. For example, he could name as targets specific children in the room, pictures on the walls, or signs on the walls and chalkboards. He then directs the children to jump their flashlight beams from target to target in a designated sequence.

## Look and Touch / Game 43

Numbers, shapes, or similar targets are arranged to form a circle on the top of a table. Duplicate targets are placed opposite each other, for example, as shown in Figure 17, the number "1" at both north and south. In time to the beat of a metronome (tempo can be varied), the child alternately touches the duplicate targets with his index finger; finger and eyes are to arrive at the target simultaneously.

**Figure 17.**
**Eye Saccadics in Look and Touch Game**

The children can work together, one performing, the other observing. Our experience at the Tyler Thinking School has proved that even first grade children can successfully and happily team up this way to help each other.

## Catch My Thumb / Game 44

This game is played by two children, the first thrusting his thumb upward and within reach of the second child. The second child has to catch the first child's thumb while the first child attempts to tuck away his exposed thumb and thrust his other thumb up for the second child to catch. The children switch roles when a thumb is caught or when the teacher directs.

The interaction in this game, like that in the other paired games, had an interesting by-product at Tyler. The children learned responsibility as leaders, tolerance of each other's strengths and weaknesses, and patience to await their turns.

### OCULAR CONVERGENCE GAMES

In *ocular convergence,* the eyes move toward and away from each other as an object is moved toward and away from the child. This type of eye movement plays an important role in the academic functioning of the child—for example, in tasks such as copying a printed paragraph or transfering graphic material from chalkboard to paper and vice versa. In the act of changing fixation between far and near, two visual mechanisms are involved: the focusing of the eyes and the convergence of the eyes. Both mechanisms must function simultaneously. Ocular focusing means adjusting the optical power of the eye to accommodate to the distance of an object. Ocular convergence means adjusting the position of the two eyeballs to the relative distance of the object of regard so that both eyes point to that object. We describe three of the many games which may be used to develop ocular convergence.

## String Cross / Game 45

A white shoelace is used in this game as in string tracking (Game 37). One end of the shoelace is inserted through a small hole in a square of black cardboard or through a large colored button. Holding the cardboard in the far hand and the end of the shoelace in the near hand, the child positions one hand at the tip of his nose and the other hand directly in front of him. The child directs his eyes to the point where the shoelace goes through the hole in the cardboard. He should see a "V" coming to a point at the far end of the shoelace. He slowly moves the cardboard toward his eyes and away from his eyes. The aim of the game is for the child to continue seeing the image of the "V" as he moves the cardboard toward and away from himself. The point of the "V" should remain where the shoelace passes through the hole in the cardboard.

Inexpensive red-green goggles add interest and tell the child where he is actually fixing his eye. The goggles have a red filter for one eye and a green for the other; the child should be able to observe the image of a red string coming from his "green eye" and the image of a green string coming from his "red eye." These "strings" intersect at the actual point where the child's eyes converge.

Follow the bug (Game 36) can be incorporated with string cross to form an interesting variation. The child holds one end of the shoelace in each hand, positioning one hand before his nose and the other in front of it. He then moves the far hand to one of the nine positions described in this chapter under "Mental Map of Eye Movement Games." Holding the shoelace stationary, the child is to imagine a bug crawling along it. As the child chooses, the "bug" stops, moves forward, moves backward, and so on. The goal is to control eye fixation at any point along the string. His string images should form an "X" at the point where his eyes are fixated—unless, of course, he fixates on the very end of the string, in which case, he will see a "V." To help the child become more aware of the shoelace doubling, it may be marked at intervals with black ink, or small objects such as buttons may be placed along it.

String cross does not lend itself to objective evaluation, for the teacher can rely only on the child's verbal response. In addition, some first graders have difficulty understanding and following the rules. The game is, nevertheless, valuable for developing the child's control of his own eye movement.

### Far and Near Eye Jumps / Game 46

This is a game which helps to develop "far to near" and "near to far" eye fixations. A flexible four-to-five-foot rope such as string, cord, white shoelaces, or nylon or plastic clothes lines is required. The rope is marked at intervals with knots, buttons, small clothes pins, or ink. The child is instructed to look from marker to marker in various sequences; for example, he may be told to look from the nearest marker to the farthest, or from the second mark to the fourth.

A variation similar to string tracking (Game 37) is that the child looks at a point on the rope and attempts to see both sides of a "V" converging at this point. Another variation similar to follow the bug (Game 36) is where the imaginary bug would be moving on the rope, toward and away from the child.

Pegs and a small pegboard are used in another variation. Three pegs are placed diagonally from corner to corner of the pegboard as illustrated in Figure 18. The child holds the pegboard at eye level and sights along the line of pegs. He is to change fixation by jumping his eyes from peg to peg—far to near and back again. The child is usually fascinated because the pegs he has *not* fixated will seem to be double. This doubling image is the result of the process previously defined as physiological diplopia. While one child plays, another child may observe the positions of his eyes while expressing commands like "Closest, furthest, middle, closest." In this situation, both children are active. Rhythmic convergence movements may be introduced by having the child fixate his eyes to accompany the beat of a metronome.

Figure 18.
Convergence Saccadics with Pegboard

## DIGITAL MOVEMENT THINKING GAMES

At the end of the school year all children had developed proper pencil grasp. Through the activities at school, they were made aware of their fingers and finger movements, and they could apply this knowledge to the task of holding a pencil without ever being specifically taught to do so.

Fingers are the body's tools for work, play, and nonverbal communication; it is important that the child knows how to control them accurately and efficiently. When the child has inadequate handwriting or drawing skills, the teacher should try to determine the root problem. It could be that the child does not take time to write neatly; it could be that he has not yet mastered hand or finger movement. If the child has not yet mastered this type of discriminative skill movement, mere drilling in writing or drawing will not be sufficient. The child would probably benefit more from playing the hand-finger discriminative movement thinking games that follow.

### Paper Tearing / Game 47

A broad line is drawn on a piece of unlined paper. While holding the paper in the air, the child tears along the line using his thumbs and forefingers assisted by a rotating movement of his wrists. The child should not rip the paper; rather, he should tear it along the line. When the child has mastered the technique of tearing in a straight line, he can tear angles, curves, and various combinations.

The teachers at Tyler devised an adaptation of this game. They drew columns on the chalkboard designating specific patterns to be torn from paper. A three-inch-square piece of paper with one of these patterns drawn on it was given to each child. When the child had finished tearing the pattern, he would show the results to the teacher. If he had torn the pattern correctly, he would write his name in the appropriate column on the chalkboard. The teacher would then give him another pattern to tear.

Using this technique, the teacher adjusted the assignments to the child's need; she gave him easier or harder patterns to tear and discussed the results with him.

## Folding Paper / Game 48

Whenever demarcations are required, the children should be told to fold their paper rather than to draw a line down the page. They should also be encouraged to use the fore-finger and opposing thumb when folding paper. Origami paper games are of interest and develop this ability.

## Mental Map of Fingers / Game 49

Some of the children had little or no knowledge of mental map of fingers. Activities that help children to learn placement and control of their fingers include working with clay, finding things buried in the sand, and working with finger paints.

A picture can be drawn with food coloring on the child's hand with his fingers used as a specific part of the picture. If the picture is of a turkey, the fingers can serve as the turkey's tail feathers. When the child wiggles his fingers, the feathers will move. A little ingenuity will produce many such designs.[6] Finger puppets will also help the child to know his fingers and how to control them specifically.

In another variation, the child and teacher face each other across a table and place their hands, palms down, on the table. The teacher directs the child, "Follow me" and then taps his fingers on the table alternating with fingers on one or both of his hands. The child may give an immediate imitative response, or he may wait until the teacher stops and then perform the same tapping movements in the same sequence. The teacher may also direct the child to tap by pointing to specific fingers on the child's hands. Another variation calls for the child's fingernails to be colored with water paint; he is then asked to point certain fingers or to match fingers to corresponding color spots on paper.

In a still more complex variation, pictured in Figure 19 the

Figure 19.
A Cross-handed Game of Mental Map of Fingers

**Figure 20.**
**Finger-String Play**
A string game of Cat's Cradle involving two children
to promote teach play and interdependence.

child is asked to extend his arms so that the palms of his hands point in opposite directions; he then crosses his arms and clasps his hands palm to palm intertwining his fingers. Keeping his fingers clasped, he rotates his arms down, toward himself, and up—thus bringing his clasped hands to a position in front of himself with his fingers pointing up. While the child is in this position, the teacher points to but does not touch one of his fingers. The child moves what he thinks is the correct finger. The crossed reference—left hand on the body's right side and right hand on the left—encourages concentration and further develops mental map of fingers.

### Finger-String Play / Game 50

Many books[7] are available which describe games children may play with string. Cat's Cradle shown in Figure 20 is one well-known game.

### Pincher / Game 51

Games in this category are played to develop refined thumb and index finger control. The child discovers where his fingers are and how to use them in precise movements. For example, with his thumb and forefinger, the child may rhythmically pull pegs from a pegboard and drop them into bottles. He may also pick up small objects, such as plastic bottles or small ten pins, and drop them into a bucket—checking to see how many he can place before knocking one or more of the other objects over.

## LIP AND TONGUE MOVEMENT-THINKING GAMES

Although speech therapists know the vital role of lip and tongue movements in articulation and are aware that children with severe speech problems need specialized therapy, lip and tongue movements have often been ignored in the design of programs to develop discriminative skill function. We are concerned here with those children who may have a slight speech malfunction which might cause confusion in relating the sound to the sight symbol of that sound; this confusion may cause them to have difficulty with spelling.

The acquisition of these skills begins in that stage of the infant's development when he discovers his world through oral manipulation. The tongue becomes the infant's tool of identification. The mother's breast, the fist, a toy, anything picked up from the floor—all are explored with the mouth. The child tastes, squeezes, feels texture, and stores the acquired information for later reference.

This early mouth and tongue knowledge can be of help to the child in eventually knowing both lateral and directional movement. No place else in the human body is there a movable confined internal organ which by explorative thinking movements can confirm a body location as being top (up), bottom (down), sides (right and left). This same organ can track, fix, thrust, and grasp. All these movements occur before the child has developed any language concepts. If the child has developed good tongue play, lip control, and oral space knowledge, he has an advanced start on the thinking skills he may later apply to academics, specifically to diction, reading and spelling, and the articulation of sounds peculiar to foreign languages.

### Peanut Butter / Game 52

The teacher places peanut butter on a section of the child's teeth and has him remove it with his tongue. He should run his tongue around his top and bottom teeth on the inside and outside—all the while thinking about his tongue. A variation is to have the child watch himself in a mirror as he moves his tongue right, left, up, down, and diagonally without allowing it to touch his lips. The tongue movements should be made both inside and outside the mouth.

## Follow with Your Tongue / Game 53

Before a child begins tracking with his tongue, he may practice by moving his tongue back and forth while watching himself in a mirror. The child is then ready to track various objects. For example, the teacher may move his index finger back and forth in front of the child urging him to watch with his eyes and follow with his tongue. Because the child cannot check himself by touching the object, the teacher or another child provides feedback.

## Point with Your Tongue / Game 54

This game is similar to eye fixations in that the child attempts to point to a specific spot with his tongue. He may do this while observing himself in a mirror, or he may point to designated objects while another person observing him provides the necessary feedback. The child may also point his tongue rhythmically by following the beat of a metronome.

## Tongue Forms / Game 55

Small, plastic, geometric forms are attached to pieces of nylon fishing line from eight to ten inches in length. These forms should be stored in a mild antiseptic solution when they are not being used. The child closes his eyes and the teacher inserts a form in his mouth, holding the other end of the string to prevent the child from swallowing the form. The game may be varied by the use of templates. The child then moves his tongue around the inside boundary of the template to identify the shape. Both geometric forms and templates may be varied in size and thickness. The child may verbally identify the form, visually match it to a line drawing, make a graphic representation, or find its identical mate in a feel-and-find box.

Tongue form recognition often provides reinforcement for the child who has difficulty recognizing forms through vision or hand thinking.[8]

## Comic Faces / Game 56

To develop a mental map of the lips, the child stands in front of a mirror and is directed to make specific, but unusual, lip movements. This game can also be played in groups without a mirror.

## Button Battle / Game 57

This game is played by two children and requires a twenty-four-inch long piece of strong string with a large, flat button firmly attached to each end. One button is inserted between the lips and teeth of each child; the button should *not* be placed behind the teeth in the oral cavity. The goal of button battle is for one child to pull the button from the other child's lips. Repeated sterilization of the buttons is, of course, important.

## String Race / Game 58

Several children may play this game. Each child should have a sturdy twenty-four-inch string with a knot on one end and a button or similar object on the other. The child places the knotted end of the string into his mouth. He is then to work the string into his mouth only by moving his lips and tongue. The first child to gather the entire string and button into his mouth wins. The load may be made heavier by adding weights onto the button.

## Straw Carry / Game 59

One or more children may play this game which requires only pieces of paper and strong straws. The child holds the straw in his mouth and places its other end on a small piece of paper. Without touching the paper, he sucks the straw so that his breath draws the piece of paper against it. He then carries the piece of paper to another place in the room. A variation may incorporate this activity into a relay race. To complicate the task, the paper also can be replaced by heavier objects such as small metal disks.

## Straw Polo / Game 60

The child propels a ping-pong ball by blowing against it through a straw. Individuals or groups may play, and an element of competition can be introduced by having the children race to see who can cross the finish line first. Both straw carry (Game 59) and straw polo develop an awareness of breath control.

Throughout this chapter we have emphasized the interrelations of the three discriminative movement systems of eye, hand-finger, and lip-tongue. These subsystems are part of a total action system. In this total action system, general and discriminative movement thinking play distinct but complementary roles. General movement involves the transporting and positioning of the body so that discriminative movement can occur accurately and efficiently. Discriminative movement involves the use of precision "tools" that enable us to explain our thoughts to others—by talking and writing—and to receive thoughts from others—by observing and reading.

When a task seems too high for a child, the problem may be the result of the child's having difficulty with either his general or his discriminative movement thinking. At the Tyler Thinking School, the teacher was freed from the conventionally structured system of class periods, required textbooks, and exams, and she quickly became attuned to the needs of individual class members. She became adept at on-the-spot analysis; she could pick up the nonverbal clues that indicate a child's needs: squinting, squirming, clenching fists, holding the head too close to the paper, refusing to perform specific tasks. These were specific actions which told the teacher when, and sometimes how, to vary her approach.

The teacher in a Thinking School is aware that a child's failure to perform a task is often due to poor integration of discriminative subsystems. We have referred to this poor integration as "noise on the circuit"; it includes improper eye focusing, poor finger control, and poor articulation. The confusion and stress stemming from noise on the circuit can prevent or interfere with the learning process. The alert teacher will not be satisfied merely with noting the end result, the child's solution of a problem. Rather, he will observe the way in which the child performs the task and will then be able to discern whether the various discriminative movement subsystems support or interfere with the child's activity. A School for Thinking involves the whole teacher and the whole child.

# 8. Visual Thinking Games

An individual is constantly receiving information both from his own body and from the external environment. Information received through the senses from the environment must be processed, decoded, encoded, and integrated with body knowledge if it is to be meaningful to the individual. Education is constantly appealing to and utilizing the various information processing systems, the best known of which are visual, discussed in this chapter, and auditory, to be discussed in Chapter 9. There are, however, other systems which are important: the olfactory, which we will not discuss; the tactile-kinesthetic-manipulative (sometimes called the haptic) which we shall refer to as hand thinking in our discussion on Chapter 10; and movement thinking which has been discussed in Chapters 6 and 7. As emphasized in Chapter 7, the organic impairment or inadequate functioning of any of these information systems could cause "noise on the circuit" and confuse the other thinking systems—thus handicapping the learning process in academic and preacademic situations.

Let us take, for example, the seemingly simple task of copying a square by drawing or making a construction using small sticks. The function of the vision mechanism as a pathway for incoming information is of primary importance in this task as in many other academic tasks. A child may look at a square, recognize a square, and visually select a square from a group of forms. This same child may not be able to draw or construct a square because he lacks the necessary body knowledge. At least three body and sense thinking processes are involved in this task; they can be applied to any graphic or manipulative task.

1. *Movement thinking*—"I can direct my arm, hand, and fingers to move a specific distance and in specific directions, stopping, starting, and turning as I dictate." This type of movement thinking, more fully discussed as graphic thinking in Chapter 11, underlies a child's adequate drawing of an object.

2. *Hand thinking*—"I can direct my hands and fingers purposefully to manipulate or construct an object for meaningful communication." Only if hand thinking is properly developed, can the child construct a design suitable to his age, using materials appropriate to his age.

3. *Visual thinking*—"I can look at several objects and without making any other body contact with them, determine their similarities and differences." If visual thinking is properly developed, the child can successfully match similar designs.

While visual thinking plays a prominent role in the performance of many tasks, it is only a part of a total information processing system, and integration of all parts of this system is of primary importance. The vision process itself cannot feel texture, weight, pain, nor pressure. Nor is the vision process able to smell flowers, new mown hay, or freshly baked bread. The visual mechanism cannot taste ice cream, apple pie, or a lemon, nor hear a siren, a laughing child, or a church bell. All these sensory experiences are conjured to consciousness by a picture, a design, or a printed word processed through the visual mechanism. Knowing through vision implies knowledge that has been previously obtained or is presently confirmed by other information processing systems.

Malfunctions of the vision mechanism may affect the child's visual knowing. Imagine an improperly synchronized movie or a double exposure photograph; they illustrate some of the types of visual confusion that can ensue from a faulty vision mechanism. At the Tyler Thinking School a specifically designed vision screening[1] helped us to identify vision malfunctions and minimize their potential interference with the child's learning process.

In Chapter 6 we have already discussed the important role of vision in relation to body thinking, but some review of the relation between visual thinking and sight may be in order. The word sight is limited to the physiological process of radiant energy entering the eye and being transported to the visual cortex of the brain. Vision, in contrast, includes the visual thinking necessary for meaningful interpretation of these neural impulses.

Light enters the eye through the pupil and is scattered onto the retina where it is transformed into neural energy. A unique aspect of the sight mechanism is that two systems (a right and a left eye) must work simultaneously and with precise synchrony in order to send an accurate message to the brain. Two mechanisms are involved: the focusing mechanism and the eye movement mechanism. The focusing mechanism is controlled by the ciliary muscle, a small muscle system within the eye; the eye movement mechanism is controlled by the extra-ocular muscles, a group of separate but interrelated muscles externally attached to the globe of the eye. Although these two systems vary in function and nerve supply, they must be coordinated. If this coordination does not occur, sight will be impaired and the observer may not see objects clearly. This sight malfunction may distort vision such that the observer may have trouble identifying objects and centering them in his visual world.

The thirty-five games described in this chapter are divided into four categories according to the type of equipment used: parquetry blocks, pegboards, a tachistoscope, and miscellaneous materials. The games emphasize the visual thinking concepts of parts-whole, figure-ground (discrimination between a design and its background), and time perception.

A similar developmental sequence is used with all materials.[2] Before having the child attempt the games, the teacher should be certain that he can perform basic *manipulation of materials*. For example, the child should be able to stack parquetry blocks on the broad and the narrow sides, and he should be able to build three-block bridges with them. The child then plays *matching* games in which he uses actual material to construct copies of models; the models are first constructed with parts touching, later with spaces left between parts. The child then constructs models from *memory*. Next his constructions are copied from *pictorial representations* of actual models. He then constructs from *outlines*, first with, and then without, directing lines. Next we have the child perform *reversals* in which he rotates the model along environmental-spatial axes which correspond to the body axes described in Chapter 6.

The child then plays games to develop his sense of *perspective;* the knowledge to translate from vertical to horizontal planes is developed through *chalkboard match.* Games such as Me and minutes develop the child's *time perception.* At the highest levels games are played involving *receptive and expressive communication* where the child gestures, draws, speaks, writes, or reads. Throughout we emphasize the *integration* of visual thinking with all visual thinking activities.

## PARQUETRY BLOCK GAMES

Parquetry blocks may be purchased in most toy departments; they are an excellent educational toy. The blocks are of various sizes, colors, and geometric shapes. One of the first activities a child should master is stacking the blocks; he should begin by stacking them on the broad side and then attempt to stack them on the narrow side. The next step is constructing a bridge from three blocks. This establishes the child's knowledge of manipulating blocks with his fingers and hands. Also, the "reach-grasp-hold-release" cycle described in Chapter 7 is developed when the child plays with the blocks in this manner. We describe ten games which exemplify the developmental sequence utilized in all visual thinking activities.

### Block Match / Game 61

In this game played by the child and teacher, only parquetry blocks are required. There are three variations ranging from the simple to the complex. In the first variation, a pile of parquetry blocks is placed between the teacher and the child. The teacher selects a block and holds it up before the child. He is asked to select another block which matches the teacher's block in shape. This variation continues to develop the child's concept of same—not same; the body thinking foundation of this concept was discussed on p. 82. If necessary, various visual discrimination games are played to develop the child's knowing of objects as same or not same. The sameness concept must be established for each of the sensory input systems: movement, vision, auditory, hand, olfactory.

In the second variation, the teacher constructs designs from the parquetry blocks and the child is to construct matching designs. The blocks may be placed on the table or floor in the horizontal plane or on top of one another in the vertical plane. Two or three blocks are initially used; as the child becomes more proficient, additional blocks are added. Because of its diagonal construction children will probably have more difficulty with a diamond than a square or a triangle. In addition, some children find it difficult to match a shape that has been rotated to a different position such as an inverted triangle or a tilted square. They must understand that shape remains constant regardless of position.

The third variation is the most complex. The child is to match a pattern in which the parquetry blocks have been separated slightly. Then increasingly wider spaces are left between the blocks. This variation helps the child to visually develop the concept of pause or separation.

## Take Away and Add On / Game 62

In this game there are two parquetry block designs on the table: the teacher's model and the child's copy. The teacher shields the block designs from the child's view while he adds one block or removes one block from either design. The child then determines what change has occurred and adds or removes a block from the unaltered design so that they once again match. Later two or more blocks may be added or removed.

## Picture Match / Game 63

The child is shown an illustration of a design constructed from parquetry blocks. This acts as a symbol for the blocks themselves. The child then uses actual blocks to match the illustration; the blocks he uses in his reconstruction should be of the same color, shape, and size as those in the pictured design. First the child can match the design by placing his blocks on top of the picture. Later he can construct a duplicate design on the table beside the picture. The picture may be placed in various locations around the room; the child remains at the table and reconstructs the design. This helps to develop an awareness of constancy of position. The child should realize that the relative positions of the elements in a pattern remain constant regardless of where the pattern is placed in the child's visual world. By applying his knowledge he discovers that the teacher's right hand stays on that side whether he faces the child or stands with his back toward the child; the position of an object placed above a line on a vertical chalkboard remains above the line when the configuration is transferred onto a horizontal table surface, even though the child now sees the object as further away than the line.

At Tyler, each child was free to choose both the picture to copy and its placement within the room. This is characteristic of the Thinking School's freedom-within-a-structure. The teacher's role was to encourage the child to attempt more complicated tasks. The teacher facilitated the child's choice but did not impose his own choice on the child. It was not uncommon for a child to reject a suggested pattern because it was "too hard" or "too easy." A group of children may compete to see which child can finish his copied design first. This type of competition and discussion generally gives the child an opportunity for positive self-evaluation.

### Memory / Game 64

The child observes a parquetry block design for a short time. The design is then covered. Without uncovering the design, he is to recall and reconstruct it. The child verifies his effort by removing the cover from the model design.

### Outline / Game 65

To improve concepts of parts-wholes, the child matches a drawing in which the individual blocks have been clearly demarcated

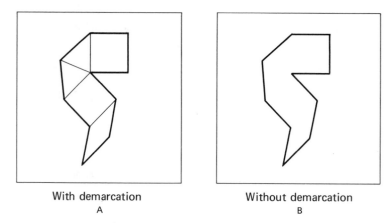

With demarcation
A

Without demarcation
B

**Figure 21.**
**Outline Designs for Parquetry Block Games**
The two outlines are identical. (A) has the demarcations which clearly
indicate the individual blocks that fit into the outline.
(B) lacks these interior demarcations

as in Figure 21A. He first matches by constructing his design on
top of the picture; later he constructs on the table beside the picture; and still later he matches the drawing after it has been positioned in various places around the room. In a more complex
variation as shown in Figure 21B, the individual blocks composing the design are not clearly demarcated.

## Reversals / Game 66

In this game, the child is asked to create parquetry block designs
by reversing the parquetry block design model. These reversals
occur along the various spatial axes which correspond to the axes
of the body described in Chapter 6. The reversals are performed
on designs which range from simple three-block patterns to more
complex five-to-six-block patterns. As the child masters the technique, he may be asked to reverse patterns in which spaces have
been left between the blocks. Children usually find it most difficult to manipulate mentally diamonds and squares that have been

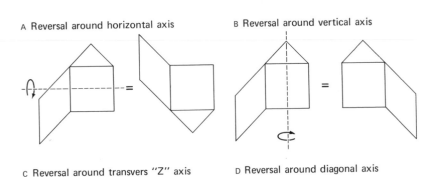

A Reversal around horizontal axis
B Reversal around vertical axis
C Reversal around transvers "Z" axis
D Reversal around diagonal axis

**Figure 22.**
**Diagram of Four Types of Parquetry Block Reversals**
Reference should be made to rotation around the
body's axes (Figure 3).

placed at an angle. Sticking the blocks to a transparent overlay and allowing the child to flip the transparency provides helpful feedback; it allows him to see the blocks rotate in three-
dimensional space. The four ways in which reversals may be
performed are sketched in Figure 22.

1. The child reverses along the *horizontal axis* transposing
the top and bottom of the pattern; this environmental spatial axis
corresponds to the body axis extending through the hips (Figure
22A).

2. The child reverses along the *vertical axis* transposing the
sides of the pattern; this corresponds to the body axis extending
up and down through the top of the head and center of the body
along the midline (Figure 22B).

3. The child reverses along the *transverse* or *"Z" axis* ro-

tating the pattern in a clockwise and counterclockwise direction. This corresponds to the body axis extending from front to back through the center of the body, Figure 22C.

4. The child reverses along the *diagonal axis* transposing upper left to lower right, lower right to upper left, and so on. This corresponds to a diagonal movement utilizing two body axes such as the movement of the right shoulder toward the left knee, Figure 22D.

## Chalkboard Block Match / Game 67

The purpose of this game is successful transfer from chalkboard activities which take place on a vertical plane to desk or table-top activities which take place on a horizontal plane. A parquetry block design is drawn on the chalkboard, and the child reconstructs it at his desk. This activity enhances the "copy from the chalkboard" concept and demonstrates that "up" on the chalkboard translates to the "top" of the paper which is "away from" the child when he is working at his desk. (See also Picture Match, Game 63.)

## How Would It Look From There? / Game 68

This game is the first one that deals explicitly with the child's development of visual perspective. The child sits at a table in the center of which a two-block pattern has been placed. A square and a triangle are used because of the arrow-like directional attribute of the apex of the triangle. The child is to determine how the design would appear to a person sitting somewhere else around the table; then, on a tray in front of himself, he constructs the pattern the way the other person would see it. He can evaluate his decision by picking up the tray, holding it in an unchanging position in front of himself, and walking over to the other location. This dynamic movement type of activity strengthens and further enhances the child's integration of movement thinking and visual thinking. For additional visual perspective games see Games 149 and 150.

## Me and Minutes / Game 69

This game is designed to develop the child's judgment of the speed with which he works and his perception of time. The game has three phases: How long will it take you to solve this problem? How much can you get done in this amount of time? Can you solve this problem after having had only a glimpse of it? This game is applicable to all thinking games.

## Communication / Game 70

The child may communicate with others in four major ways—through gesture, graphic signs, speech, and writing. We specifically played parquetry block games which utilized these four modes. Gesture, as a basic mode of communication, pervaded all our activities. Some children drew designs (graphic signs) which other children then constructed with actual parquetry blocks. From "sign" language, the children progressed to "verbal" language. One child, playing director, verbally described a simple parquetry block design, visible to him but hidden from the other children; the other children had to construct their designs according to his description. The children took turns playing director. In a more advanced variation, the children were given written instructions to follow. Finally, they wrote their own instructions for others to follow.

As the children took turns playing the role of the speaker or writer (expressor) and the role of the listener or reader (receptor), they developed the process of linguistic communication. The expressor must give accurate instructions, and the receptor must follow these instructions accurately.

## PEGBOARD GAMES

The four games described in this section utilize pegs and pegboards or other materials which serve a similar function. We prefer

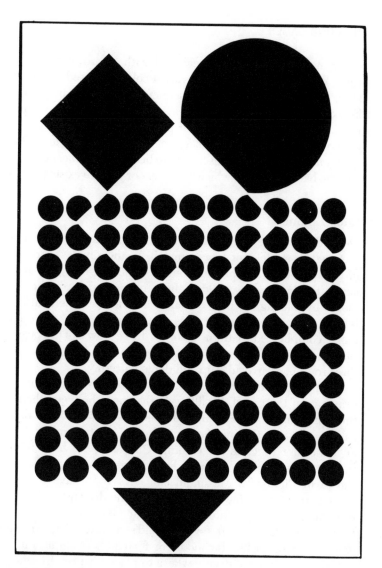

**Figure 23.**
**Cassiopeia. "A Figure-Ground Effect"**
Visual concentration on the various flattened edges alters the
forms from squares to rectangles and other configurations. The
mind, not the retina, produces the visual effigy. In all cases, retinal
stimulation is the same, but the mind alters the projected image.

a five-inch-square wooden pegboard with ten rows of ten holes each; knobbed wooden pegs of varied colors are used. Where suitable, the same developmental sequence described in parquetry block games is followed. Whereas games played with parquetry blocks emphasize the concept of parts-whole, games played with pegboards emphasize the concept of figure-ground. The child acquires the knowledge to discriminate between an object or pattern and the background on which the object or pattern exists (Fig. 23).

### Peg Match / Game 71

Depending on the child's level of thinking, different line patterns are used as models for him to match. In the simplest form, pegs of the same color are placed along a single row one after another across the board. The child is then encouraged to duplicate the model by placing the pegs one after another into the board from left to right. Subsequently pegs of different colors are used. A more complicated pattern involves three rows. The pegs are placed one after another in a single line which traverses these three rows in an irregular up and down pattern.

Some children may need the additional visual clue of a line drawn onto the board. By filling in the space between the holes, the confusion of the "separation effect" is eliminated, making it easier to discern the specific figure from the total ground. This is an important function for reading. Clinically, we have found a specific sequence for using a line drawn on the pegboard as shown in Figure 24. Maximum clue (A) is to have the model placed on a drawn line and a duplicate line drawn for the child's reproduction. In the intermediate clue (B), the line is erased from the model but left for the child's reproduction. Minimum clue (C) uses no line for model or for child. In duplicating the model the child must decide where to place his pegs by choosing the appropriate unmarked holes.

When the child had trouble following the color sequence of a pattern, his perception of color was investigated. He was presented with a peg and asked to give the teacher one that was

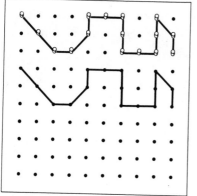

Maximum clue
A

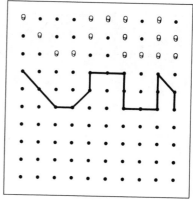

Intermediate clue
B

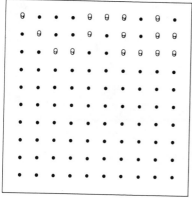

Minimum clue
C

**Figure 24.**
**Pegboard Patterns in**
**Developmental Sequence**
In each pegboard the upper area is
the model; the lower area indicates
where the child is to place his pegs.
In (C), blank lower half indicates total
absence of any guide for child except
pegs of the model.

"the same"; the teacher was careful not to use language that
would label any color. If the child continued to confuse colors
and if the teacher was certain that he could make a "same–not
same" judgment, he was referred for more comprehensive professional evaluation.

**Figure 25.**
**Acoustical Tile with Paper Attached for Chalkboard**
**Peg Match Game**

## Chalkboard Peg Match / Game 72

The pegs for this game are golf tees. The pegboard is an old-fashioned acoustical tile with vertical and horizontal rows of holes. The child begins by folding a piece of eight by eleven inch paper twice so that the creases divide it into four equal rectangles. The paper is then unfolded and mounted on the pegboard by a peg in each of the four corners as shown in Figure 25. A rectangle drawn on the chalkboard is subdivided by horizontal and vertical dotted lines which represent the folds in the child's piece of paper. The teacher then draws a design on the chalkboard rectangle. The design may be contained within one or more of the quadrants. The child must duplicate the design by punching holes in the paper attached to his pegboard. He should attempt to place the proper design within the proper quadrants or the proper parts of the design within the proper quadrants. To do this he must be able to judge the relative position of the chalkboard design on the paper as well as the position of the hidden holes. In a more advanced variation, the child may copy overlapping designs. Finally, he is asked to copy the design by reversing the quadrants along the vertical, horizontal, "Z," or diagonal axes. As in Games 63 and 64, the child develops transformation thinking; in this case, he translates the vertical representation of the design on the chalkboard to a horizontal representation on his pegboard.

## Wireform / Game 73

This game affords the child the opportunity to discover that shape of an object remains constant regardless of its position in space. An acoustical ceiling tile covered with paper may again be used as a pegboard. Wire coat hangers are bent into squares, triangles, rectangles, and so on. These bent coat hangers are shown to the child, one at a time, at an angle. The child tries to determine what the shape and size of the wireform would be if he could see it in its straight ahead position. Then, on the pegboard he punches out the projected shape and size. After he has finished, he checks his work by placing the wireform on top of his punched-out paper. This enables him to evaluate whether he interpreted the shape and size correctly.

### Pegboard Communication / Game 74

Pegboard communication games may be played with the entire class or in small groups. The teacher or a child gives verbal instructions such as, "Place a blue peg in the first hole in the first row on the right." After the child has placed his peg, another instruction follows: "Now place a red peg in the top row—third hole from the left side."

When this game was introduced at Tyler, some of the children resorted to interrupting techniques such as dropping pencils, asking to go to the bathroom, or stating that they could not hear. To counter these tactics, we devised the game of "robot" and used it with all verbal expressive-receptive games when we felt it would be beneficial. The group was told that the leader was a "robot" programed for a task with which it proceeded regardless of the interruption. The robot-machine could answer no questions and make no judgments. Like a tape recorder, it just went on and on. Thus the children were required to pay attention and not make noise lest they miss an instruction or disturb their fellow classmates. The game worked; the children were enthralled. Many eagerly requested to play the robot. Everyone attempted to follow instructions, and those children with questions waited for the robot to "turn off" before asking them. We were careful not to overuse the robot game, but its magic make-believe appealed greatly to our first graders.

## TACHISTOSCOPE GAMES

Games played with the tachistoscope generate high interest and develop rapidity in visual thinking. There are near point and distant tachistoscopes. A translucent screen may be used; the children sit on one side of the screen watching the image flashed on the other side. To help them retain the image, they are instructed to continue watching the spot where the image appeared for a few seconds after it has disappeared. Before flashing the image, the teacher alerts the children by saying, "Ready, Set, Now!"—raising rather than lowering his voice on the final word "Now." Most of the targets can be flashed in $\frac{1}{75}$ of a second, but sometimes it is necessary to reduce the speed so the children can better grasp the targets. The entire class, small groups, or individuals may play. At Tyler, we used only distant tachistoscope projections.

Eleven games are described. The teacher should remember to work within the ability of the group. Patterns flashed on the screen should be presented again later for confirmation; this repetition builds both the child's efficiency of visual processing as well as his span of attention. He must be able to take in visual information, integrate it with information from past experience, and communicate it to others by some form of expressive effort.

### Digit or Letter / Game 75

There are two variations of this game. In the first variation, numbers, or letters, or a combination of both are flashed on the screen. The children are asked to copy them, say them aloud, or arrange them in proper numerical or alphabetical order. They may also be asked such things as "What is the third number in that row?" "What letter is second from the last?" This activity helps the children to develop concepts of span and combination and also long and short term memory.

In the second variation, the children learn to concentrate on the above activity while disregarding the presence of "noise." They are told to create noise by repeating their own name (or specific letters or numbers) while images of letters or numbers are flashed on the screen. The children continue saying their own names aloud as they record on paper the letters or numbers they see on the screen. This develops high-level concentration.

### Tell A Story About The Picture / Game 76

Pictures are flashed on the screen. The children are asked to describe what they see or to answer questions such as "How many legs did you see on that dog?" "Which direction was the car going?" A further challenge may be added by flashing pictures with letters hidden in them such as on the side of a horse or the branch of a tree. The children are then asked to find the hidden letter in the picture.

### Forms and Shapes / Game 77

Complete and incomplete forms are flashed on the screen and the children are asked to draw an exact copy of them on paper in the same sequence and position in which they have been flashed. In a variation the children may be asked to draw only the missing parts. In another variation they make completed drawings of the flashed incomplete forms.

### Chalkboard Tach / Game 78

A form is flashed on the chalkboard, and one child is asked to draw on the blank chalkboard, in the exact spot where it was flashed, the form identical in size, shape, and position. The other children draw the form at their desks. To check the child's drawing, the tachistoscope is set at constant exposure and the form is projected onto the chalkboard. In a class discussion, the results are evaluated and the child who has been at the chalkboard gives a self-evaluation. The child then traces with chalk the projected image on the chalkboard. This movement thinking activity of tracing the projected image provides feedback for improvement of visual spatial positioning and of graphic responding.

### Arrow / Game 79

There are three phases to this game as illustrated in Figure 26. In the first variation (A), patterns composed of arrows with arrowheads but no tail feathers are flashed on the screen. These patterns may range from two or three arrows in horizontal or vertical arrangement to four or five arrows in random arrangement. In the second variation (B), tail feathers are added. In this

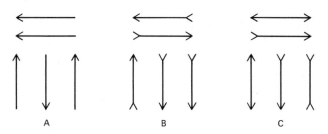

**Figure 26.**
**Arrow Patterns in Developmental Sequence**
(A) shows arrows with points but no tails; (B) shows
tails added but each arrow is directionally consistent;
(C) shows tails and points that vary in direction.

variation, the direction of the tail feathers is constant with the
arrowhead in each arrow. In the third variation (C), the tail
feathers and arrowheads point in various directions. This is most
complex and requires acute visual discrimination.

The children may play the game in two different ways. In
one version, they are given a set of the pictures to be flashed and
asked to select the correct picture after the flash. In another version, they draw the picture which was flashed.

## Geometric Dot Patterns / Game 80

A pattern of dots some of which are connected by lines is flashed
on the screen. The children have paper imprinted with the same
dot pattern but without the connecting lines. They are to draw
the lines to match the flashed pattern. Reversals and changes of
position may be introduced by asking questions such as "How
would it appear if you were on the other side of the screen?"
Complexity of patterns follows the same variants described in
dot patterns (Game 87).

## Bead Positions / Game 81

Small Indian beads or the smaller wooden beads are placed on a
transparent surface with a circle drawn on the middle of it, or

the transparent surface could be divided into quarters by vertical and horizontal lines. This transparent surface is then placed on the working surface of the tachistoscope or overhead projector; the resultant bead pattern is then flashed on the screen. The children are provided with five or six beads and a pattern drawn on paper to match the background of the tachistoscope slide. The children may match the design, or they may answer such questions as "How many beads are inside the circle?" "How many beads are below the circle?" "How many beads are outside the circle?" "How many beads are on a line?" or—"not on a line?" To vary the image on the screen, both transparent and translucent beads may be used. Also, a bead may be placed on its side so the center hole is not exposed. The child would then search for a particular bead. Different designs can be easily created by shifting the position of the beads. Not having to change slides and the versatility and ease of altering the design makes this a popular game for teacher and child.

## Mosaic Tile Flash / Game 82

Small mosaic tiles or parquetry blocks are placed on the tachistoscope surface. The children have matching tiles or blocks, and they attempt to duplicate the flashed design. Here again, add on, take-away, reversals, and changes of position are possible.

## Flash Fog / Game 83

The tachistoscope is deliberately cranked out of focus before it is flashed. Gradually the picture is brought into focus and the target is periodically flashed on the screen. The first person to identify the target correctly is best in "seeing through the fog." All previously mentioned targets can be used in this tachistoscope game.

## Dominoes / Game 84

Domino images can also be flashed—single or double. As directed, the child must arrange his actual dominoes in the same or in a reversed position.

## Tic-Tac-Toe / Game 85

Several typical tic-tac-toe patterns are printed on paper and given to the child. Flashed on a screen are projected models of other tic-tac-toe patterns. In some of the spaces of each flashed pattern, there are vertical, horizontal, or diagonal lines going in various directions; not all of the spaces need to be filled. The patterns should, of course, range in difficulty from the simple to the complex. The child must fill in his tic-tac-toe patterns to match the others which are being flashed on the screen. At first, only one or two spaces may be marked; gradually more spaces are filled. Later, reversals and changes in position are introduced.

## MISCELLANEOUS MATERIALS

In this section, we describe ten games which develop the previously mentioned visual thinking concepts of parts-whole, figure-ground, and time perception. The developmental sequence used throughout this chapter is also appropriate here.

## Construct-O-Line / Game 86

In this version of a popular thinking game, the child experiences that a line is more than a mark on paper, that it is a graphic representation of a concrete element. He also gains the knowledge that overlapping lines have a continuity and sequence pattern at the intersection; the lines do not randomly progress to the intersection and then alter their course.

Equipment for construct-o-line includes (1) a wooden board, four-inches-square and a half-inch thick with four rows of four holes each; (2) sixteen No. 6 penny spikes which have been cut to three-inch lengths with the cut ends rounded and smooth; (3) flexible but strong transparent plastic cut into four-inch squares.

On a transparent piece of plastic, the teacher marks four rows of four X's each to correspond to the holes on the small wooden board. He then punches holes in some of marked places; the holes should be large enough to fit over the heads of No. 6 penny nails. The child puts nails into the board to correspond to the holes which have been punched into the plastic. To evaluate his placement of the nails in the proper columns and holes, the child places the plastic sheet over the nails onto the board. If he has performed the task incorrectly, the plastic sheet will not fit or some of the holes will not have nails protruding through them. This aspect of the game helps the child to develop basic number concepts because he must move "so many" holes over from "such and such" a side in the row "this many" up from the bottom. The child can perform this activity even before he has learned the numeral labels of "one," "two," "three". . . .

In the second phase of this game, the teacher draws lines on the plastic sheet to fill in the spaces between the holes. The child is to duplicate the line pattern by stretching rubber bands around the appropriate nails on the wooden board. Some programs require the child to make the desired forms with the rubber bands by stretching open a single rubber band. The child grasps the rubber band in both hands, stretching it open and placing its outline over all the specified prongs. A circular or oval shape in his hands becomes a triangle or square shape on the board (Figure 27A). We do not recommend this approach. We have the child loop one end of the rubber band around the first peg and wind and twist that one rubber band from peg to peg until the design is completed (Figure 27B). Thus his arm, hand, and fingers are involved in the movement thinking necessary to reproduce a duplicate of the model. In the first approach A, only a visual match is obtained, but in our approach B, a visual match of the model is developed through a movement match of arm-hand-finger thinking integrated with visual thinking. The transference to graphic thinking (discussed in Chapter 10) is obvious.

The patterns the child is to duplicate may range from a straight line to many lines in overlapping or separate patterns. The lines may be of various colors and the child may use colored rubber bands to match them. When using colored rubber bands, the child must be able to determine the sequence of the lines:

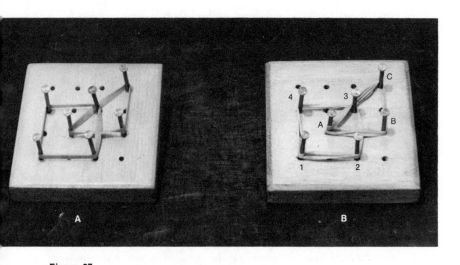

**Figure 27.**
**Placement of Rubber Band on Construct-o-Line**
(B) In constructing the square this child started by looping
the rubber band around nail 1 and proceeded sequentially to 2, 3, and 4.
The expected path is 4, 3, 2, 1. In constructing the triangle,
this child went from A to B to C. Children usually
proceed from A to C to B. Note that the end result of (A) and (B)
is visually similar but motorically quite different.

which is to be constructed on the bottom, in the middle, and so on. Again the child may check his performance by placing the plastic sheet over the board.

In another variation, thin, plastic-coated wire is substituted for the rubber bands. The wire is extremely flexible and is available in various colors. The child twists the wire around the nails on the board. To check himself, he lifts the wire pattern from the board and places it on top of the plastic sheet which he has used as a model. The child can then examine the design he has constructed by viewing it in a vertically held position. Perceiving it from a totally different plane he begins to understand that shape and design remain the same regardless of position. Construct-o-line, particularly significant in hand thinking development, lends itself well to previously mentioned sequences such as "memory," "chalkboard," and "communication."

## Dot Patterns / Game 87

In this game, the same graphic patterns used in such things as pegboards, construct-o-line, and marble boards may be used. The simplest pattern consists of sixteen dots arranged in a square pattern four rows of four dots each. A more complicated model has five rows of five dots covering the same area as the sixteen-dot pattern. There are two basic phases to dot pattern: match and reversal. These are utilized in many varied dot pattern thinking games.

Two four-inch-square dot patterns are made on a long sheet of poster board, oak tag, or other such paper product. A clear transparent plastic sheet is placed over the dot patterns. A slanted drawing surface is preferred; Getman's School Skill Tracing Board described in Chapter 11 is excellent for this purpose.

A model is drawn on the transparent overlay by connecting specific dots of the first dot pattern. The child is to match the model by drawing a line connecting the appropriate dots of the second dot pattern. The transparent plastic overlay is used because the child can write on it with wipe-off crayons or wax pencils. More important the child can wipe off, and thus totally eliminate, an improper choice. The temporary aspect of the wax pencil mark encourages the child to attempt to copy the design.

Similar benefits are obtained when using chalk and chalkboard.

To evaluate his work the child may use another transparency of the model and slide it on top of his own reproduction. A mismatch indicates an improper choice and the child is free to wipe off and make the necessary correction to obtain an accurate match.

The simplest dot pattern is composed of straight, horizontal, or vertical lines. Diagonal lines are more difficult, and intersecting diagonal lines are even more complex. Figure 28 shows different dot patterns. Once the child can match a complicated intersecting pattern involving almost all of the dots, a second color can be introduced.

The complicated concept of pause or separation is conveyed by having the child skip or omit segments of lines. To do this, he must start and stop with the proper dot. This phase of dot pattern requires intelligent orientation in space.

In the reversal phase, the child may first reverse the pattern on the horizontal or vertical axis: The top becomes the bottom or the sides are transposed. Again, the child perfects this technique by reversing patterns ranging from the simple to the complex and utilizing the previously mentioned variations. These are evaluated by his reversing the model overlay onto his reproduction and observing the match or mismatch. He is then ready to reverse on the "Z" axis by making clockwise and counterclockwise rotations. Finally, he is shown a diagonal reversal in which, for example, the upper left-hand corner becomes the lower right-hand corner. Again, the patterns to be reversed may vary in complexity.

In still another variation, the child must match or reverse linear patterns drawn without the dots which previously acted as clues. Or he is shown a pattern and asked to duplicate it from memory. Or he must translate a pattern from a vertical surface to a horizontal surface: chalkboard to paper on desk. The pattern may also be flashed on a screen. In addition, the child may be asked to think of the pattern from different points in space: "How would it appear if I were standing on my head?" "How would it appear if it were on a window and I were on the other side of the

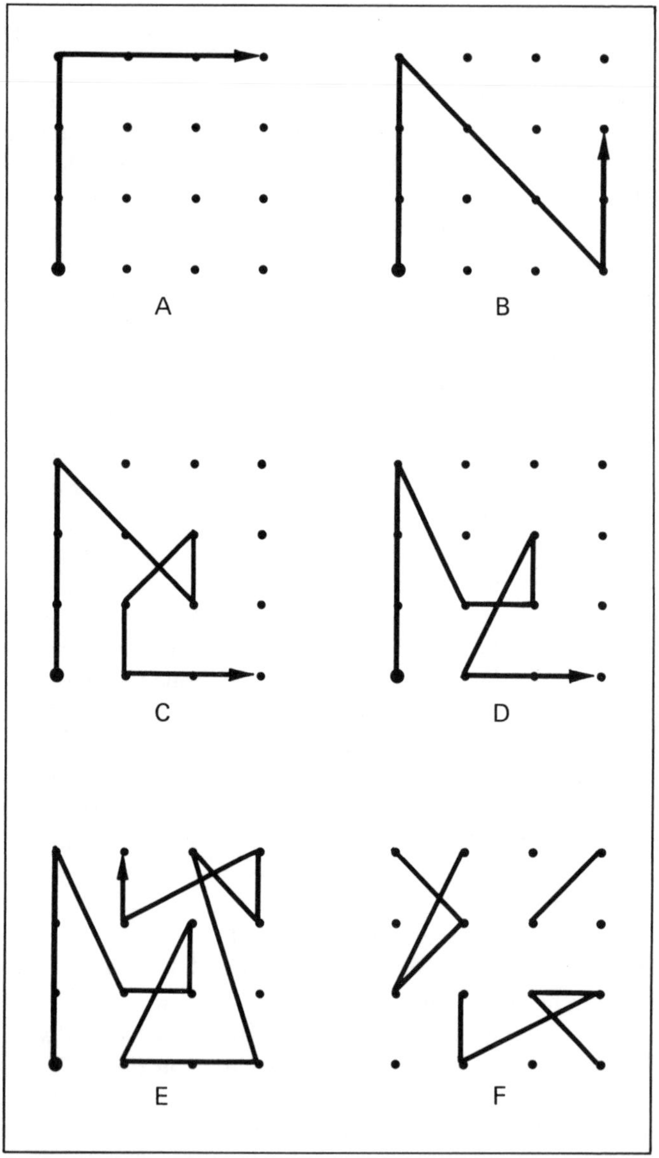

**Figure 28.**
**Dot Patterns in Developmental Sequence**

window?" In extremely complicated versions, reversals of vertical, horizontal, and diagonal patterns are attempted after these patterns have been flashed onto the board.

## Camouflage / Game 88

This game helps to develop the child's visual discrimination thinking.[3] The teacher should prepare five overlays by drawing combinations of squiggly lines and intersecting angular lines. On smaller pieces of paper, he then draws simple patterns of lines, letters, or shapes. The overlays are placed on one of the patterns to "camouflage" it. The child is to identify the hidden pattern. If an overhead projector is used, the game may be played in groups.

If no one is able to discover the camouflaged pattern, the teacher may jiggle it so that motion may make it more visible. If the children are still having difficulty, he may remove the camouflage overlays one at a time. The task may be made even simpler if the hidden pattern has been drawn in a contrasting color. If the teacher wishes, the child who discovered the hidden pattern may trace it on the overlay or draw it on the chalkboard.

## Perception Bingo / Game 89

This is a basic game that develops visual discrimination of form and design through visual matching only. The cards for this game can also be used in Chapter 6, Game 5-2. Pieces of cardboard the size of bingo cards are divided into six sections with visual designs drawn on each of the six sections; each card should have a different combination of designs. The designs drawn in each of the sections can be of varying complexity, and some should be similar without being the same. Small cards should then be marked with each of the designs used on the large cards, and these are placed in a large container. One of the small cards is taken from the container and shown to the children. If this design is on the child's card, he places a marker in the appropriate section. The goal is, of course, to see who can fill his card first.

In a more difficult variation, the single designs can be flashed by a tachistoscope so that the children have only a fraction of a second to determine the configuration of the model. Understanding the complexity of the design requires increasingly acute visual discrimination.

## Fit-A-Space / Game 90

Several different games may be played with this inexpensive toy.[4] It contains about a dozen four-inch pliable plastic disks. The disks vary in color and have a different texture on top and bottom. Three small geometric forms are prepunched out of each disk. They are easily removed and reinserted. In order to match a geometric form to the proper disk, the child must discriminate color, texture, and form.

In one game we played, all of the punched-out pieces were placed in a heap on the center of the table. In turn, each child chose a punched-out shape and placed it into his disk. If the child made a wrong choice, he lost his turn. After a certain number of rounds, the child who had filled the most disks was declared the winner.

In a more difficult variation, the geometric forms are irregularly cut in half. The child is asked to select half a form on his first turn and wait until his next turn to select the other half. Again, a wrong choice results in a lost turn.

In a still more complex variation, three disks are placed on a geared-down turntable. As the disks slowly revolve, the child is to decide which form fits into which disk. He then fits the form into the revolving disk. The forms must be viewed from several constantly changing positions which encourages the child to develop form-constancy in visual thinking. Accurate hand-eye coordination is required in order to place the geometric form in its proper place.

## Memory X's / Game 91

This game, played by the entire class or in small groups, develops the child's knowledge of *spatial-temporal relations*. This knowledge serves an important role in reading, mathematics, and other academic skills. *Spatial* refers to placement and relations of the

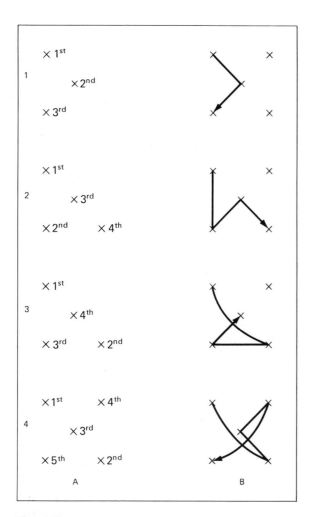

**Figure 29.**
**Memory X's Game**
(A) Developmental sequence of Memory X's as shown on
the chalkboard. (B) The child's response of connecting
the X's in correct recall of the order in which they were drawn
by the teacher. Note in (3) and (4) the center X is touched
only once as specified by its drawn serial order.
The teacher could have superimposed a second X
on top of the center X, and it then would have been
touched twice by the child's lines.

parts within the total pattern in a specific configuration: The parts may be randomly selected and placed but when completed, they form a specific pattern. For example, the spatial arrangement of numbers to be added may be changed without the final sum being affected: $2 + 4 + 3 = 4 + 2 + 3$. In contrast, the component digits of a number must follow a specific serial sequence: 243 is not 423. This specific and orderly serial arrangement is known as *temporal* relation. A child with inadequate temporal sequencing may pronounce spaghetti as "pasgetti." All the sounds are there but they are in improper temporal order.

To help develop and utilize intelligent spatial and temporal relations, each child is given a sheet of paper upon which are printed patterns of X's. The X's in each pattern are placed like the five-pattern in dominoes: two dots above, two dots below, one in the middle. X's in this same pattern are drawn on the chalkboard in a specific sequential order. For example, the one in the upper left is drawn, next the one in the lower right, third the one in the center, fourth the one in the upper right, and fifth the one in the lower left. The children draw lines connecting the X's on their paper in the same temporal sequence as the X's were drawn on the board. Thus the child would start with his penciled line at the X in upper left, proceeding to the lower right, then to the center, and so on. His final drawing would appear as shown in Figure 29-4. In its simplest variation only three X's are utilized. Gradually more X's are involved. Also the speed with which the X's are placed on the board is gradually increased. In the most advanced phase, five X's are placed rapidly on the chalkboard.

When appropriate, one of the children is encouraged to reproduce the sequence on the chalkboard, and the class then evaluates what he has done. This game encourages children to make accurate decisions rapidly. Reversals and How would it look from there? games previously described can also be played with memory X's.

### Size Blocks / Game 92

This game[5] may be played in small groups or individually; it is well adapted to the development of mathematical skills. The two by two-inch blocks vary in thickness from one-quarter to three inches. Using the blocks, the children explore building ascending and descending steps. They discover the concepts of variation and order. The child is asked questions such as "Which two blocks put together make one of these blocks?" "How many of these small blocks do you see?" "How many different ways can you arrange these blocks?" The size blocks were used for matching, sequencing, seriation, and permutation. Arranging them vertically and horizontally demonstrates the constancy of temporal

$$\begin{array}{r} +\,6 \\ +\,7 \\ +\,3 \\ \hline \end{array}$$

or spatial ordering; the child learns that $6 + 7 + 3 = 16$, also

c

that a is the same as cat.

t

## Puzzle Talk / Game 93

Several variations may be played with one or more children. In one, a child is given a number of small, odd-shaped, varied-colored pieces of plastic and a small rectangular box. He is to arrange as many pieces as possible within the box according to specific instructions. Examples are, all yellow pieces touching, no yellow pieces touching, all triangles touching.

Another approach is to present to the child the outline of a pattern drawn on an index card and have him discover which pieces were used to compose that pattern. If he has difficulty, he may be directed to place the pieces on top of the pattern. The solution to the puzzle talk should be drawn on the back of the card so the child can evaluate his own performance.

Later, the child may make his own pattern, trace around its outline, and present it to one of his group members who has in turn composed a puzzle for the first child to solve. The children then solve each other's puzzle; we call this nonverbal puzzle talk. The children alternate playing the roles of expressor and receptor.

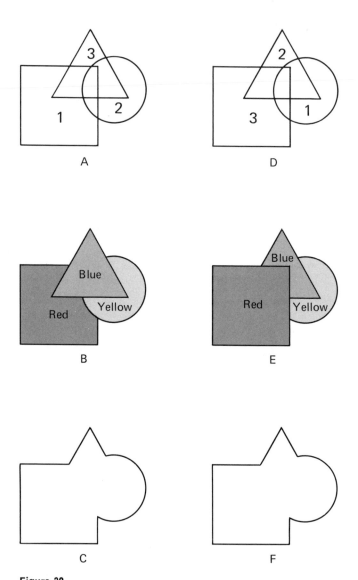

**Figure 30.**
**Three Overlapping Forms**
The child follows instructions [models (A) and (D)] regarding
order of placement of colored tiles, and discovers
that in spite of different appearances his overlapping constructions
[(B) and (E)] have the identical outline as shown in (C) and (F).

## Overlaps / Games 94

This game demonstrates for children that an outline of overlapping forms does not always make clear which piece has been placed on first. It emphasizes the importance of temporal ordering, discussed in memory X's (Game 91). A series of overlapping forms (triangles, circles, squares) is drawn on a card. Each form bears a number which indicates whether it was drawn first, second, third, and so on. The child is given similar forms cut out of cardboard or plastic. He follows the instruction of the model to discover that the pieces can be arranged in various orders of overlap to create entirely new patterns which retain the original outline (Figure 30).

In a variation, a concrete pattern constructed from the cutout forms becomes the model, and the child selects the proper card to match it. Later the child may construct and draw his own patterns. This can be considered as a permutation-combination task. The game can be varied by asking the child to transpose the parts of the pattern or attempt to think of how it would look from different positions.

## Parts-Whole Puzzle / Game 95

In this game, a series of four-inch squares, such as sample linoleum tiles, are subdivided into varying shapes and placed on top of each other in a box. The child is to determine how to replace them in the boxes. The goal is to determine alternate approaches to combining the various shapes to fit into the box. For example, he may compose the first layer of four two-inch squares, the second of two triangles, the third of two four-by-two rectangles, and so on.

In this chapter, we have discussed sight as the input system, and distinguished it from vision and visual thinking as the information processing system. The reader is encouraged to investigate further the workings of this complex organ—the eye—its integral interrelation with movement, and the role it plays in the thinking process.

However, we also wish to emphasize that all sensory inputs are of importance to the thinking child. Each sense input should be developed through a series of high-level thinking sequences from simple to complex activities, integrated with each other, and finally utilized in receptive and expressive communication functions. As illustrated with the games in this chapter, these communication functions can be subdivided into gesture, graphic signs, speech, and writing. That the latter two involve language and their transfer value to academic skills is obvious. The former have just as much transfer value, but are less obvious.

# 9. Auditory Thinking Games

Although the auditory function is closely related to speech and language, the auditory activities that we discuss in this chapter are primarily of a nonlanguage nature. The fifteen games described develop the basic processes of hearing thinking and listening thinking, and can be considered the prerequisites of acquired written or spoken language in the mother tongue of the child's culture.

At the Tyler Thinking School an audiometric evaluation helped identify children with problems who should be referred for specialized care. This type of screening should take place in the early weeks of the child's first year in school—kindergarten or first grade.

Any teacher of phonics is familiar with the child who has difficulty discriminating or sequencing sounds. The inability to cope with phonics could result in his being labeled as having a specific auditory learning disability. Usually there is no problem with the structure or mechanism of the ear; rather, the child has not developed the capacity to interpret the sounds he hears. His difficulty has to do with thinking in relation to the information received through the auditory mechanism. The games described in this chapter are designed to enhance the child's auditory thinking and to correct auditory processing deficiencies which may interfere with the child's learning to read and spell.

The children discriminate pitch and intensity and can relate this knowledge to the concepts of duration, pause, and nonsense word elements. Working with acultural sounds or nonsense words, they code and decode both written and verbal sounds and symbols. In the latter part of the program, culturally oriented language symbols in the form of meaningful words, rather than nonsense words, are used. The purpose is not to teach the language symbols themselves but to develop skill in the use of language to follow directions or instructions.

The program differs from the approach traditionally used in teaching phonics in that it emphasizes the integration of auditory thinking with other thinking activities. The program is based on the premise that thinking precedes language, and we encourage the playing of auditory thinking games before a child is placed in a formal written-language program.

Sequential activities in the auditory thinking program are similar to those followed in the visual thinking program described in Chapter 8. There are many parallels between visual thinking and auditory thinking; both involve similar components such as laterality-directionality, figure-ground, overlap, reversals, and sequencing. There are, however, significant differences. Auditory input immediately fades away; visual input is relatively more permanent and the object is usually available for re-evaluation. Additionally, the ears, as the auditory information entrance port, are themselves nonmobile. The whole head must move to direct an ear toward a sound. The eyes, as the sight input mechanism, are quite mobile. Eye movement is relatively independent of head movement.

Our visual thinking and auditory thinking programs utilize concrete objects in the early stages. For example, such things as buttons or sticks are used by the children to represent the kinds of sounds they hear. The objects are later replaced by written symbols which represent the sounds. This replacement serves a twofold purpose: It emphasizes the value of a coding system and it provides a transition to the auditory-visual decoding of written symbols which is the reading process.

Before presenting the games themselves, it is important to emphasize again that they should be discovery rather than instructional experiences. Group instructors should allow the children's auditory thinking skills to develop naturally in response to the games; they should never give the children the "right" answer.

Children should be encouraged to evaluate their own nonverbal or verbal responses as well as the responses of their classmates. (A tape recorder is useful for this kind of auditory-verbal feedback.) When the games involve a nonsense language, the children are expected to discover the code themselves and to respond by sending their own messages to the teacher or their classmates.

To further ensure that the playing of the games would be a discovery experience, we recorded them on cassette tapes. The use of a tape recorder freed the teacher from the role of group instructor and allowed her to circulate among the children. While the tape recorder was giving task instructions, the teacher was able to assist individual students, giving praise and preventing the frustration of failure. The teacher could help when and where needed without keeping the other children from moving ahead. Children having difficulty with auditory tasks frequently create some sort of disturbance; for example, they drop their pencils as an excuse for having the teacher repeat the sound. The use of a tape recorder, like playing robot in Game 74, helps to eliminate this type of behavior. In addition to increasing the teacher's efficiency, the use of tapes also promotes standardization.

The auditory thinking games develop the child's ability to discriminate variations of several basic components: (1) *pitch*—the variation of a sound from high to low; (2) *intensity*—the loudness or softness of a sound; (3) *duration*—how long a sound lasts; (4) *pause*—the length of time between sounds; (5) *elements*—variations in the component sounds of the nonsense words used.

Different conditions in the manipulation of nonsense sounds help develop an adequate interpretation and utilization of sound sequencing—a prerequisite for reading and spelling. (1) *Recall* (immediate and delayed)—numbers, letters, and nonsense sounds (not nonsense words) are recalled in various sequences; (2) *Location*—where is a given sound: beginning, middle, or end, or in multiple locations of the nonsense word; (3) *Identification*—given only a nonsense word, what is the beginning, middle, or end sound, or combination thereof; (4) *Innovation*—the child creates a nonsense word with a given sound in the beginning, middle or end, or in multiple positions; (5) *Add-On, Take-Away, Substi-*

*tute*—specific sounds within the nonsense words are manipulated. All of the games may be played individually or in groups. In any game requiring identification, discrimination, or location of sounds, the teacher should "hide" his mouth to prevent the child from lip-reading; the primary sensory input in these games is always auditory.

## High-Low / Game 96

This game develops the child's auditory thinking of pitch discrimination. A series of high and low pitched sounds are presented verbally to the children. A nonsense word, "BO" for example, is chosen for the code word. The tasks might range from a simple two-unit problem in which the child is asked to discriminate high "BO" from low "BO" to a more complex problem involving several "BO" sounds of high and low pitch presented in random order.

The child may respond by vocal imitation. Or a horizontal line may be drawn on the chalkboard or pegboard, and high-pitched sounds can then be represented by marks or pegs placed above the line, low-pitched sounds by marks or pegs placed below the line.

In a more advanced variation of this game, the syllable "BO" in varying combinations of high and low pitch is presented in sentence-like formation. Each unit is given a number as shown in Figure 31. The teacher, or a child acting as expressor, reads aloud one of the "BO" units; another child responds by giving the proper numerical designation. Conversely, the child may be given the numerical designation and asked to respond by giving the appropriate "BO" response verbally. In sending and receiving messages, the children are acquiring the basic foundation of written communication: the encoding and decoding skills which are used in the process of reading.

Some children who perform chalkboard activities, such as the recording of high and low pitch, have difficulty performing the same activity on paper. Traditionally, children are taught that a piece of paper has a top and a bottom. Adults often assume

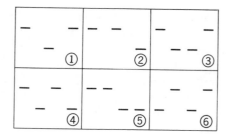

**Figure 31.**
**Graphic Representation of Various High-Low Auditory Sequences**
Sequence 1 is decoded as "high-low-high," sequence 2
as "high-high-low," etc.

that children are relating the vertical direction "up" with the "top" of the horizontal page of paper. This is not always the case as was discussed in Game 67. Intelligent transition from the vertical plane of the chalkboard to the horizontal plane of the paper can be a slow developmental process.

One of the students at the Tyler Thinking School had been selected to be the subject of one of our staff teaching demonstration lessons; she usually performed capably. When we proceeded from the chalkboard activities to pencil and paper tasks, she could not relate the up-down of the vertical chalkboard to the up-down of the horizontal paper. We tried to convey this concept in several ways: by slowly tilting the chalkboard until it was horizontal; by using a portable chalkboard; by working with paper held in a vertical position on the chalkboard surface. None of these methods worked well. On a verbal level, our student understood that the top of the paper represented "up" and the bottom "down," but she could not utilize this concept when asked to make high- and low-pitch representations. To her, the "top" of the paper was the top surface, rather than the top edge.

We finally resorted to making an up-down representation on the table using small wooden cubes and a small box. Cubes on the top of the box were to represent high sounds; cubes on the table along the bottom edge of the box were to represent low sounds. By working with a vertical plane on a horizontal table, the child soon gained the necessary insight. After having internalized the concept, she could use any working surface to play the rest of the auditory thinking games.

Children having difficulty translating the auditory concept of pitch may also be encouraged to drop down to the level of movement thinking. While vocally repeating a high-pitched "BO," they raise their hands upward; they lower their hands while repeating a low-pitched "BO."

### Loud-Soft / Game 97

Activities for developing the ability to discriminate between loud and soft sounds are essentially the same as those described in high-low, Game 96. Instead of having the children indicate pitch differences by varying elements of pegs in a pegboard or marks on a chalkboard, we had the children represent loud sounds by drawing wide marks or placing thick pegs and soft sounds by narrow lines or thin pegs.

Sensory-motor reinforcement is provided by having the children make tight fists to represent intense or loud sounds; the children relax or open their hands to indicate less intense or soft sounds.

### Duration / Game 98

After the children have gained some proficiency in discriminating pitch and intensity, the concept of duration is introduced. The child can express duration graphically by elongating the mark representing pitch or intensity. When the child is ready to play this game, he no longer needs the reinforcement provided by actual objects such as pegs or buttons. His representations can be graphic.

### Pause / Game 99

To have the children discriminate varying lengths of time or pauses between sound elements, a technique similar to that used in duration, Game 98 is used. The difference is, of course, that the pause rather than the duration of the sound is now being studied. The children indicated the length of the pauses by leaving longer or shorter spaces between the marks or the objects that represent the sounds.

## Elements / Game 100

In this game, two nonsense code words are used, for example "BO" and "BEE." The children create a written symbol for each "word": "BO" could be represented by a straight line, "BEE" by a wiggly line. These two elements are then used in games which combine other auditory discriminations. A sequence such as the following could be graphically represented (Figure 32) by the

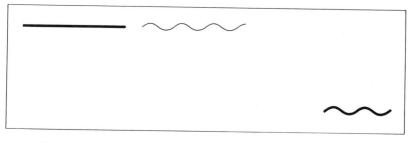

**Figure 32.**
**A Complex Graphic Representation of an Auditory Sequence**
**Involving High-Low, Loud-Soft, Pause, Duration, and Elements**

child; a long loud high "BO"—short pause—a long soft high "BEE" —long pause—a short low loud "BEE."

## Buzzer Boards / Game 101

Buzzer board games can be played individually by having the children use a cassette recorder, or in groups of six to eight children, where competitive groups may play under the direction of a leader.

An ideal and inexpensive buzzer board can be constructed by anyone who has a little skill in electronics. The box contains a buzzer and a light component operated with the button-type doorbell switch. Because children often take their cues from the movement of the instructor's finger, the switch should be obscured from their view.

In buzzer board games, the children can respond through concrete representations (utilizing objects such as buttons and cubes) or graphic representations (lines drawn on the chalkboard or paper).

The object of the game is to represent different stimuli through proper placement: A button might represent a buzz, a stick a light. Graphically, the varying elements can be represented by letters and lines. For example, a child might be asked to write a "sentence" such as, "Long light—short pause—short buzz—long pause—short light." It would appear as

L_____ B_____ L_____

## Rhythm / Game 102

Although rhythm games are more properly placed in the category of movement thinking, we have included them with auditory thinking because of the importance of rhythm in music and speech. Rhythm cannot be considered as solely dependent on auditory input; it requires primarily an internal timing process.

Following the pattern set by an electric metronome, the children perform rhythmic activities such as clapping hands, stamping feet, nodding heads, blinking, sticking out the tongue, and tapping their hands on a surface. The metronome flashes a light or clicks to set the pattern. For those children having especial difficulty, the sight-sound clue of light and click is sometimes helpful by simultaneously reinforcing each other.

The most advanced activity presented under rhythmic movement thinking is rhythm walk (Game 13) described in Chapter 6.

## Clap Patterns / Game 103

This is an auditory movement communication game requiring responses ranging from simple imitation to the production of a complicated graphic code.

In the simplest form, the teacher claps his hands in two successive patterns and the child responds by stating whether the patterns were same or not same. The clap pattern is presented to the child via three different processes. In *auditory only,* the teacher's hands are hidden from the child's view; he can hear, but not see, the clap pattern. In *auditory-visual,* the child facing the teacher can both see and hear as the teacher claps the rhythmic pattern. In *visual only,* the teacher moves his hands as though clapping but stops just prior to their striking. Thus the child sees the rhythmic pattern but hears no sound. Clap patterns should progress from the simple ( clap–short pause–clap, clap) to the complex ( clap, clap–short pause–clap, clap, clap–long pause–clap, clap–short pause–clap ).

The child should be encouraged to respond to the rhythmic pattern rather than to the number of claps per unit. Hearing, understanding, and interpreting clap patterns is a response to rhythm–pause–duration. Once the child can perceive similarity and uniqueness in clap patterns, he is asked to reproduce the clap pattern by clapping his own hands. At this point, the game integrates auditory thinking with movement thinking. Difficulty in imitating clap patterns usually indicates that the child is having difficulty with movement thinking, particularly coordination of the body's axes. The child must know that the body is symmetrical and be able to coordinate right and left sides of the body intelligently.

Symbolic representation is introduced by having the child draw marks on paper or the chalkboard or place objects such as chips, sticks, or blocks. For example, the symbol "/  //" represents "clap–moderate pause–clap, clap." The symbol "/  //    /  ///" represents "clap–short pause–clap, clap–moderate pause–clap–long pause–clap, clap, clap." As in previous games, the child can alternate as receptor, making the symbolic representations, or expressor, performing the clap pattern.

A tape recorder can also be used advantageously in this game. Individual clap patterns can be presented for the group to reproduce, represent graphically, or construct with sticks or blocks. A series of patterns may also be drawn on the board. The child is asked to reproduce one of these patterns, or the leader claps one of the patterns and asks the child to designate the correct pattern. Clap patterns may also integrate the child's perception of intensity; he would be asked to discriminate between loud or soft clapping sounds.

Clap pattern games integrate auditory, visual, and movement thinking from the simple level of same—not same to the more complex level of receptive and expressive written symbol communication. Clap pattern games develop prerequisite skills vital to the reading process.

## Nonsense Word Discrimination / Game 104

Children in all cultures share a common development pattern in their auditory thinking. Understanding of spoken language evolves from the common ability to discriminate, differentiate, and sequence specific auditory components of a composite sound pattern. If the child has mastered auditory thinking and discriminative movement thinking of lips-tongue-vocal cords, he will be able to produce sounds not native to his mother tongue, such as the French "R." For the sake of developing generally applicable techniques as well as avoiding confusing sound elements with recognized words, the auditory thinking games utilize only nonsense words and sounds.

In the nonsense word discrimination games, either a single nonsense word or a series of nonsense words is introduced, depending on the difficulty of the game. At Tyler, we began with English sounds and progressed to less familiar foreign sounds, but we always used acultural nonsense words. The children were to indicate whether two sounds were identical or not identical (expressed to the children as same or not same), then whether two words were identical or not identical. The children were also asked to reproduce the sounds and words. Sometimes it was helpful to use a tape recorder to monitor their responses.

## Sound Patterns / Game 105

As with all auditory thinking games, the sound pattern games can be played with the teacher and a group of six to eight children, with the teacher and one child, or with one child and a tape recorder. The object of the sound pattern games is to determine the location of a specific sound within a nonsense word.

In the simplest variation, the teacher vocally presents a specific sound which the children repeat. Before playing the next variation, the children must understand the concepts of beginning, middle, and end. The teacher presents nonsense words such as "BAL," "LOM," "ILZ." They contain the "L" sound which the children have been alerted to look for. They must designate the location of the specified sound in the word (beginning, middle, or end) either verbally, by placing a peg or block in the appropriate place, or by making an appropriate mark on paper or the chalkboard.

In a more complicated variation of this game, the instructor presents the nonsense word first and gives the sound to be listened for afterward. The children are given the word "DRIZIM" and asked such questions as "Was the specified sound (Z) at the beginning, middle, or end of the word?" "What sounds followed or preceded it?" In still another variation, the nonsense word is presented and the teacher asks, "What sound was in the beginning of the word?" "In the middle?" and so on. The child should always respond with the phoneme; he should not use letter labels. Finally, the child is requested to compose his own nonsense word with a specified sound in a specified location within the word.

In another sound pattern game the child is asked to say the nonsense word with a specific part added, removed, or substituted. For example given the nonsense word SPLIMIK: (1) What would be left if the sound "im" is removed (the answer is SPLIK). (2) Now add the sound "er" between the sound "s" and the sound "p" (the answer, SERPLIK.) (3) Now substitue the sound "ub" for the sound "ik" (the answer, SERPLUB).

The use of nonsense words demands higher level auditory thinking than the use of cultural words which are already familiar components of the child's vocabulary. Performing this difficult acultural task helps the child to develop auditory-verbal thinking as differentiated from cultural language use.

## Sound Location / Game 106

In this game, a noisemaker is sounded, hidden from the child's field of vision so that he can hear but not see it. The child is then asked to locate the sound by saying where it is or by pointing to it. Then the noisemaker is moved and the child is to describe the direction of the movement using himself as the point of reference: "It is above me." "It is below me." "It is moving away from me." The child then visually checks the location of the noisemaker, thus confirming his auditory response by visual input. This matching of sight and sound helps establish a more integrated space world and provides another reference point for efficient movement thinking.

## Number and Letter Recall / Game 107

In these games, a series of numbers or letters are orally presented to the children. There may be as few as two items or as many as five. At first the child repeats them in the same sequence they have been presented; later he reverses the sequence. Sometimes the child is requested to "draw" the numbers or letters in the air in front of himself and then the teacher directs him to point to the imagined letters or numbers in random order or in forward and reverse sequence. This activity helps to establish the recall of numbers and letters and aids development of the reverse concept through the use of the auditory thinking mode.

In more complex variations of the game, numbers and letters are mixed. The teacher asks questions such as "What letters did I name?" "What numbers followed the letter _____?" "What were the last three letters I said?" "What did I say between _____ and _____?"

Nonsense sound groups can be substituted for numbers or letters and a recall game can be played. Given the verbal presentation of "ro, ba, dip, sig," the child responds by repeating forward, reverse, or other aforementioned variations.

## Syllable Blocks / Game 108

For this game, nonsense syllables are printed on one side of parquetry blocks, one syllable per block. The game is easier if different forms are used for different syllables. The teacher arranges two or three blocks on the table with the printed side down and verbally names each block with its printed syllable. When the teacher later points to each block, the child must respond with the syllable name; the naming may occur in series or in random order according to instructions. The teacher then rearranges these blocks, and the child is to verbalize the newly formed nonsense word. The child thus creates nonsense words from the component syllables.

Syllable blocks helps the child to understand that several sound sequences can be combined to create a complex word and that complex words can be subdivided into component sounds. It provides a beneficial transition to the time when the child is ready for academic reading instruction.

## Do What I Say / Game 109

The auditory thinking games discussed so far have all dealt with listening for discrimination, perception, recall, or movement. More complex listening games can be played which combine all of these functions and require focalized auditory attention over a longer period of time. These games can be recorded on a fifteen-minute cassette tape and are suitable for groups of six to eight children as well as for one child.

In this context listening can be defined as extracting information from extended auditory input. In the Do what I say games, the children are given a series of commands to move body parts, manipulate blocks, place pegs, draw forms, and perform other action tasks. In the simple tapes, the instructions are repeated; in the advanced tapes, however, instructions are presented only once. Instructions are spoken loudly and clearly. The range of complexity is from simple two-unit commands to more difficult four-unit commands. For example, a two-unit command from a general-movement sequence tape describing activities that require large forms to be placed on the floor might be: "Jump into the circle; then jump into the diamond." As the children become more proficient, more complex instructions are added. A highly complex command might require the child to fold a piece of paper so that the lower left corner meets the upper right corner or to make a specific placement of a peg in a pegboard, such as "in the hole in the second row from the top and two columns from the right."

The use of tapes requires a heightened measure of attention from the child. The tape should be replayed or the task should be simplified for those children who find tapes confusing.

### Hidden Sound / Game 110

This figure-ground listening game develops the ability to discriminate a specific sound from a background of sounds or from an overlapping sound. The children are instructed to listen for a given word, number, or sound as the tape is played. Whenever they hear the specified sound, they are to respond by making a mark on paper or dropping an object into a container. If there is a dispute over the number of times a specific sound occurred, the tape can be replayed.

For the auditory thinking games to be effective, it is necessary that the initial clue to the identity of a sound be purely auditory. At first some children may require a visual clue to aid them in understanding the auditory input. With others, sight input may evoke "noise on the circuit." The games should be structured to stimulate thought, not to reward rote learning.

A Thinking School philosophy considers the development of auditory thinking discussed in this chapter as being foremost in importance in the primary grades. Such development will enhance the child's understanding of phonics. The games presented are designed to promote auditory thinking skills which will prepare a child to cope with the complex tasks of reading and related academic subjects.

In the same manner that the tachistoscope aids visual thinking, the listening games develop the child's ability to focus attention on, and derive information from, auditory stimuli. The auditory thinking games have been designed to integrate all phases of thinking. The fifteen games described in this chapter are not intended to be an exhaustive compilation; they are examples that we hope will stimulate teachers and parents to develop other games of their own.

# 10. Hand Thinking Games

Most academic information is presented through visual or auditory channels; teachers use lectures, reading, or audiovisual aids to convey information. The philosophy implemented at the Tyler Thinking School emphasizes a commitment to the development of the child's *total* thinking. Thus all modes of thinking are encouraged, and all types of information input are utilized. Hand thinking is a quite basic function of man; it plays a major role in the intellectual development of the child. In this chapter, we describe eight games to develop the child's hand thinking.

The hand is a source of input information not readily available to the eye or ear. The child feels texture, then matches it with vision. Roundness, smoothness, sharpness, and pliability are first felt with the hand, then matched with vision and, in some cases, sound. Merely hearing the words "rough–smooth," "flexible–rigid" does not assure adequate knowledge of texture or plasticity. This is best learned by fondling and manipulating with the hands. The constant violation of DO NOT TOUCH admonitions gives evidence of our need to handle objects to confirm what our eyes see. We want to touch things that appeal to our aesthetic sense. We use touch when we cannot identify an object. We discard things which have an unpleasant feel. In short, we receive information through our hands. We "think" with our hands.

Hand thinking implies processing information received through two types of sensory input: *tactile* and *proprioceptive-kinesthetic*. Tactile refers to our sense of touch; proprioceptive-kinesthetic (more fully discussed in Chapter 6) refers to our awareness of both the body's location and the movements of bones, joints, muscles, and tendons. We must have both types of sensory input in order to "know" an object hidden from sight; passive touch by an object will not provide us with sufficient information about such things as texture, form, and sharpness.

For example, if a blindfolded person extends his arms palms upward, and two balls of comparable weight—one slightly rough and the other smooth—are placed in his palms, he will not usually be able to discriminate between the balls. If, however, he is permitted to move his hands and fingers, he will quickly perceive the difference in texture. A similar test can be performed with small parquetry blocks; form differentiation is almost impossible unless the person can actively handle the blocks. Thus, to determine such attributes as texture, form, and plasticity, we must have a combination input of touch and movement. We call it hand thinking.

Hand thinking can be considered as a reinforcer for integration of visual thinking and auditory thinking. The hand acts not merely as an input source for information received. As output expressor the hand can, for example, draw what the eye sees; as input confirmer it can verify through touch what vision thinks it sees. Transformations, permutations, combinations, classifications, number concepts, and letter recognition are but a few of the many thinking activities which are enhanced and reinforced by the development of hand thinking to an intelligent level.

Thinking games should never be played in sensory deprived environments, and the player should not be artificially restricted or handicapped. His arm movements should not be hampered, and his eyes should not be shut or blindfolded. The individual should learn how to extract incoming information of his choice from the totality of environmental information impinging on him. If he is directed to shut his eyes, for example, he is actively depriving himself of visual input from his environment. This active deprivation could in itself cause confusion.

The feel-and-find box is ideal for our purposes because the child's information input systems are not artificially restricted: He works with his eyes open and is able to move freely. When playing games involving the feel-and-find box, the child is encouraged to use both hands—not just his preferred writing hand. This promotes the full extent of interrelated thinking in a bilateral organism.

The feel-and-find boxes used at Tyler were made with both ends removed. One end had a cloth draped over the opening; objects were placed into the box through the nondraped end. The children played the games by alternating in the roles of expressor and receptor. They discussed, argued, agreed, and disagreed. As the Tyler teacher was free to roam, she could readily facilitate the children's creative endeavors.

The following hand thinking games utilize the developmental sequence which is fully explained in Chapter 8 and exemplified in the parquetry block games. Beginning with the crucial concept of same—not same, the games progress through reversals to the high level of receptive-expressive communication, both verbal and written. For ideas to increase the number of hand thinking game variations, the reader is referred back to Chapter 8.

## What Am I Where? / Game 111

The teacher may play with the child, or two children may play. If there are three or four feel-and-find boxes, the game can become a small group activity. What am I where? enhances the child's recognition of forms and spatial relations.

A thin layer of plastic clay is spread on a large sheet of cardboard. This sheet is portable and can be inserted and removed from the feel-and-find box. Depending on the development of the child, from one to five parquetry blocks are pressed into the clay in various positions—some upright, some flat. It is advisable to use a square piece of cardboard; a single parquetry block pattern can then be used four times. The clay-covered cardboard can be removed, rotated ninety degrees, and reinserted into the Feel-and-Find Box without displacing the parquetry blocks.

Through the curtain, the child inserts both hands into the box. He must determine the shape of each parquetry block, its position within the confines of the box, its location relative to the other blocks, and the amount of space separating the blocks.

In the first variation, the child is to reproduce on top of the box the exact pattern that his hand tells him is inside the box. He is encouraged to confirm his pattern by reaching into the box again. When the child is satisfied that his duplicate pattern is accurate, the curtain is lifted and he evaluates his duplicate pattern by visual comparison. Hand thinking and vision thinking are thus integrated. If his duplicate pattern is inaccurate, he makes the necessary adjustments on top of the box.

Should actual match from hand thinking to vision reproduction prove difficult for the child, the teacher could build a pattern on top of the box and have the child reproduce it inside the box. Here the child is matching visual thinking to hand reproduction.

In the next variation, the child reproduces a pictorial representation of a block pattern. The picture is placed on top of the box and the child builds the pattern inside the box. Conversely, a pattern is constructed inside the box and the child is asked to select from a number of pictures the one which matches the pattern inside the box. The teacher can draw the block patterns himself, use commercially prepared pictures, or take Polaroid photographs. If photographs are used, the concept of perspective can be easily introduced.

Tachistoscope flashing, chalkboard drawing, transformation, and communication games are suitably incorporated as variations of this game. The developmental sequence should always move to the more complex with the child beginning at the level where he is most comfortable.

## Dominoes Touch / Game 112

Commercially marketed dominoes are pressed into the clay sheet to form the type of patterns discussed in what am I where? (Game 111); the same developmental sequence is used.

The child rubs his fingers over the depressed dots on the dominoes to determine how many dots there are on each. In addition, he determines the spatial relation of each domino to the total pattern of dominoes inside the box. The child's concept of number is developed, and his knowledge of figure-ground discrimination is increased.

This domino game prepares the child for mathematics in much the same way that clap patterns (Chapter 9, Game 103) prepares him for reading.

## Feel-and-Find Beads / Game 113

Large, wooden beads of various shapes are placed inside the feel-and-find box; the child strings the beads while keeping his hands within the box. He begins by stringing beads to match a model of a string of beads which has been placed on top of the box. In the next variation, the child handles a strand of beads which has been placed inside the box and then attempts to string a similar strand outside on top of the box. Stringing the beads correctly develops the child's recognition of shapes and temporal relations. In addition, vision thinking and hand thinking are integrated and reinforce each other.

There is a variation in which the child is both expressor and receptor. A string of beads is placed in the feel-and-find box along with loose, assorted beads and a piece of string. Without removing his hands from the box, the child must reproduce the pattern of the strung beads by composing a new string of beads. Again his knowledge of temporal relations is enhanced. The understanding of temporal relations is basic to reading and other academic skills.

## Form Board / Game 114

Form board is a deceptively simple game which challenges the child's hand thinking.

Adaptations of the Seguin form board may be used here; it is a board with a circle, square, and triangle cut out so that they can be removed and replaced. Other boards may incorporate a cross, rectangle, and oval for a total of six removable units. The

**Figure 33.**
**Feel-and-Find Box**
The child explores with his hands the form board within the box
in order to arrange the forms on top of the box accordingly.

board may also be constructed so that the same six forms are divided into twelve pieces with each form being split in half. The fit-a-space disks described in Chapter 8, Game 90 are also suitable for use here.

While keeping his hands within the feel-and-find box, the child places the cutout forms into the correct spaces. In another variation, illustrated in Figure 33, the child arranges the cutout forms which have been placed on top of the box in such a manner that their locations and shapes correspond to spaces in the form board (or disks) concealed in the feel-and-find box. Spatial positioning and form recognition are emphasized here.

## Seriation and Comparison / Game 115

These games develop and reinforce the classification and seriation concepts discussed in Chapter 12 and help the child to make the subtle distinction between things that are same in one way and different in another.

Squares of sandpaper ranging from smooth to rough are placed within the box. The child is to arrange the squares in series; for example, he covers the roughest piece with the next roughest and so on.

Forms such as triangles and squares can be cut from the sandpaper. Then the child would sort and arrange them according to both shape and texture. The triangles would share the attribute of being three sided; in this sense, they would be the same. Their texture would, however, vary; in this sense they would be not same.

The same variations used in What am I where (Game 111) may be introduced here. In these variations, the child will be reinforcing the integration of vision and hand thinking to develop an intelligent knowledge of texture. In addition to its practical value, this knowledge of texture enhances the individual's aesthetic appreciation of art, photography, architecture, and nature.

The feel-and-find box can be used to play other games which develop the child's awareness to make subtle discriminations. For example, plastic golf balls can be filled with varying quantities of buckshot. Size and shape remain constant; the child is asked to determine relative weight. Length and width discrimination can be developed by having the child manually explore nails, popsicle sticks, wires, and string. Size blocks can be used for three-dimensional comparisons of size and volume.

### Familiar Objects / Game 116

Pairs of familiar objects such as combs, marbles, spools, vegetables, and fruits are used in this game. One of the paired objects is placed on top of the box, and the child is asked to find its mate from among a group of different objects in the feel-and-find box. When both of the paired objects have been placed within the box, the child sorts and pairs the objects. Plastic letters and numbers are also used in this manner.

This hand thinking game also can be played by placing an object in the child's hand while he is holding his hands behind his own back. The same rules apply. A ring-formation game can be played by having the children reach behind their backs to pass objects to each other.

### Construct-O-Line Hidden / Game 117

The same games played in Construct-o-line, Game 86, may be played here, but now the hand thinking techniques introduced in what am I where? (Game 111) are applied. The child's knowledge of what a form is, how forms appear in varying spatial transformations, how to draw or construct a form, and how to position points in space is enhanced. The concepts of number, figure-ground, temporal and spatial sequencing, and linear form recognition are involved. These concepts are applied to the academic subjects including reading, writing, and arithmetic.

### Hidden Draw Me / Game 118

A template made by routing a design in a six-inch-square masonite section or linoleum block is placed inside the feel-and-find box.

Various template signs should be made of geometric or simple linear patterns.

The child inserts both hands into the feel-and-find box. One hand holds the routed template, the other hand traces and explores the design. The child is encouraged to use his index finger as the tool for exploration of the design. The teacher should observe which hand the child seems to prefer. If he chooses the hand opposite to the one he generally prefers when writing, there is probably movement confusion involving coordination of the body's axes (discussed in Chapter 6, p. 84).

When the child thinks he has interpreted the design, he attempts to duplicate it on a sheet of unlined paper; he is to draw it exactly as his hand determines it to be. It is important that he make size, shape, and position the same. When the child has finished his drawing, he removes the template from the box and places it on the table. To evaluate his performance, he places his drawing on top of the template and moves the tip of his index finger along the grooves of the template while he holds the template in a stationary position with his other hand. This results in an indentation of the paper conforming exactly to the grooves of the template design. If the child's drawing is accurate, the drawn lines will correspond to the indentations in the paper. The child may repeat the procedure to perfect his results. As the child's skills improve, the templates increase in complexity.

In a variation, the template is no longer used, and the child copies a specified picture with his hands obscured from view in the feel-and-find box. The picture can be placed in various locations around the room.

In a less abstract task, the child duplicates a design by manipulating clay rope within the feel-and-find box. He may also be directed to shape clay in a specific design or to inscribe a design in a flat piece of clay with a metal stylus or a carpenter's nail.

This hand thinking game improves the child's graphic thinking (discussed in the next chapter) and develops speed and accuracy in hand thinking feedback. Efficient hand thinking feedback enhances the child's knowledge of how to stop, start, and change direction of hand movements. It will improve activities involving precise manipulation: drawing, tearing, cutting, writing, and painting.

As stated previously, communication games involving both giving and following instructions have proven necessary and valuable in the Tyler Thinking School program. Our experience has shown that these communication games should be introduced early in the first year; appropriate, uncomplicated instructions are given to direct the children to manipulate parquetry blocks, pegboards, and other actual objects.

After carefully observing the receptive–expressive cycle, the teachers became more aware of their crucial role in the communication cycle constantly occurring within the classroom. Language usage with first year children is particularly important. It is not enough to use simple, uncomplicated words; the words should not have a dual meaning. To a child, "like" may mean "the same as" or "enjoy"; children can not always discern the difference in meaning from the context. The child often interprets "bottom of the paper" to mean "the under surface." Verbal instructions should always be conveyed in short, specific sentences. Language should be meaningful. The words used should be already part of their vocabulary or they should be new words which have been precisely explained.

Older children who came to the Thinking School in their second year were less attentive when first exposed to expressive-receptive games. During initial exposure, they participated half-heartedly and sometimes confused themselves through their own elaborate misinterpretations. We suspect this confusion was an example of adult-induced failure stemming from casual and inappropriate use of language.

Hand thinking games of expressive-receptive communication (written or verbal) are especially valuable when visual input is absent, in which case the importance of precise verbal communication becomes even more evident. The task demands that the child match his auditory input with the input obtained through hand thinking. In a high-level thinking activity he is challenged and must concentrate on the instructions in order to interpret the objects he is to use. If he is casual about paying attention, he will not be able to solve the task.

Recognition and identification of familiar objects through hand thinking develops an awareness of small detail. The goal of these games is to increase the child's curiosity, his ability to probe for detail. When he looks at a button, brush, or sea shell now, he may be more aware of specific, minute detail. He will be able to "feel" through his eyes.

# 11. Graphic Thinking Games

There are two components to graphic thinking: movement thinking and visual thinking. Vision guides and directs movement. Knowing where to stop the total body or any of its component parts is as important as knowing when and where to start. For example, children may have difficulty coloring outline drawings and staying within the lines. The problem may stem from their inability to look at and predict the beginning and end of a line or space, or they may lack efficient coordination of ocular and arm-hand-finger movement. The individual must make a match of these two movements for accuracy and efficiency of skills such as writing, drawing, cutting, and folding. If there is a mismatch of vision and movement, the child may be confused. Until he sorts out and corrects his mismatch, he will function at a low developmental level on any graphic task.

Any activity involving arm-hand-finger-vision match, we call a graphic thinking activity. This includes writing, drawing, coloring, cutting, threading, and carving. The following eleven graphic thinking games have self-evaluation built into them and can be played individually or in groups.

Ocular movement control, well integrated with digital movement control, will ultimately lead to intelligent graphic thinking. It must be emphasized that anything written or transcribed is merely a translation of a movement: A stylus has been placed in the fingers and that stylus is in contact with a surface which may be visibly marked or inscribed. The mark is only the concrete translation of the movement of arm, hand, and fingers.

Developmentally, it is advantageous to initiate graphic thinking activities on a vertical surface. If the child is working on a chalkboard, the bottom of the board should be tilted out approximately eleven to thirteen degrees so that it conforms to the skeletal structure of the vertebral column and its supporting substructures as the child stands upright in front of the chalkboard.

During seated graphic thinking activities, the child should work on a plane surface tilted twelve to fifteen inches upward from the horizontal as in a drafting table. Harmon's research indicates that this degree of tilt matches the natural curve of the spine when an individual is seated while performing a contained, near-point task.[1] Body stress is thus minimized. Less body stress increases the efficiency of all thinking processes.

## Graphic Tracking / Game 119

For optimal graphic performance, the child should function as a well-balanced, integrated, bilateral thinking person with the two sides of his body united in a single thinking action. He should be in a position to use one arm for performance and the other to support his body weight on the writing surface.

This game of tracking develops the child's knowledge of how to trace on, or track along, a line. As mentioned previously, this discriminative movement is analogous to tracking, or following an object with eyes, hand, or tongue.

At the most basic level, the child traces along a path approximately one-inch wide and eight-inches long, solidly chalked in on a chalkboard. Polychromatic Alphasite (triple size) chalk is preferred for this task. If a chalkholder is not available, chalk breakage is minimized by masking tape which may be wrapped in two layers around the hand-held portion of the piece of chalk. The child holds the chalk in his preferred hand (placing his other hand on the chalkboard for support to emphasize bilateral coordination) and draws a line through the solid path from one end to the other without going beyond its lateral borders. At first only straight paths are used, but later angled and curved ones are introduced.

Once a child can track along a solid one-inch-wide path, the path can be decreased in width until the child is eventually tracing a single, thin line. This thin line may then be drawn in angles and curves. Intersecting lines are introduced next. When tracking an intersection, the child must realize that the line continues; he must be able to plot and plan his movements in advance, knowing that he has to cross the intersection in order to get to the end of the line. The last variation is to track an overlapping spiral. The child should master the overlapping spiral before attempting the prewriting sequence (Game 129).

## Dots / Game 120

First graders sometimes have difficulty, computing how to draw a straight line in a direct path between two dots. This is fundamental to the eventual emergence of handwriting skills. In sequence of increased difficulty, two dots are laterally placed, then three dots in triangular position, and finally four dots in diamond-shaped fashion. Figure 34 shows how the four dots can be connected so that the concept of intersection is introduced. The child is instructed to draw a line from here, to here, to here, and so on. This game enhances the child's understanding of how to follow the sequence.

## Hare and Hound / Game 121

One child, the "hare," attempts to place "X's" on the chalkboard faster than another child, the "hound," can connect them by draw-

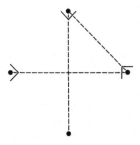

**Figure 34.**
**Four Dots Connected with an Intersecting Line**

ing a line from "X" to "X." When the "hound" catches the "hare," the children change roles.

## Dot Picture / Game 122

Two children play this game. The first draws "X's" on the board and the second draws a connecting line between them. When the "X's" are connected, they should form a picture, for example, four connected "X's" to form a square, three to form a triangle, many to form a circle. The first child may think of more complex designs such as a fish or a house. Both children are developing graphic thinking, and the first child is also learning how to preplan.

## Templates / Game 123

Using templates increases the child's knowledge of the movement necessary to create the basic forms upon which writing and other graphic arts depend. The best templates are made with a large section for the child to hold the template against the chalkboard with his nonwriting hand while his preferred drawing hand tracks within the template on the board.[2] The exact manner in which the child tracks the form is not important; it is important that he develop kinesthetic-proprioceptive knowledge of how the form is graphically constructed.

The child should track the form several times without stopping. The template should then be removed and the child should trace over the lines he has already drawn on the chalkboard. After tracing the drawing several times, the child should then draw the same form directly under the template tracing—without using the template, however. He repeats the entire procedure three times. This results in three template tracings and three free-form drawings directly underneath.

He should then be encouraged to evaluate his free-form drawings by telling which he likes best, next best, and least. In the final step, the child selects a different colored piece of chalk and traces the template over his free-form drawings to check his previous evaluations. Thus he is able to determine the areas in which he needs to improve. The evaluations can also be made in groups with all children benefiting from the discussion.

Templates should be used in the following sequence: circle, square, triangle, rectangle, diamond. The rectangle and the square should be compared so that the child discovers that things can be similar yet not the same. He should be shown both the similarities and differences.

## Chalkboard Tach / Game 124

A design is flashed onto a screen from an overhead projector by rapidly covering and uncovering it or from a tachistoscope. The designs should vary from single forms to multiple forms, to overlapping forms, to forms in different positions. (See chalkboard tach, Chapter 8, Game 78).

A group of children watch the projected design while one child tries to reproduce it in size, shape, and position on the chalkboard. After the child has drawn the design on the chalkboard, the group may discuss it; the teacher can reproject the design over the child's drawing to check for accuracy in size, shape, and position. Those children who remain seated at their desks can also reproduce the design on a piece of paper folded to represent an area of the chalkboard.

The design is then once more projected and the child can trace over the projected lines for double feedback. He can see how well he has drawn the design the first time, and he gets graphic thinking feedback from reproducing the design a second time. The same technique may be employed using clay as a writing surface and a carpenter's nail as a stylus.

## Electro-Trace / Game 125

This is a simply constructed battery operated game.[3] A flexible but sturdy wire is connected to flashlight batteries which operate a light or a buzzer. The child holds a loop which surrounds the wire. He attempts to move the loop from one end of the wire to the other without allowing the loop to touch the wire. If the loop

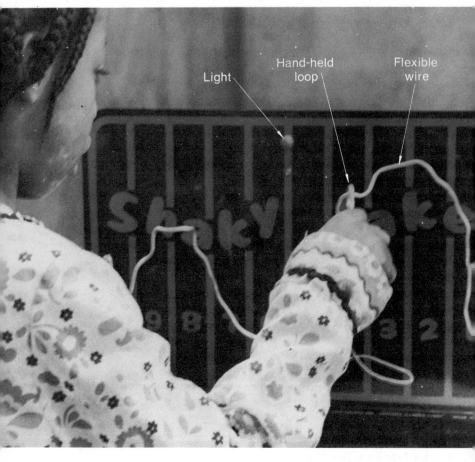

**Figure 35.**
**Child Playing Shaky Jake**

touches the wire, it activates the buzzer or the light or both. The flexibility of the guide wire allows it to be bent or straight. The goal is to develop hand-eye skills in moving the loop from one end to the other without touching the guide wire (Figure 35).

Another technique is to place a piece of masking tape on a larger piece of tin foil. The child is to trace the tape line with a metal tool held by a wooden handle. If he leaves the tape and touches the foil, a buzzer sounds or a light goes on or a counter clicks.

These battery operated electronic games can be homemade or purchased commercially.

## Getman School Skill Tracing Board / Game 126

This is an appropriately slanted drawing surface approximately eighteen-inches square.[4] One edge of a plastic overlay is attached to the upper edge of the tracing board so that the plastic may be lifted up freely. A series of prepared designs such as lines, geometric forms, mazes, and letters are placed under the plastic. Various graphic thinking activities are played such as tracing, connecting dots, drawing forms, following mazes, and tracing manuscript letters. Wipe off crayons or wax marking pencils are used. Both of these are easily removed which increases the child's willingness to attempt the task by reducing his fear of making a mistake.

## Near-Point Tasks—Multiple Forms / Game 127

Using a near-point tachistoscope, the child flashes a design and then draws it from memory on tracing paper or on a transparent plastic sheet. For comparison and evaluation, the card is removed from the tachistoscope and the child's drawing is placed on top of it. The child is able to see the model through his tracing paper or plastic sheet. If the match is not good, the child reinforces the desired result by tracing the form onto his overlay and then proceeds to the next tachistoscope card.

## Graphic Puzzles / Game 128

In this game, the child traces intersecting lines with either his eyes only, a flashlight, or a crayon. Given the beginning of the line, the goal is to discover where the line ends. Although puzzles like these are commercially available,[5] the teacher can also make them by drawing overlapping and intersecting lines. To make the lines more obvious, different colors are used. The teacher's drawing is then covered with transparent paper on which the children trace with wipe-off crayons or wax marking pencils. In this manner, the puzzle may be used repeatedly.

The designs may be varied from the simple to the complex—for example, a thin line and thick line of the same color may be drawn, then two colors may be introduced, then equally thick or thin lines, then additional lines, curves, and angles may be drawn.

## Prewriting Sequences[6] / Game 129

Before attempting this game, the child should be fairly proficient in all the preceding graphic thinking games.

A sequence of graphic linear designs has been devised to promote the flexibility that will help the child to print, write, or draw. See examples of these designs in Figure 36.

The children must try to duplicate all of the above drawings. The last design in Figure 36 is a free-form design which the child is also to duplicate. The goal is exact and specific reproduction of the intersections, sizes of loops, and positions of angles. Exact reproduction of sections and spaces is encouraged.

The teacher helps the children to discover where their drawings differ (not same) by questioning them or by coloring a section of his own drawing and having the children do the same to theirs.

When the children have improved their graphic thinking and are able to make the designs, the designs are gradually changed to take on the form of cursive writing, as shown in Figure 37.

Proficiency in reproducing designs is enhanced by having the children hold a screen (a sheet of oak-tag will do) over their

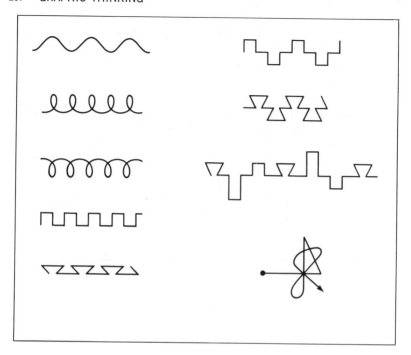

**Figure 36.**
**Prewriting Graphic Designs in Developmental Sequence**

drawing hand. This minimum clue situation emphasizes the mental integration of vision thinking and hand thinking and helps to internalize graphic thinking so that it becomes an intuitive mental process. With visual confirmation completely excluded,

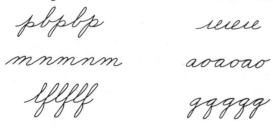

**Figure 37.**
**Prewriting Cursive Designs**

the children must have even greater control over hand-arm movement thinking. When the screen is removed, the children have the visual feedback necessary to evaluate their accuracy.

A mark on paper, an inscribed mark on clay or stone, a chalk written message, a painting—all are translations of an arm-hand-finger movement. The movement is made by holding a stylus against the surface to be marked. It is the movement thinking, not the stylus, that creates the graphic design.

If the child has difficulty with graphic thinking, his general movement thinking and his discriminative movement thinking should be evaluated first. This should be followed by evaluation of his visual thinking. Only if these are adequate should he be actively involved with writing and drawing skill development.

# 12. Logical Thinking Games

The games described in this chapter, like all thinking games, are played for the thinking that the child must do and not for the learning of specific subject matter or of rules for solving problems. The activity of the child and the child's comprehension of what he is doing and why he is doing it are all important. Results are not stressed for their own sake but for the feedback they provide to further the child's thinking.

From this viewpoint, the games of this chapter differ from a mathematical program, even though most of the exercises clearly fall within mathematical thinking. Ideally, the games illustrate how a psychologically suitable curriculum of mathematics or science would be a natural continuation of activities that characterize all human thinking. A major benefit of a School for Thinking is the easy transfer of general habits of thinking to special fields of academic knowledge and the child's realization that these special fields are not unconnected bits of knowledge imposed upon him.

Shortcut rules to obtain results on problems, such as mathematical formulas, are useful to the child when he has the capacity to comprehend the problem in a high-level fashion. If rules are given prematurely to the child they are likely to be more a hindrance than a help to his natural curiosity and development of thinking. Knowing how to execute a rule correctly is at best a low level performance in contrast to knowing how to explore the task. Exploration means mentally moving within the thinking system that the child has interiorized and applying the system to the task at hand. Knowing how to multiply by means of memorized multiplication tables does not automatically imply that the child has interiorized the underlying logical mathematical system. However, once he comprehends the system and can freely move about within it, solving of arithmetic problems clearly is facilitated by knowing the multiplication tables.

In short, the child is encouraged by the teacher for the activity of the thinking game and is not pushed for obtaining a result he does not himself discover. The cues that guide the child's activity come primarily from the task and not from the teacher's verbal or nonverbal behavior.

Many thinking games use artificial objects or artificial language, such as geometric blocks, logical symbols, and numbers. For a proper comprehension of what thinking is, it is imperative that the child does not confine the application to the artificial school situation. Therefore, whenever possible, materials from the physical and social environment are brought into the Thinking School for use in the games.

## CLASSIFICATION

All classification involves a grouping or sorting of objects into classes according to some rule or principle. Girls can be grouped into blondes, brunettes, and so on; or into unmarried, married, divorced, widowed; or into levels of education. Within each of these groupings or dimensions there are levels or subclasses which exemplify the dimension. For example, levels of education range from grade school to graduate school. Some of the attributes within one dimension are measurable in a continuous quantifiable manner, such as length (in inches) and age (in years), others are continuous, frequently from one extreme to another, but not easily measurable, such as beauty versus ugliness, sleepiness versus wakefulness; finally, others are discontinuous or discrete, such as sex and nationality. A person belongs unequivocally into the masculine or feminine gender; but there are many graduations to the classification of beauty and they arbitrarily vary as the opinions of the beholder.

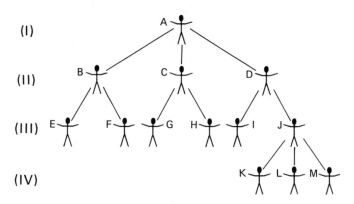

**Figure 38.**
**A Family Tree of Four Generations (I) to (IV)**

The examples given so far deal with classification on a horizontal level, that is, the different dimensions have no intrinsic relation to each other. Hair color, marital status, and education are unrelated characteristics into which people can be classified. However, this horizontal level is only the beginning of classification.Classification has its most significant aspect when one considers its vertical or hierarchical direction.

We shall use as example an existing family tree as illustrated in Figure 38. All true classification involves, at least theoretically, the possibility of a hierarchical classification. The grandfather A has three children B, C, D each of whom has in turn two children E to J. Finally, J has three children K, L, M.

This is a perfect example of a hierarchical arrangement of classes insofar as all classes stand in a necessary relation to each other. In the context of Figure 38 the class of sons at level (II) implies the presence of the class of father at level (I) and of the classes of children and grandchildren at levels (III) and (IV). A child who comprehends this system can mentally move up or down a level (vertically) and across a given level (horizontally) or up or down and across (obliquely) within this system. He understands that a person J can be at the same time father, brother, son, and grandson. Moreover, I and J are alike as being related children of the same parent D, whereas H and J are alike as being related grandchildren of the same grandparent A. These relations characterize the respective classes of siblings and cousins and show how the two classes are different and at the same time alike.

When a child responds to the well-known similarity problem "In which way are a cat and a mouse alike?" with "One is big and one is little," he demonstrates his difficulties with coordinating horizontal and vertical moving within the classification system. That is, being asked to compare cat and mouse, he focuses on the horizontal level of the classification system and answers incorrectly with the dimension of size. For the correct answer he has to move along the vertical direction. "Animal" is the *common* dimension that lies at a higher level than the *differentiating* dimension of size.

For the person who comprehends the system, the relative distance of one element to another within the system, does not appreciably affect his performance. But for a child the question "In which way is a cat and a tree alike?" is considerably more difficult than "In which way is a cat and a mouse alike?" The reason for this difference is clear. Life—the common dimension for cat and tree—is two levels removed from cat and tree, whereas animal—the common dimension for cat and mouse—is only one level removed.

All classifying implies quantification. As soon as we speak of roses we exclude from the number of things belonging to that class anything that is not a rose. Moreover, with regard to the class of roses, we can make the following statements without having to verify them by observation: "There are more flowers than there are roses." "All roses are flowers (which really means all roses are some of the flowers)." "Not all flowers are roses." The criterion which allows us to make such statements without the need of external evidence is a logical certainty that follows from our comprehension of what a classification system implies.

Children have difficulties with clearly separating three things that go with all classifying. First, they confuse the thing and the class. They do not clearly understand the difference between the mental construct of a class and the physical objectivity of a thing. Classes do not exist in the physical word but are constructed by the inquiring mind. When a five-year-old child has a bunch of flowers in his hand, ten roses, two tulips, and one daisy, and he is asked, "Are there more roses or flowers?" his answer is likely to be that there are more roses than flowers. Of course, this child generally knows what flowers are and what roses are. But he fails to understand adequately that the criterion for the correct response is to be found in mentally moving within the classification system and not in physically moving his eyes through the number of flowers he holds in his hands. Mentally he says to himself "I have here many roses and a few flowers (the two tulips and one daisy)." Note that these are correct statements. But the child, who has not yet clearly separated classes and things, classifies the things in front of him as if the two classes of flower and roses were on a horizontal level. Distracted by the physical sight of many roses, he neglects the vertical direction in which the two classes are related.

Apart from the basic difficulty of clearly separating the physical object and the mental class to which it belongs, the use of language in classification creates confusion between the class and its name and the thing and its name. When young children deny that a doctor can be a father and still be a doctor, they get confused because they think that when the label changes the situation changes. On the other hand, where one label can be used in two different meanings, that is, can correspond to two different classes, children will have difficulties accepting the narrow meaning as included in the broad meaning. For many young children the class "school" is the elementary and secondary school. College and university have a different name and consequently are not included in the class of school. They find it difficult to comprehend that the name "school" is not limited to their own experience. They have experienced the word "school" and the word "university" as belonging to two different classes of things. They are confused when the name of one thing is now used to designate the class that includes both things.

These are not merely linguistic difficulties, as some would say, that can be overcome by teaching the child words or phrases. The linguistic difficulties are symptoms of the immaturity of the child's thinking. The difficulties are thinking difficulties. When a child develops to the stage that he can readily comprehend (has the criterion for) the relevant properties of a class (What is it?) and the entire range of things included in the class (How does it belong?), then he dominates the thinking system in a high-level fashion. As a result he will dominate the linguistic medium and use language intelligently.

Classificatory thinking permeates all intellectual activities. The discussion so far can be readily applied to all logical thinking games. These games are meant to give the child the opportunity for high level experiences. The child of primary school age is just beginning to interiorize the system of classification and other systems of logical reasoning such as seriation, combination, and quantification. Interiorization here means that the child acquires the ready use of the internal criterion that the thinking system provides. Knowledge can then be used where appropriate. The games are high-level activities to the extent that the child uses the thinking system at his highest developmental capacity. This is the purpose of all logical thinking games.

## SORTING BY DIMENSIONS

### Matching Properties / Game 130

On the easiest level the children are given objects that differ only in two or more attributes within one obvious dimension, such as objects of different colors or of different texture. In addition, the property by which objects are sorted is also shown by the container. A ready example are two containers, blue and red, into which blue and red objects, respectively, have to be placed.

Similarly, different textures can be sorted: rough styrofoam balls are put into rough styrofoam cups and smooth balls into smooth cups. In another game wooden objects go into wooden boxes and metal objects into metal boxes.

## Class Sorting / Game 131

This game differs from the preceding in that there is no matching of properties and that sorting is done into a container of whatever nature, later without any container, simply by putting objects of one class onto a sheet of paper, within a circle, or just on one side of a table. If the dimension is not so obvious that it can readily be discovered by the children, the teacher can verbalize the class to be sorted. For instance, in picture sorting, the teacher suggests that things that move go here, things that stay stationary go there. However, it is decidedly better to let the children discover and spontaneously verbalize the class into which they sort objects. In all these games what is important is not so much the discovery or the linquistic aspect but primarily the child's comprehension of classification. This comprehension is exercised in the child's actual sorting of objects.

One variety of this game shows the children that the number of classes need not be two, for example, three colors, three shapes, and four sizes. Sorting out one class from the rest of the items is also instructive: "Put all things that are round into this box and leave the other things on the table." As children take turns to perform this game they form the class of roundness (exemplified by the objects in the box) and the complementary class of things not round (exemplified by the objects left on the table).

This game also can readily be adapted to all kinds of everyday things and help children to clarify their thinking about these things. Things that break, tear, burn, rust are different ways of classifying. Children can be asked to collect things of one class and bring them to the classroom. If appropriate, the objects collected can be further subdivided according to some dimensions, such as leaves sorted into various shapes.

## CLASS SWITCHING

In the previous games we played with distinct nonoverlapping attributes, e.g., objects that differed in the attribute of shape only: They were round, square, triangle, rectangular, either one or another. But now we have objects that can be sorted into more than one obvious attribute, for instance objects that differ in shape and at the same time in color and size.

## Class Discovery (2 attributes) / Game 132

Children are presented with nine geometrical cutouts: three triangles, three circles, three squares, of three colors, blue, yellow, red. They are told to sort them as seems natural and best to them. Only if necessary are the children told to sort into three classes. Such instructions can be indicated nonverbally by handing the children three boxes into which the objects are to be sorted. Probably most children pay attention to one dimension only and group the cutouts according to color. Once they succeed with this, the children are applauded and told to do another sorting. No pressure is put on them to discover the second dimension, namely shape; but they are given many opportunities and when children work in groups it is likely that one or another child discovers the possibility of sorting according to more than one dimension. Through several games of this kind and without much talk the children realize a vital principle of classifying—its arbitrary character. In other words, it is just as correct to say that these cutouts are blue, yellow, or red as it is to say, they are triangles, squares, or circles.

## Class Discovery (3 attributes) / Game 133

This game is as the preceding, but a third potential dimension is added, such as size in addition to color and shape. This addition makes the task considerably more difficult, and children need plenty of unpressured and unhurried opportunities to discover and practice the principle of switching of classification principles. This game is readily applied to things in the child's environment: sorting of buttons by shape, size, color; of cutlery; of books.

## OVERLAPPING ATTRIBUTES

A further step in classification recognizes explicitly that an object can belong at the same time to two or more classes.

### Overlapping Circles / Game 134

As a preparation we played this game first with two hoops lying side by side. Blue objects were sorted into one, yellow into the other, and outside the hoops were all other colored objects. Then we put small (versus large) objects into hoop 1 and yellow (versus nonyellow) into hoop 2. What should children do with objects that are both small and yellow? They go into both circles and the only way to accomplish this physically, is to place the two hoops partly one on the other. The intersecting area marks the space where a small yellow object belongs. When the game is ended the child has sorted all the objects into four groups: small, yellow, small and yellow, and—outside the hoops—neither small nor yellow. Here, as before, the introduction of the overlapping

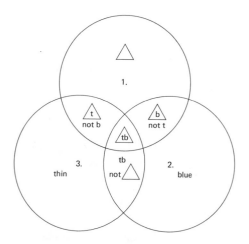

**Figure 39.**
**Three Overlapping Classes: triangle (△), thin (t), blue (b).**

hoops is done slowly to give the children plenty of time to assimilate the principle of intersecting classes.

After children perform the double classification readily, the addition of a third overlapping hoop makes the task a little more complex. We deal now with three different dimensions, such as shape, thickness, and color and choose one attribute of each of these dimensions as relevant, say—triangle, thin, blue. Figure 39 shows these dimensions assigned to three hoops which have four overlapping areas: Thin (not blue) triangles; blue (thick) triangles; thin, blue (not triangles); thin, blue triangles. In the three nonoverlapping spaces are: (1) triangles that are neither thin nor blue, (2) blue objects that are neither triangles nor thin, (3) thin objects that are neither triangles nor blue.

### Discovery of Overlapping Classes / Game 135

In this variation of the preceding game the teacher displays all the items in front of the children and puts a certain number of them into the respective spaces of overlapping hoops. On the basis of this initial display the children continue the sorting and are corrected by the teacher until they discover the appropriate principle of classification. While in Game 134 the children are either instructed to sort according to two or three attributes or are left free to choose as they please, here the task is to infer from the given display the underlying principle. The last example in Game 134 could be modified by the teacher putting at once one thin blue triangle into the triple intersection. From this one item the entire principle of classification is determined except, of course, that it is quite irrelevant which hoop is assigned to which attribute.

### What Can a Thing Be / Game 136

In this game, which can be played with the entire class, a child shows a certain object, say, a pen and asks what it can be used for. "To write," is the natural answer, that is, "It belongs to the class of writing utensils." But what else? The children take turns or are called upon, depending on circumstances. A pen can be used to point, to tap, to break, to spank, to tear, to make a hole, to search for something, to throw like an arrow, to turn something around, and so on. An ashtray can be a container, a plate, a window, can be used as a template to draw a circle, and so forth.

At other times the teacher would show the children the picture of a person and ask them in turn what this person could be. The children start by suggesting different vocations, such as postman, shopkeeper or miner; then the teacher encourages an alternate classification: a father. Children have difficulties with switching dimensions on the same object. Finally, another child volunteers: an uncle, a grandfather, a husband. What else? A son, a grandson. Are there other dimensions? He can be a Democrat, a friend, a churchgoer, a tennis player, all various and different dimensions that intersect in one person.

## ORDERING AND SERIATING

In this task the child's attention is focused on the sequential pattern in which items are placed. That is, an item is correctly placed when the child simultaneously takes into account the placement of neighboring items and the sequence or pattern that the items form within the whole.

Sequencing is as ubiquitous as is classifying. When we identify or recognize objects and when we know how to use them or how to act in certain situations, we assimilate the objects or situations to general schemes. Such an assimilation is at the least an implicit classifying of so many particular events into general mechanisms of acting that are hierarchically interrelated, not unlike the family tree of relations depicted at the beginning of the chapter. Sequencing, on the other hand, is inherent in the nature of all external actions that always take place in time and hence manifest a temporal coordination. For sense and body thinking, proper sequencing is essential, and the challenge of many games in earlier chapters resides precisely in the exercise of a coordinated sequence. In the chapter on auditory thinking a number of rhythm or pattern games were described because the auditory sense is particularly characterized by its temporal dimension. The relation of auditory sequencing and language can be recognized by the difficulties some children have with differentiating "spaghetti" from a "pasghetti" sound sequence. This illustrates how sense, body, and logical thinking interact and mutually benefit from a healthy development of each interrelated aspect of sequencing.

All systems of numbers are of course based on the operation of seriation insofar as each number is meaningful and determined by its relative position within the sequential system. Similarly, mathematical concepts of "greater than" or "smaller than" imply an ordered sequence and the logical inference, if A is bigger than B and if B is bigger than C, then A is bigger than C, is recognized by the child as valid and necessary once the operation of seriation is fully developed. Here, as in other games, mathematical and logical thinking are closely related. We stress again that the logical games described in this chapter are not meant to take the place of an adequate program of mathematics or science but illustrate logical operations common to all types of thinking.

## Patterns / Game 137

The patterns games described here are limited to visual patterns and relate to sense thinking as well as to logical thinking. As sense thinking they all have a perceptual support, which enables very young children to grasp some patterns. For example, a pattern green–blue–green–blue is readily continued by green; four blocks of obviously different sizes are placed in descending order from large to small. As the perceptual support becomes less obvious, the logical comprehension takes on greater importance. The teacher can vary the level of difficulty, up or down, on a logical thinking task simply by modifying its perceptual support.

Pattern and sequence games can be played by groups of children with blocks, pictures, drawings, on the blackboard, or with paper and pencil. They frequently admit of more than one appropriate solution. Given a pattern such as xxox, one may complete and continue as xxoxxoxxo . . . , but equally well as xxoxoxx depending on whether an open or a closed pattern is intended. The first given pattern is open-ended; it continues without limit. The second pattern is closed and exists in its present form as a symmetrical whole. Generally, closed patterns are closer to perceptual thinking, open patterns to logical thinking.

### Seriation / Game 138

To insure logical thinking the items to be seriated must differ from each other in not too obvious a manner. Consequently, the child must use some form of measurement, if only lining up one item against another. The child is presented with ten sticks of different lengths and asked to properly arrange them. Any ordering, any grouping is accepted and simply observed. Some children take the sticks and make the outline of a figure; others group the sticks into groups of small or big ones. On a subsequent day the children are given not ten sticks but ten disks of different size. Now the child is unlikely to make an outline and more likely to sort them into small groups. At this point the teacher can introduce the stick task by explicitly instructing the child to arrange them by length in an ascending order from little to big. The teacher observes whether the child lines the sticks up against a straight line, such as the edge of a table or a box. Eventually the teacher suggests a descending order as well as introduces other items to be seriated, such as circles of different sizes, sandpaper of different roughness, colors of differing shades, blocks of different thickness.

A more difficult variation of this game is interpolation which requires that the children first have completed placing several sticks in series. The children have completed a series of seven sticks. The teacher has kept back three sticks which are now handed to the children to be placed in the appropriate spots within the series. Here the teacher can observe how intelligently the child interpolates these sticks, whether by perceptual trial and error or by logical preconception.

## Lining Up / Game 139

In this game ordering and seriation is applied to persons and everyday objects. When children line themselves up according to height, they behave with their bodies in a manner analogous to the seriation of sticks: They have to compare themselves against the neighboring children and make sure they stand between the one child just a little taller and the one child just a little smaller. Other ways of lining up are in alphabetical order of first names, by hair color, by chronological order of birthdates.

## PERMUTATIONS

In these games the children learn to pay attention to the various ways in which a fixed number of items can be arranged. Take the numbers 1, 2, and 3. One can arrange them—with no duplication of numbers using the standard permutation formula $3 \times 2 \times 1 = 6$ patterns or permutations: 123, 132, 213, 231, 312, 321. Notice the systematic sequence of these numbers, first the two triplets starting with 1, then those with 2, and finally the two triplets starting with 3. This is an example of one possible systematic approach. With four items the standard formula for possible arrangements would be $4 \times 3 \times 2 \times 1 = 24$ permutations: 1234, 1243, 1324, 1342, 1423, 1432, 2134, 2143, . . . and so forth. These tasks are given to the children with a view towards having them freely discover a systematic method of achieving a complete set of possible arrangements.

## Arrangements / Game 140

Four children Tom, Mary, Jim, and Sam sit around a table. "In how many different ways can you arrange yourselves?" The answer is 24, as shown above, but all we are interested in here is to give the children the opportunity to experience several possible arrangements. To help keep records and to compare the results of several groups of four children, the four sides of the table are each marked with a different color as illustrated in Figure 40. The chil-

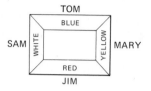

**Figure 40.**
**Placement of Four Children**
**around a Table**

dren write their names or initials after the color on a sheet of paper. For instance, one group's record may begin like this:

| Blue   | T | M | S | J | J |
|--------|---|---|---|---|---|
| Yellow | M | J | T | T | S |
| Red    | J | S | M | S | T |
| White  | S | T | J | M | M |

By actual movement of themselves around the table, the children do with their own bodies what in other permutations they do with physical objects. Note also that the children can realize that change in an arrangement does not require the change of all items: J T S M is different from J S T M even though J and M have not changed position. A variation of this game is to have children make different arrangements with concrete objects, colors, or numbers. If a sufficient number of items are available there is no need to keep records since the children can simply line up one arrangement under another.

When the children are just beginning to pay attention to the method of construction and the total number of possible permutations, it is advisable to have only three different objects to arrange. Six is a number the children can feasibly grasp in contrast to the 24 possible permutations of four items.

Another way of limiting the number of arrangements is to ask for different pairs of two only. Given three items, 1, 2, 3, such as three objects or three colors—not fixed items as before but three items that can be used more than once—how many different pairs can be formed? One method of constructing pairs looks like this: 11, 12, 13, 21, 22, 23, 31, 32, 33; that is $3 \times 3 = 9$ pairs. With four items one can make 16 pairs: 11, 12, 13, 14, 21, 22, 23, 24, 31, 32, 33, 34, 41, 42, 43, 44. For five items we could apply the standard formula of $5 \times 5 = 25$. At no time does the teacher tell the children the rule for arriving at the total number or for constructing the pairs in a systematic fashion.

## Graphic Permutations / Game 141

This game is no different from the foregoing except that it is done on the chalkboard without the use of concrete objects. The teacher puts a short sequence of items on the board, such as, L X O T U. Then he draws a line under it and leaves the group of children alone to play the permutation game. Their task is to take turns and write as many different permutations of the given items as they can think of. Colored lines or geometrical forms can be substituted for letters or numbers.

## CROSS CLASSIFICATION

A complete cross classification requires that all given items are classified according to two or more dimensions at the same time. As the following games will show, cross classification adds to simple classification the further requirement of a consistent sequential order. The result of a cross classification is a matrix in the shape of a square where the horizontal rows indicate items belonging to distinct attributes of one dimension and the vertical columns indicate items belonging to distinct attributes of another dimension.

## Matrix / Game 142

Use a matrix board, that is, a square piece of cardboard or wood, evenly divided into four spaces as shown in Figure 41. The child has to choose from numerous items having two dimensions, for instance, shapes (with the attributes triangles, circles, squares, diamonds) and colors (with the attributes blue, yellow, red, white).

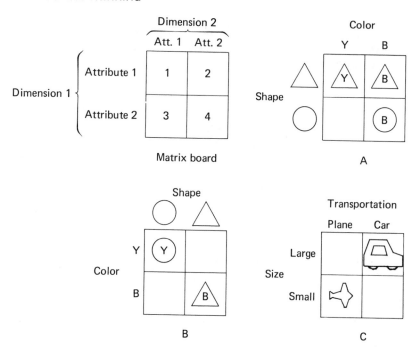

**Figure 41.**
**Placement of Classes on a Matrix Board**

A. The first step is to complete a matrix with one free choice. For instance, the teacher puts a yellow triangle into space 1, a blue triangle into space 2, and a blue circle into space 4. The child's task is to realize that the logical choice is a yellow circle for space 3 (Fig. 41A). Here, as always, the teacher is careful not to impose a correct solution too quickly. It is better to leave the children alone, to let them observe and to talk to each other and to give them plenty of opportunities for different types of construction and thinking.

B. A next step is to have the child complete a matrix with only two items given that share the attribute of one dimension and differ in the attribute of the other dimension. The teacher puts a yellow circle in space 1 and a blue circle in space 3, in other words, he determines the designations of column 1 as circles and of rows 1 and 2 as yellow and blue, respectively. It is up to the child to determine the designation of column 2, by putting in spaces 2 and 4 a yellow and blue triangle, or square, or diamond. Each of these choices would be equally logical and result in the completion of a matrix where column 2 would be triangles, or squares, or diamonds, respectively (Fig. 41B).

C. A more difficult variation is to fill in the matrix with two items that differ in two attributes. For instance, spaces 2 and 3 are occupied by a big toy car and a little toy plane respectively. Note that in this game diagonal spaces are filled, whereas in (B) horizontal or vertical spaces were filled. In this case, the child may choose a big plane for space 1 and a little car for space 4 (Fig. 41C). In other words, he determined the dimension of the columns as transportation (plane, car) and of the rows as size (big, little). The other solution would be the big car in space 4 and the little plane in space 1.

## Graphic Matrix / Game 143

In this version of the matrix game children work on the blackboard and take turns in constructing or completing a matrix. This game can turn into a free discovery: One child starts by drawing a circle in the middle of a nine-square matrix. Another child continues by making a bigger circle in the right adjacent square. With this step the dimensions and the attributes of the column are practically determined: Column 1 is little, column 2 is middle sized, column 3 is large, and the dimension is size. (Note that this involves a natural sequence or seriation.)

What if the child instead of a large circle had drawn two circles? Can another child discover the attribute for column 1? Column 3 has two elements, column 2 one element and therefore column 1 would have to have half an element, in this case, half a circle. At this point the choice of the rows is still undetermined. If a third child draws a triangle in the square just above the middle, that would determine the designation of triangle for row 1, circle for row 2 and possibly square or crescent for row 3.

As children get used to this game they will discover that form and quality of lines lend themselves well to cross classification. For instance, columns 1 to 3 have straight, wavy, zigzag lines, respectively; rows 1 to 3 have thin, normal, thick lines, respectively. This game also can be handed out on ditto sheets with the teacher letting the children freely construct matrices or complete those that have been started.

### Natural Matrix / Game 144

Children collect objects that can be cross classified, such as leaves, shells, buttons, food, screws, stones. Preferably small groups of three to four children work together and discuss with each other what objects and what attributes they would look for. In this manner they get to know things in their natural environment and find those regularities and relations which the logic thinking games have helped them to discover and construct.

## SYMBOL-PICTURE LOGIC

Games of logic symbolization are particularly suitable for the age corresponding to grades one to three and can be continued up to grade six. They combine many thinking activities that are practiced in other games and provide a good opportunity for the teacher to observe whether a child is ready for formal learning, that is, for dealing in an artificial symbol system of logical relations. The logic we are dealing with is closely related to the logic of classification; but in addition to classification there is the primary problem of the symbol-object relation which creates many high-level challenges for the young child.

### Symbol Picture Logic / Game 145

This game is described in detail in Chapter 8 of *Piaget for Teachers*. Here we give only a brief outline. Children come to the blackboard and in turn complete logical problems within the system that the teacher introduces. As a general rule, the teacher gives no verbal explanation of the logical meaning of the symbols.

Briefly, a logical expression consists of three parts: a symbol expression of a class, an arrow indicating a judgment of truth or falsehood, and a drawing as a concrete sample of a class. For instance,

$$H \rightarrow \text{⌂} . T \rightarrow \text{♀} . S \rightarrow \text{✮}$$

would be one way to begin. The teacher can verbalize, "H goes with this, T goes with this," etc. and, if suitable, can add that the letter-symbols are the first letter of the respective words. First letters are not really essential, and other arbitrary letters or graphic symbols can be used as well and are at times preferable.

Now the child is shown that not only:

$$H \rightarrow \text{⌂} \text{ but also } H \rightarrow \text{⌂ ⌂} \text{ and even } H \rightarrow \text{⌂ ♀}$$

because H symbolizes the class of house and this class is verified by one concrete house as well as by two or more concrete houses and is still verified by a house that has a tree next to it. On this point the child is encouraged to understand by means of written symbol problems the difference between a symbolized class and a particular object of that class.

The teacher can pose problems to complete in three different ways: $? \rightarrow \text{⌂}$, $H \, ? \, \text{⌂}$, $H \rightarrow ?$
To illustrate the first way, children are shown that a particular object situation, e.g., a star and a tree, can be symbolized truthfully in different ways: $S \rightarrow$ is acceptable and so is $T \rightarrow$, but with H one has to put $H \nrightarrow$, where the crossed arrow indicates "H does not go with that." ("That" refers to the entire situation to which the arrow points, here, a star and a tree. See Fig. 42.)

We are practising here a most essential aspect of thinking. There is not just one true way in which one can think about (in this case, classify) an objective situation, just as there is not just one way in which one can exemplify a class. Generally, a symbolic expression can be verified by more than one situation, and a situation can be symbolized in more than one symbolic expression.

**Figure 42.**
**Symbol Picture Logic**
One pictured situation within the circle, and three different symbolic expressions.

This aspect of an essentially arbitrary perspective is characteristic of all thinking. Children in the School for Thinking got this message implicitly by all thinking games, but most explicitly by this symbol-picture logic where different solutions to one problem are the rule.

A further step in this game is to illustrate by means of examples the meaning of $\overline{\ }$, the negation sign. $\overline{H} \rightarrow$ means, show me an example where the absence of the house is verified and, consequently, any drawing except a house would be appropriate. Further, the teacher can attempt to introduce the logical connective of conjunction that is placed between the symbol letters, such that H • S means both the presence of house and the presence of star while T • $\overline{H}$ means both the presence of tree and the absence of house and $\overline{H}$ • $\overline{T}$ means both the absence of house and the absence of tree.

With older children the teacher can add another logical connective, namely disjunction, by means of the sign v. Disjunction, in contrast to conjunction, means "either . . . or, or both," such that T v $\overline{H}$ means "either the presence of tree or the absence of house or both." Consequently, T v $\overline{H} \rightarrow$☆ would be a correct statement since the absence of house ($\overline{H}$) is verified: the arrow points to a situation that does not include a house.

Finally, one can put the negation sign over the conjunction or the disjunction indicating the denial not of the class but of the logical operation. $\overline{H} \bullet \overline{T}$ differs from $H \overline{\bullet} T$; in the first case one affirms the conjunction of two negations, in the second case one denies the conjunction of two classes. Therefore, $\overline{H} \bullet \overline{T}$ ("not a house and not a tree") $\not\rightarrow$ ⌂ , but $H \overline{\bullet} T$ ("not the combination of a house and a tree") $\rightarrow$ ⌂ ; likewise $\overline{H} \vee \overline{T}$ ("not a house or not a tree") $\rightarrow$ ⌂ , but $H \overline{\vee} T$ ("neither a house nor a tree") $\not\rightarrow$ ⌂ . These more advanced operations are close to formal thinking and would not normally be found in children below age ten.

## PROBABILITY

The children in primary grades slowly develop a stable and objective view of the world. The preschooler's world presents a curious mixture of incompatible viewpoints. On the one hand, the little child sees regularities and necessities that are out of place. A child may think that all optometrists' offices *must* be in the lower level of their house because he has seen this arrangement in one or two cases. On the other hand, he sees randomness and chance where adults see necessity and regularity. Thus he thinks that it is sheer luck that his daddy gets a monthly paycheck, not realizing the connection between work and salary. The misinterpretation of this work-salary relation is expressed in the child's saying, "I know who is the richest man in town. The bus driver, because he collects all the money."

Probability deals with understanding of chance, greater or lesser likelihood, necessity, impossibility, and equal odds. We remember the seven year old who only knew of three alternatives, sure yes, sure no, and maybe (which he called 50–50). He failed to recognize the possibility of any further distinction within the maybe category. The games in this section are designed to provide the children with the experience necessary to develop a more mature understanding of probability.

### Marble Probability / Game 146

In this game the child has to predict the color of a marble he happens to take from a container with marbles of two colors. If there are eight yellow and four blue marbles there is a 8/12 (2/3) probability of yellow over the 4/12 (1/3) probability of blue: Yellow is of course the more reasonable guess even though the chance outcome may be blue.

Children sit around a dish in which eight yellow and four blue marbles are placed. The children in turn are asked to guess which color they are more likely to find. As the child reaches for a marble the dish is screened from his eyes. The other children can observe what is happening. In the beginning the marble that was removed is always replaced in order to give the children the opportunity to play with odds that stay invariant. After one or two turns some other odds are presented, 8 to 2, 7 to 4, 6 to 5. The closer the odds are to 50–50, the less clear is the feedback for the child, and consequently the task is more difficult.

Later on the same game is played, but the taken marbles are not put back into the dish. This means that the odds are continuously changing. To make this game more challenging children can be asked to take two marbles and guess the colors. The problem of predicting the colors of two marbles counteracts a spontaneous tendency to alternate judgments. With eight yellow and four blue marbles, the more reasonable prediction for two marbles is two yellow, not one yellow, one blue.

Once the children begin to show some understanding, the task is made more difficult: The marbles are shown to the children and then hidden in a bag. The children must keep track of the changing odds as the bag is handed from one child to another and each child predicts the color. At first the children keep score by recording the color of the marbles that are taken out successively. Later the game is played without keeping record. Now memory plays an important part in the game which makes it more challenging.

## Spinner Proportion / Game 147

Instead of marbles of different colors, this game uses circles divided into sectors of different colors and sizes, for instance, 3/4 of the area is black, 1/4 white. A spinner is attached to a 1/4 inch transparent plastic sheet of the same size as the varicolored circle. It is then placed on top of the circle and spun. The children predict on what color the spinner will stop. There are many ways to increase the complexity of this game. One can split a color area into two or more parts, for instance, two separate white sectors each covering 1/8 of the circle area instead of one white sector covering 1/4 of the area. One can also use three colors instead of two colors (just as one can have three colors of marbles in the preceding game).

A final version includes the use of two circles with different color sectors. For instance, 3/4 black and 1/4 white versus 2/3 blue and 1/3 red. The problem is: Which is more likely to occur, the white on circle 1 or the red on circle 2; the black on circle 1 or the blue on circle 2? If the same two colors are on both circles in different proportions children find this task even more difficult: Which is more likely to occur, the black (3/4) on circle 1 or the white (2/3) on circle 2?

## Prediction / Game 148

How many Ford cars will one see within the next twenty cars that pass by? How many cars will pass by before one sees a Chevrolet? How many out-of-state cars will pass by in the next minute or the next five minutes? What is the first letter on a page of a book randomly opened? How many words will be on a page before one finds a specific word such as "the, and, is, a, but"? In which grade is a nine-year-old child most likely to be? Could an eight year old or a seven year old be in that grade also? How many peas are in a pod? A great variety of everyday situations or objects can be used to illustrate intelligent probability thinking. Children who are proficient in the "artificial" games will also be found proficient in the "natural" situations. It is important that the child makes this connection between school and real life, and it is useful for the teacher to observe how skills exercised in school are applied to everyday situations.

## VISUAL PERSPECTIVE

A child does not easily realize that a given visual configuration is seen differently depending on one's viewing position. The development of spatial thinking is required before a child understands some of the more obvious principles of visual perspective. The four coordinate points: front, right, behind, and left shift with the perspective of the viewer. Simple to complex games can be played in which the children exercise spatial-visual thinking. These games are visual thinking games, see particularly Chapter 8, Game 68. How would it look from there? In Game 68 a child reconstructs the spatial arrangement of block patterns, but in visual perspective games the child constructs separate objects in relation to a visual background, e.g., a room or a nature scene.

### Object Perspective / Game 149

Four children, A, B, C, D, sit around a square table on which an open doll house with various rooms and furniture is placed. Each child has a cardboard tray and duplicate pieces of furniture. Child A is asked to arrange the position of the furniture for one room on his cardboard tray the way B sees it; child B is to arrange the furniture of another room the way C sees it, and so on. Once the children have done so, they carry their cardboard tray, as in Game 68, to the position of the respective child and evaluate their construction from the other child's position.

While the previous version of this game concentrates on position and spatial transposition, another version deals with the perspective of partially hidden objects. As an example, three pieces of furniture—a sofa, a lamp, a television set—are lined up against a wall of the doll house. The child who views this arrangement from the side has to reconstruct on his tray the proper sequence of the furniture. He confirms his construction by carrying the tray to a position where he has a front view of the furniture.

In another version of this game, we use a cardboard on which is painted a simple landscape: a lake (blue), a road, and a wooded area (green). A car and a cow are placed in this scene. The scene is set in the center of a table where it is viewed by children at different positions. Again each child has a duplicate cardboard of the scene. The children place a car and a cow on their cardboard as seen from another child's perspective and evaluate their arrangement as previously indicated. The position of the scene, the absolute placement, and the direction of the two objects are important for an adequate understanding of perspective.

## Picture Perspective / Game 150

In this game the principles of left-right and front-behind reversal, and the resulting visual overlap are exercised. A simple scene is concretely presented, say, a large building in the middle, a tree on its right side, and a factory in the rear left-hand corner. The children viewing the scene from in front are to choose one of four schematic drawings that show this scene from the opposite perspective. The four drawings include the correct perspective, a drawing of the front perspective, and two other drawings that do not have the appropriate left-right or front-behind reversal. After each choice, the child compares the drawings with the actual view from the other side. In another scene a reversal perspective includes partial or complete overlap, due to reversal of front-behind, when a tree is seen in front of a large building, but would be invisible if the building is seen from behind.

Subsequently, other than opposite perspectives are practiced. First, what would a scene look like from the left or the right side? Later one can also ask for a diagonal perspective from the four corners on the scene rather than from the midpoint of the four sides.

This game can be turned into a graphic thinking activity in which children are required to make a schematic drawing from different perspectives, including visual overlap. However, this is perhaps beyond the developmental level of primary school children but it indicates how easy it is to drop and raise the difficulty level of perspective games so that they are a high-level challenge.

# 13. Social Thinking Games

Piaget's insistence on the unity of intelligence and knowledge is evident in his proposition that the intelligence that deals with the physical and the logical world is basically not different from the intelligence that deals with the social world. He holds that logical operation and social cooperation are more than just semantically related. A child cannot develop one without the other and they mutually influence each other. Search for truth and respect for another person or another person's opinion are two facets of a healthy attitude that is as conducive to the intellectual as to the social aspects of a developing child. A School for Thinking can be evaluated on both aspects as was done in Chapter 5. For the furthering of thinking in its concrete physical and logical application, acting and manipulating on the part of the child are required. Likewise, for social thinking, active participation is essential. However, the more important part of developing a mature social personality should be the spontaneous outcome of an overall healthy experience of life and work rather than a specialized focusing on social problems.

Within this overall program some activities should be primarily directed toward encouraging the children to experience another person's viewpoint. This chapter groups these activities under the name of experience games.

## EXPERIENCE DRAMA[1]

When we use the terms dramatic play and drama games we do not mean the performance of a rehearsed program. The theatrical play is concerned with a communication between the actors and the audience. Drama in the classroom is concerned with the players themselves and the experiences they have while playing. Drama games are unrehearsed, relatively short pantomimes and improvisations, usually given something of a structure by the teacher-director. Costumes, props, and especially sets need not be used. Indeed, they can be a deterrent in the early sessions when a player may rely more on a special hat or cane to express for him what he should be experiencing and showing on his own. The process of experiencing can be explored at any time and in any available place. Drama games can be played in libraries, multi-purpose rooms, music and art rooms, stairways, hallways, lunch-rooms, playgrounds, as well as in classrooms.

Drama is basically a task-oriented group activity. As a consequence, the players express many different ideas and opinions during the course of one game. Each player has the chance to be unique and to be respected for bringing a new idea to his play-mates. In turn the player learns to pay attention to and respect the unique contribution of other members of the group.

One of the best features of drama games is the constant exposure to varieties of social behavior. In one of the schools a tough little girl hit a boy hard enough to make him cry. The drama resource teacher asked all the children in the class to sit down, close their eyes in order to concentrate more easily, and remember a time when someone hurt them. Then volunteers told their stories and saw them acted out by other members of the class. During one scene this teacher had the tough girl playing a gentle one coming to the aid of someone who had been hurt. Later when the children and the teacher discussed all the fighting and hurting they had witnessed, this girl drew the conclusion that if we thought about it first, we would never fight. She became more gentle during future drama sessions, usually sitting next to the teacher in the watching group and always eager to play. What she learned by being experientially involved in a dramatic problem solving situation she would not have learned by simply being told, "It's not nice to hit other people. Don't do that again."

The teacher encourages the players to understand and appreciate the differences as well as the similarities in human behavior they are seeing and experiencing. When asked, "How do you do that? Is there another way?", the children soon learn that there is more than one way to do most things. For example, one boy captured a butterfly in a jar during a drama game. During a discussion afterward he learned that during the same game one child had used a net, another had used her hands, and a third had been unable to capture a butterfly. All the players, however, had discovered that they had to move slowly and carefully in order to get near the butterfly. Next they did a turnabout, with the players acting butterflies being chased by children. One activity naturally led to another. Afterward the teacher capitalized on the children's excitement by asking them to go to the library to find out more about butterflies and make drawings of them. By the end of the day several children in that class knew quite a bit about butterflies.

Children show their fears and their special likes as well as their more casual thoughts and feelings during drama games. The game of Tell me what happened usually produces tales of cuts, blood, and bandages the first few times it is played. When asked to find something nearby in a desert during Walking, a shy seven year old found a witch doctor dressed in diamonds and rubies, while two other players found an Indian and a lake, respectively.

Children are also able to enjoy kinds of experiences that might not be offered them outside of the dramatic play situation. Children in the southern part of the country may not have really played in snow, but can do so in a drama game. Children in the city can experience what it feels like walking through a wheat field just after a rainfall. "It was all sticky," exclaimed a seven year old. Children can ride in the pocket of a kangaroo, be one-inch tall, climb a mountain, see a ghost, pick apples, drive racing cars, and drink salt water. This is certainly all very stimulating to the children.

There are no rights or wrongs in drama. All experiences are valid. In this atmosphere of low competition the shy child can surmount his self-consciousness. A child attended a certain school for two months without uttering one word, not even responding to the taking of daily attendance. One day he joined a game in which children were making a living tableau of a picture they had found in a book, bringing it to life. It was a scene in which maple syrup was being taken from trees on a snowy day in Vermont. This boy volunteered to hold a bucket under a tap on a tree. He interacted with the other children for the first time that year and continued to do so, although very shyly, after the game was over.

Drama games provide an ideal medium for the self-conscious child. Because there is no audience in a formal or critical sense, no child feels pressured. Since the emphasis is on solving the problem of the game (crossing a busy street, getting to shore in a leaky boat) the player easily loses his awareness of playmates who are watching at this particular time. In order to avoid feelings of self-consciousness, it is advisable to initiate children into drama games by playing group games of high concentration, such as Listening, in which everyone is a player.

In the early stages of creative work the players frequently experience a kind of fear of freedom. Perhaps they are uncertain what to do because they have never played dramatic games before. Certainly most children have played "house" and "cops and robbers" at home, but everyone played, no one just watched, and no one held a discussion afterward. The participation of the teacher, sometimes as a fellow player, may be a new experience for many children. They may hold their trust in reserve the first few days until they are sure that the teacher really approves of the things they are saying and doing in the improvisations. "Oh-oh. Now you're gonna get it," said a girl when a boy shouted during a drama game. But the shouting was completely in character for the person he was playing, a store owner who just had a window broken by some naughty boys. The teacher encouraged him to go on and the children relaxed and enjoyed themselves. At that moment trust entered the classroom and set the stage for the rest of the school year.

The teacher of experience drama is not an authority figure of the traditional sort but emerges as a playmate and coach. He joins in the activity, sitting or standing within the group, and will ask visitors and observers to join too. The children are delighted and relaxed in such an atmosphere of openness.

At this point the problem of noise arises as it does in other activities of the School for Thinking. The universal fear of most teachers is losing control of the class. Noise could be the signal that it has happened. At some time every teacher must make the distinction between creative noise that signifies learning and the noise of a class that has for the moment no direction. There will be noise during drama games. When it occurs it will reflect life, sharing, creation, growth, and excitement about learning something. As long as the noise is part of the problem solving of the game there is no reason to be dismayed. If the noise has nothing to do with the game and is coming from a source outside of it, the children have lost their concentration. Stop the game. Without too much fuss begin another game, not the same one, or start an entirely different activity. Make sure the children do not think you are punishing them by stopping the drama game and going to another activity. You have simply thought of something better to do at this time.

This is why the children do not play unassisted but with a teacher-director coaching throughout the game: He helps the players to maintain their concentration on solving the problem of the game without imposing his own interpretation, so that the children have their own experience while playing. At the same time he helps those watching in the audience to discover and evaluate how the problem is being solved. The teacher talks softly to the player whenever he observes that the player is losing his concentration. When coaching at the time of the first drama session, and for many sessions afterward, the teacher will remind the players to "Listen with your ears, but not with your eyes." This means listen to the teacher, but in doing this do not look away from the scene in which you are playing or you will lose your concentration completely. The players must continue to play while they are being coached unless they are told to "freeze." Coaching suggestions will accompany some games on the following pages.

The teacher-director sits with the children who are watching and not playing. His coaching keeps the watcher interested in how the players are solving the problem and hopefully sparks ideas in the group watching to explore other ways to solve the same problem. These ideas are discussed or acted out when the current players have finished. Each game can be played as many times as interest warrants. Often an experience in one game will suggest another game, as in the previous story of the butterflies. After the teacher gathers a little experience he will instinctively know when to stay with a game and when to change games.

At the end of most games a discussion and evaluation follows. It can be brief—this is usually best—or lengthy according to the demands of the particular game having been played. The players will want to know if the children watching understood what happened and the children or the teacher will want to tell how they would have played the game. The aims of the discussion are to discover the problem acted out, how it was solved, and how else it could have been solved. For example, the problem was to cross over a big mud puddle. The player jumped, slipping and getting dirty in the process. The children sitting in the audience made several alternative suggestions: making a walkway with a board, finding large stones to put across the mud, or simply walking around it. Someone noted that the last was not valid because it would not have solved the problem of crossing *over* the puddle. Someone else discovered two stones were adequate because while standing on the first he could place the second in position, then stand on the second to place the first, and so on.

In conclusion, since young children often are able to show what they know long before they can write or adequately verbalize, dramatic play in the classroom provides a unique opportunity for the developing child to "show off" his thinking. A seven-year-old girl acted so well the role of a small baby in How old am I that she even had a wobbly head. "Babies have weak necks," the girl explained later. Verbalizing as a consequence of personal experience, and experience as a consequence of personal acting is the appropriate order of psychological priorities which dramatic play brings to the fore.

The ideas for some of the games in this section can be found in *Improvisations for the Theater* by Viola Spolin.[2] Many teachers of elementary school children have difficulties using the Spolin games since they were written for training students of the theater. Some of Spolin's games are simplified or adapted here for elementary school classroom use. Other games are original or based on ideas that children suggested.

## TUNE UP GAMES

The body is the actor-player's instrument. The first games to play are those that help the child discover the possibilities of this wonderful instrument that he may never have considered.

### Blindfold Hello / Game 151

Child A is blindfolded. Child B stands before him and says, "Hello A (name of blindfolded child), who am I?" Child A may make three guesses, each guess preceeded by the "Hello" question. Child B is the next to be blindfolded and another child comes before him. This game may be played as long as the children express an interest in playing. It is an excellent way to learn names at the start of the school year.

### Touch Hello / Game 152

When the children are experts at playing Blindfold Hello try this variation. Child A is blindfolded and must touch the face and head of child B to discover his identity. As in Game 151 each child may make three guesses. Child B is the next to be blindfolded.

### Listening / Game 153

The children sit with eyes closed and listen to the sounds:
  a. outside the building (example follows);
  b. outside the room (hall, other rooms);
  c. inside the classroom.

When variations of the game have been played during the course of several days one adds another specification:
  d. try to concentrate on only one sound you hear;
  e. imagine a person connected with one of the sounds you hear.

In sum, there are nine variations of one game: a, ad, ae, b, bd, be, c, cd, ce.

Discussion—Ask individuals to make a sound that was particularly interesting. Where did the sound come from? What made the sound? Did anyone else hear that sound? Do you agree with what he said? Who heard another sound?

*Example (Game 153a)*

| Teacher: | Players: |
|---|---|
| Close your eyes and listen to the sounds outside the building. | Players listen for three minutes before some begin to act restless. |
| Open your eyes. A, what did you hear first? Can you make the sound? | A: (makes a bus sound). |
| Exactly where did the sound come from? | A: Outside that window (points). |
| What made the sound? | A: A bus. |
| Did anyone else hear that sound? | Several: Yes. |
| Do you agree with A? | Several: Yes. |
| Who heard another sound? | B: I heard a dog. |
| Can you make the sound? | B: Barks. |
| What kind of a dog was it? | B: A puppy. |
| | C: No it was a chihuahua. |
| Do they sound the same? | C: A puppy is more quiet. A chihuahua has a high voice like a puppy but he is loud because he is all grown up. |
| | B: It did sound loud. |

## Sounds / Game 154

This variation of the listening game uses recorded rather than natural sounds.

a. Play sounds you have recorded on tape for the children to identify. At first record familiar sounds. Later add sounds that are less familiar to the particular environment of the children. City sounds such as an elevator bell, a street drill, and a patrolman's whistle could be used with a class of rural children, for example.

b. Play professional sound effects records which can usually be obtained from the public library.

c. Play sounds that belong to one particular classification.

Water sounds, for example, might include a drippy faucet, a garden hose turned to full force, a water pistol spraying, and water going down a bathtub drain.

d. Let half the class record sounds for the other half to identify. A few days later reverse the assignment.

## Talking Body / Game 155

The problem to be solved is expressed as follows: "I am going to ask you to talk without using any words. I want you to let your body talk for you. Everyone stand up. Ready? Say:

*It hurts* with your thumb;
*Goodbye* with your hand;
*No* with your head;
*No* with your foot;
*I'm waiting* with your foot;
*I smell something rotten* with your nose;
*I'm happy* with your legs."

Discussion—Was it difficult to talk with just one part of your body at a time? Is that the way you usually express yourself? One part at a time? Let's play the game again using the whole body to express each idea, but still no words. (Repeat the game.)

*Example (Game 155)*

| Teacher: | Player: |
| --- | --- |
| Say "no" with your head. Just your head. Remember, no words. | Some children shake their heads slowly but emphatically, some quickly. Some forget and say the word "no." |
| Say "it hurts" with your thumb. Just your thumb. Feel the pain in your thumb. Feel it. | Some children wiggle their thumbs, some hold them stiffly, and others suck or blow on their thumbs. |
| Say "hooray" with your whole face. | Big smiles. |
| Say "I don't like you" with your eyes. Let your eyes do the talking for you. | Harsh stares, glares, some blink. |

**Figure 43.**
**Mirror**
A—A preschool child plays mirror for the first time by reflecting her teacher's actions.
B—Two preschoolers play mirror without the acting assistance of a teacher who merely sits nearby giving verbal encouragement.
C—Third graders play a more complicated mirror. The scene is a barber shop. The boys on the left are the reflections, those on the right are the barber and his customer. The teacher sits on the center background side coaching.

## Mirror / Game 156

Two children face each other. One is the mirror, the other is the person using the mirror (Figures 43A, 43B). The player using the mirror should have a definite chore to perform in front of the mirror, such as getting dressed to go to a party, getting ready for bed, getting a haircut (Figure 43C). As a preliminary to this game a real mirror can be used in front of which a child performs certain tasks.

Discussion—What did the mirror reflect? Tell me some of the things the person using the mirror did and if the mirror reflected those things. If you had been the person using the mirror would you have done anything he did not do? What? Why?

*Example (Game 156)*

| Teacher: | Players: |
|---|---|
| A will be the mirror and B will use the mirror as he gets ready to play a football game. Okay. Go. | A reflects B putting on a shirt, helmet, and shoes. |
| Know how much football player's shoes weigh. Show us. Feel the weight. | B takes more time with the shoes. |
| Look in the mirror and see if you are ready. | B stands still looking confused.<br>B shakes his head "yes" to the mirror and walks away. |
| | C: He forgot the pads. |
| | D: Shoulder pads. No shoulder pads. |
| | B: Oh no! |
| Can you think of any reason why a football player might not put on pads? | E: Someone stole them.<br>F: He didn't even look for them. |

B: I forgot to.

Why might a football player forget?

G: His wife just had a baby and he was so happy he forgot the pads. My daddy forgot his keys and got locked out of the house when my baby brother was born.

## GAMES FOR THE ENTIRE CLASS TO PLAY

### What Am I Doing / Game 157

One player pantomimes a simple activity—frying an egg, hitting a baseball, going down a slide. The teacher asks volunteers to join the first player one at a time and do the *same* activity. When five to ten players are doing the pantomime the players "freeze." Starting with the most recent joiners to the game and working his way to the first player last, the teacher asks each child what he is doing (some may not be doing the original activity but one that uses a similar motion). Finally the first player is asked what he was doing. Usually no discussion is needed after the game.

### What Are We Doing / Game 158

One player pantomimes a simple activity, as above (making toast, catching the ball). The teacher asks volunteers to join the first player one at a time and do a *related* activity.

Discussion—Do you do that the same way he did? How else could it be done? Could all of those people have been there in real life? Who else might have been in that scene and what would he have been doing?

*Example (Game 158)*

Teacher:

Players:

Player A is talking on the telephone

B pantomimes talking to A with another telephone.

C sits between as the telephone operator.

D and E also become operators.

Let's have someone else now. Someone doing something new in the scene.

F scolds A and makes her hang up the phone.

## Mates / Game 159

The class is divided in half. A different simple activity is given to each child in team A: bouncing a ball, rolling out pie dough, putting on make-up, breaking eggs, painting a fence, setting a table, painting a scene on an easel, sewing, chopping wood. The same list of simple activities is given out to the members of team B. No one knows what anyone else's activity is. Team A spreads out in a line or a circle and begins to pantomime their activities. Team B observes. As a member of team B recognizes his assigned activity, he joins his mate from team A and they do their activity standing together.

Discussion—Did your mate do your activity the same way you did? What did he do that made you recognize that he was your mate? Is there another way to do that activity? How? Show us?

## Blocks of Clay / Game 160

Each child pretends he has a block of clay before him (size may be determined by the teacher sometimes, by the child at other times). The child pantomimes the molding of the clay into an object. The nature of the object should be general: something you would like to have, something you dislike, something alive, something with a beautiful smell.

Discussion—What did you make? Describe it to us. Why did you make that particular thing instead of something else? Did anyone else make that too?

## From Here to There / Game 161

The children stand at one side of the room. They will go to the other side of the room while the teacher suggests an environment to them. The players have ample time to react to obstacles, objects, and weather conditions. The teacher does not give them too many things to encounter. It is important to keep in mind the size of the space through which the children travel.

Discussion—Ask the players how they felt while certain things were happening to them and how they solved any problems they encountered.

### Example (Game 161)

"Let's take a walk. Pretend this area is a field. We want to go from one side of the field to the other. Start walking slowly. There is a big mud puddle in front of you. Try to get to the other side without getting dirty. Take your time. There are some flowers. Touch one. See its color. Know its shape. If you would like to, pick some. Feel the stems in your hand. We are almost finished the walk. Just climb over that big fence in front of you and you will be all the way to the other side of the field."

The space does not have to be a field. It can be a street, a river, an ice-covered pond, and so on. This is a warm-up game for Walking; it should be used before playing Walking with young children. Once they play this game smoothly the teacher moves on to Walking.

## Walking / Game 162

As the children walk out an imaginary door the teacher leads them into an environment by suggesting noises, objects, temperature changes, etc., to which the players respond. The players act as individuals, not as a group.

Discussion—Ask players how they felt while certain things were happening to them. Did anyone else feel that way? Did someone have a different experience?

*Example (Game 162)*

"Let's take a walk. Follow me out the door. You are walking all alone. Put the rest of the class out of your mind. Try not to touch anyone else because you will break your concentration and his. Remember to listen to me with your ears but not with your eyes. Keep concentrating on what you are seeing and hearing and experiencing while I talk to you. Let's go. It's snowing. Feel the snow on your hair, on your eyelashes. Hear it under your boots. Catch a snowflake. Look at it very closely. See the design. Watch it melt. It is starting to snow harder. Know what your eyes see through the snow falling in front of you. There is something dark and large in front of you. Know what it is. Do something with that large, dark thing. The snow is up to your knees now. Feel it against your legs as you walk. Run. Know how it feels to run in snow this deep. . . ."

The directions in the above game are given very slowly. Allow the players really to respond to each suggestion you give them before going on to the next. The teacher should be directing the players to help them tune into the environment of the particular game, not telling a narrative for the game. This game is not a story, it is an experience. The example game is not complete; it could go on much longer. For another example, see Figure 44.

## Celebration / Game 163

The children act out the roles of participants on such occasions as weddings, birthday parties, christenings, Thanksgiving dinner, and ethnic festivals, or the players may reconstruct places the class has visited, such as an airport, a library, a gas station, a bus terminal, the circus. See Figure 45.

Discussion—(Social occasions) Does your family celebrate that way? What did we do that your family does? What does your family do that we did not do? Why is it done that way? Is there another way?

(Reconstructed place) What happened to you at the airport

**Figure 44.**
**Walking**
The teacher (background left) walks among the players
as she side coaches an underwater walk. The players
are finding something of their own choosing in a
sunken ship.

**Figure 45.**
**Celebration**
A—The first passenger goes to the flight desk to find out from which gate her flight will depart. The teacher side coaches nearby (foreground right).
B—Another passenger receives directions from the flight desk clerk. The passenger of Figure A has preceeded him to the flight lounge (background left) and is greeting the stewardess at the gate.
C—The airplane begins to assemble. The boy (center) is the engine, the girls (foreground) are wings.

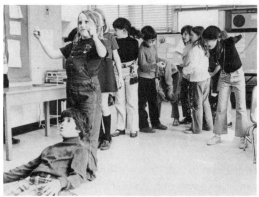

D—Passengers board the plane and take seats.
E—The plane begins to move down the runway.
F—The plane takes off.

(train station, etc.)? What did you have to do there? Did you have any problems? Could you have done it any other way?

### Example (Game 163)

"Let's play Celebration. Let's have a wedding. Who will be the bride? The groom? Who else would be at the wedding? Do you want to be the grandmother? The priest (minister or rabbi)? Who else would be there? Who else?" When all the parts have been taken the players set the scene with available chairs, tables, books—whatever. The scene is set. Begin by asking one player at a time or small groups of related players to join the scene, enter the church. The children can concentrate more easily in this free but orderly situation. The teacher might take an officiating role, such as that of the minister or head usher, in order to help along with the character of the game.

## Story Clap / Game 164

One at a time, children add sentences or phrases together to make a story. Between each sentence everyone does a rhythmic clap-clap-clap. Young children may have an easier time passing a ball with each sentence or phrase. The clapping may confuse them at first. After the story has been told (make someone end it if it gets too long or declare it the end of the first chapter and continue the same story next time) give out roles and act out the story.

### Example (Game 164)

"A big giant lived in the mountains (clap-clap-clap). He loved purple flowers (clap-clap-clap). But no purple flowers grew in the mountains (clap-clap-clap). So he decided to go into the village in the valley and pick some (clap-clap-clap . . .)."

If the children have a difficult time getting started, the teacher can begin the story. If the teacher wants the story to deal with a particular topic (illness, courage, danger) he would certainly begin the story himself. He tells just enough to get it going and does not monopolize it.

**Figure 46.**
**Tell Me What Happened**
The girl sitting on the desk tells her real life story as classmates act it out.
The girl in overalls on the right plays the role of the girl who tells the story.
She has gone to a museum with her mother and a girlfriend.
As the mother (at background left door) buys tickets for a puppet show,
the girls are lost and encounter museum guards (foreground left).

GAMES FOR SMALL GROUPS

## Tell Me What Happened / Game 165

One player tells the group about a true happening he has experienced—yesterday, last month, last year, anytime. When he has finished the group acts out the story, with the original storyteller narrating. See Figure 46.

Discussion—Has that ever happened to anyone. else? How did you act when it happened? Could anyone think of another way he could have handled the situation?

The teacher may want to ask for stories that deal with a particular subject such as trips to the hospital, summer vacation, accidents.

## Who Does This at Home / Game 166

One child pantomimes a member of his family performing an activity at home. The viewers guess who the player is (mother, baby, father) and what the activity is. The player whispers what he is going to do to the teacher, so that he can coach him while he is playing.

Discussion—Does anyone else's mom do that? Does anyone else at home do that? Can you? Are you going to do that when you are a mom?

*Example (Game 166)*

| Teacher: | Player: |
|---|---|
| Decide where you will get all the things you will need. Take your time. | Player starts to pantomime. She opens a drawer and takes something out. |
| Show us what that is by the way you handle it. Make it real. | Player folds the object carefully. She begins to diaper a pretend baby. |

Know what the new object weighs. Show us if you are moving it or if it can move by itself.

You are making it very real now. Good. Keep going.

She tries to catch the baby's flying feet. She has more difficulty doing the diapering because the baby is not cooperating.

## Who Does This at Work / Game 167

This is played exactly the same way as Game 166 except that the activity of a paid occupation is substituted for the activity at home.

## Pairs with Problems / Game 168

Two players, using dialogue, try to solve a problem. They may use available objects such as chairs to set the scene.

| Possible pairs: | Problem: |
| --- | --- |
| barber and child | child wants his hair cut a certain way |
| doctor and patient | doctor must convince an unwilling patient that she is well |
| mailman and housewife | mailman must deliver a package the housewife does not want |
| grocer and customer | customer does not have enough money to pay the bill |
| carpenter and assistant | carpenter shows assistant how to frame a door |
| taxi driver and passenger | passenger does not speak English |
| swim teacher and student | student is terrified of the water |

| cook and apprentice | cook has upset stomach |
| tightrope walker and assistant | tightrope walker has dropped her glasses |
| driving teacher and student | driving teacher has lost his glasses |

Discussion—Did they solve the problem? How? Could they have solved it another way? The teacher might have new players show rather than tell how they would solve the same problem.

## Unusual Situations / Game 169

This game is played like the preceding but involves three to five players. The players must solve their problem in a probable but unusual situation.
Some problems:

> people stranded in a leaky boat
> people in a stuck elevator
> people in a subway car during a power failure
> people having a dinner party during a power failure
> people in a balloon-and-basket that has flown loose at a county fair

Discussion—Did they solve their problem? How? How else could it have been done? Would another group like to try it another way?

## Pictures / Game 170

Show interesting pictures to the children. Let them divide into small groups to choose and discuss the picture that interests each particular group. Each group then acts out its picture while the rest of the children observe and respond.
Discussion—Who are the people in the picture? What is each doing? How? Why?

## EXPERIENCE PHOTOGRAPHY

Picture taking (still photographs or movies) can be used as a high-level activity not merely to enhance visual thinking (see the games of Chapter 8, especially communications, Game 70) but also to relate visual to social thinking. In the world of communication, reading has assumed a top priority position and audiovisual media are now extensively utilized. As with drama, photography can also be used quite effectively as both an expressive and receptive form of nonverbal communication. It is an excellent means of affording children a chance to express their ideas beyond the scope of their existent vocabulary range. Photography is an exciting form of creative, nonverbal communication and, as such, can be a learning tool for all ages.

It is easy to find a person in the community with expertise in photography and willing to help as a resource person. The magic of the camera is a fascinating study for the young child. Film manufacturers may aid by supplying materials and study brochures.[3] The children can be taught to make their own pinhole box cameras, and develop their own pictures.

For young children, the commercial cameras are generally used under supervision, but a self-constructed pinhole box camera may be taken home. This provides two additional types of social thinking experiences: first, the pride of having constructed a useful object, second, the responsibility for its care and maintenance. All photography games tie in well with experience drama and experience excursions so that a picture activity can lead to drama or an excursion and vice versa.

### Experience Picture Story / Game 171

Children, alone or in group, are instructed to tell a story with photographs. This is similar to the popular experience story technique for teaching beginners in reading. The children attempt to take photographs of interesting situations and capture the important events in sequence. They discuss the quality of the experience on the basis of these photographs. In this manner the children will show a natural interest in the chronological order of events and develop their vocabulary.

## Unusual Pictures / Game 172

Here the problem is to take an unusual picture, for instance, a scene such as a familiar spot in a fog, a busy street corner at an early morning hour, the change of scenery with snow, a familiar landscape from an uncommon perspective or distance. As the child presents his picture, the other children try to discover what the picture represents. Depending on the situation one speaks about events that led up to the scene and possible subsequent events. Children are encouraged to compare the usual with the unusual, the familiar with the unfamiliar. Throughout the games the emphasis is not on description of content but on concern with the social and personal experiences which the pictured events illustrate.

## Make an Illustrated Story / Game 173

The children's task is to look at a number, five to ten, of photographs taken by the class, decide on a theme, and come up with a story that is illustrated by the pictures. As the children listen to different themes and different stories based on identical pictures, they experience a variety of possible viewpoints and—what is most important—are encouraged to express their own personal bias and interest. This game can be played simultaneously by different groups.

## Picture Arrangement / Game 174

Selected photographs are placed before the children in random order. The photographs have a rather obvious chronological sequence. The children's task is to discover this sequence and verbalize the underlying reason.

With the entire class observing, the teacher may photograph

sequential scenes during a particular event. Later, presented with these pictures in random order a single child or a group of children attempt to sequence them correctly. In another form of the same game, a child or a group of children photograph an action sequence and later present their pictures to other children for proper arrangement. The discussion that follows exposes the children to the difficulties of communication and the importance of logical thinking for the expressor as well as the receptor.

## Picture Logic / Game 175

In previous chapters we have spoken of gestural, graphic, written and oral communication. Seeing a photograph of a scene or of one's own appearance often elicits a wonderment that the photograph is really representative of the actual visual experience. Taken for granted is the size change created by distance, the spatial awareness created by intervening objects, and the effect of shadow on contrast and contour. With photography these real life experiences can be stopped in time and studied. Logical assumptions can be made and later evaluated by photography.

For example the children can use their cameras to study and predict perspective and relate real life to Games 149 and 150 of Chapter 12. They can classify large immovable or distant objects and relate these to Chapter 12, Game 131. They can study shadows: their positions, why they are sometimes long and sometimes short, why they assume certain shapes, and many other characteristics of shadows. Photography allows the outdoors to be brought indoors for study, play, and manipulations.

## Picture Poetry / Game 176

The appreciation of the aesthetic in all things is part of the child's natural development. Awareness of the beauty of nature as well as the beauty of the various man-made things serves as a foundation for developing the child's respect for ecology, his own possessions, and the possessions of others. There is the sense of beauty in a cloud, a bridge, a butterfly, a twisted tree branch; the feel of a smooth stone or a piece of velvet; the scent of a flower or baking bread. All these experiences can enhance the child's pride in his world and in himself.

To do this the children are asked to take photographs of something that is interesting to them on account of some unique, beautiful, or fascinating aspect that they want to share with the group. They take a photograph and relate to the other children their feelings about the object that prompted their taking its picture. The teacher attempts to bring out the poet in the child through the medium of photography.

## EXPERIENCE EXCURSIONS

Excursions into the community formed an integral part of the School for Thinking. Specific preparation assured that these were not recreational trips but occasions planned for the purpose of a social thinking experience through which the children could discover and search for facts and ask reasons and conditions of these events and institutions.

The experience excursions were regularly discussed both beforehand and afterward, and the long range objective of getting to know one's environment was directly emphasized. The teacher encouraged spontaneous questions and attempted to make clear to the children that what counted was not primarily a knowledge of certain prearranged facts but an intelligent interest and concern for the social world in which the children live.

There are as many opportunities for experience excursions as there are events or places in the community. Episodes from these excursions were mentioned in Chapters 4 and 5.

### Let's Take a Walk / Game 177

The entire class spends fifteen to twenty minutes walking around the outside of the school building. They are requested to seek out various things and then return to the classroom. The instructions can ask for anything: a leaf, something living, something not living, something that did not grow there, a little thing, something interesting.

There follows a discussion supervised by the teacher. Reason is emphasized and intelligent controversy is encouraged. Reticent children are intelligently urged to present their object. This is a time to delve into mathematics, ecology, history, biology, and other sciences, man-made and natural objects, to mention only a few topics.

## Let's Learn About / Game 178

The post office, the airport, the museum, the jail, the college, the newspaper, the telephone company, the slaughter house, the cannery, the farm, the ice plant, the bakery, the dairy, all should serve as examples of the myriad of places to go.

The class chooses an event or a place in the community that is accessible and cooperative. The children experience what will occur by playing social thinking games in the classroom in preparation for the excursion. Drama techniques are particularly well adapted for this.

## Show and Tell / Game 179

This popular primary school activity is played in its customary form. The children bring something to school and discuss it. Emphasis is placed on the function of the object, its various uses, how it came to be, where it could be obtained, its shape, its aesthetic value, the feelings it evokes in the children of the classroom, especially the child who brought it, and why it particularly was chosen.

Thinking is emphasized. The teacher at first guides the discussion. As the year progresses the children are quick to catch on and allowed to dominate the conversation.

## EXPERIENCE DEMONSTRATIONS

Whereas in experience excursions we take the child into the community, here we bring people from the community into the classroom. This activity is not the same as a resource person coming in and giving a lecture. It is a way to involve the child in everyday activities and occupations that can be performed on the school grounds. Parents with various skills can come to the classroom and work with the children on small projects. Experience demonstrations are a most profitable way for parents and adults to get to know the children in the classroom.

Every effort is made to involve the children in the dynamics of the activity. Passive lecture type presentations are avoided. If a playground is to be planned, the possibilities of child participation are numerous: helping in the design, in the construction, in the original planning. Local architecture students could present various small scale models for the children to select. The children can be involved with costs, safety, durability, time estimates for construction, or simply choose which looks like the most fun. If an electrician comes in, have him help the children construct a flashlight battery energized by a simple circuit that turns a light on and off.

Telephone repairmen, carpenters, plumbers, forest rangers, biologists, members of the health care professions, fire prevention people, groups for recycling, cooks, artists, and artisans, are examples of people in the community whom growing children enjoy knowing more about. In this day of packaged products, passive television viewing, prefabricated building units, excessive use of transportation, and innumerable home appliances, the developing child needs to be exposed to the basic source and the manifold effects of things in the world around him. Otherwise, as happened with one child, they may think that heat for the room comes from the knob on the wall or that the bus driver is the richest man in town because he collects all the money.

## EXPERIENCE DISCUSSIONS

As reported in earlier chapters, classroom discussions took place whenever special problems presented themselves. These could be individual problems of certain children or problems affecting the whole class. On one occasion the teacher discussed the problem of noise during lunch time and asked the children for constructive suggestions. In another instance the children discussed how they could help a child develop insight into the antisocial effects of his actions. Another discussion focused on the rules for the free activity period.

Ideally, the children in a School for Thinking are given the opportunity for self-government as far as it is feasible. This stance is all the more important as the school aims at developing children who can make intelligent and responsible decisions. To foster this vital democratic attitude and also to prepare the desirable freedom of choice during later years at school, we suggested that the teacher assign one period a week as free. During this period the children could do as they judged best for themselves and could themselves form regulations that governed the use of this time.

# IV. Implications

# 14. A School for Thinking for All Children

The project at Charleston was by no means a fully developed "School for Thinking," if only for the obvious reason that it lasted merely two academic years. Nevertheless, the experience of these two years was beneficial and rewarding to the children and teachers of the Thinking School classrooms. It demonstrated that the guidelines for a School for Thinking, first suggested in *Piaget for teachers,* could be put into practice. In this respect the experience gained in this project has been invaluable and has provided a practical background for the Thinking School which now complements its theoretical base.

Here is a brief discussion of those factors that limited the school's positive impact and made a continuation and expansion of the project in the Charleston school district not feasible. Specifically, cooperative support was not strong enough, desirable resource people were lacking, and the push for premature academic performance was too strong.

The experience in Charleston has made it clear that a change from a traditional school to a School for Thinking cannot succeed without the constructive contribution of all parties involved—the children, the parents, the community, the administration, the teachers, and the schools of education. Since a School for Thinking requires the active support of all who play a part in it, this also means that any one significant individual or group of individuals can hinder its proper functioning. This fact is not particularly new or unexpected: To continue a system as before requires almost no conscious justification, to change a system is only possible when all parties want it and strive for it in a concerted action.

This is especially true for a School for Thinking which almost by definition can only come about through active, thinking cooperation of all people involved and can never be imposed from outside as a ready-made system to be followed.

Our project was particularly hampered by lack of adequate resource people. This included our own physical distance from the project. There was also a constant pressure to show short-term results on standard reading tests, and the constant need to justify the program not on its own terms, but in terms of the traditional philosophy of immediate results.[1] When toward the end of the second year it became clear that Tyler School would have only one first grade, so that there was no longer a choice for parents at Tyler between ours and a traditional classroom, the administrative decision not to continue with the project came as no surprise.

## Primary education

Failures of children as early as primary education is a national problem of some magnitude as well as a world wide problem insofar as the Western pattern of education has been universally accepted. One hears of numerous failures in reading in France, Germany, England, and Russia. People ask what has happened to cause failures to an extent unheard of one or two generations ago. "Unheard" is the precise word, because the failures of the past went' by the wayside at a time when the social and work structure was less demanding and the pressure for equal opportunity was less urgent. Children who failed existed all along, but society managed not to take too much notice of it.

But today these failures are expensive for society in social, moral, and monetary terms. The School for Thinking philosophy is a partial response to these failures. We believe that not a single child from whatever social environment—unless he is so seriously sick that he cannot function outside the school—need become a failure in the process of learning the desirable academic goals of elementary school. We can single out three common reasons for difficulties in the elementary classroom: (1) neurological immaturity, (2) lack of behavioral readiness, (3) absence of motivation. The ability to sit quietly and read is in part dependent on a degree of development in visual and skeletal structure that in many children is not completed by the sixth or seventh birthday. Physiological norms are hard to establish, but many investigators are convinced that a sizeable proportion of six or even seven-year-old children is not yet neurologically and anatomically developed for successful reading. Therefore, it is unreasonable to blame and punish children, parents, or teachers for the results of a physiological condition over which they have only limited control.

Many children come to school with insufficiently exercised competence of body and sense actions. Their body and sense mechanisms underlying not merely reading skill but all theoretical knowing are poorly coordinated. Some of these mechanisms are themselves prereading skills, and frequently these skills are much more meaningful to the child than the reading for which they are meant to prepare. This is because many are developmental activities that are intrinsically motivating and challenging. For example, the children at Tyler were perfectly happy to play once or twice a week the permutation games described in Chapter 12. Arranging a set of items in different linear sequences gave them the opportunity to exercise their developing comprehension of sequence. It may seem strange that children enjoyed working on an apparently abstract capacity such as discovering principles of sequential arrangements, while they would have been bored to exercise *this same capacity* in a premature attempt at learning to read. The reason for this difference is clear within the framework of the School for Thinking philosophy: The permutation game is a developmentally high-level activity which carries its intrinsic motivation whereas reading is often experienced as low-level activity.

But beyond these prereading skills there are many activities of everyday life which are meaningful and developmentally important. Any six-year-old child is ready to apply his developing intelligence to the things and events which he knows. Previous chapters, particularly Chapter 13, gave some suggestions along these lines, and we can here only refer to other authors who have written about novel ways of using crafts, art, music, as well as social and moral thinking in the elementary schools. It is here that the needed motivation for learning must be sought, if it is not already present through environmental and personal circumstances. Since the motivational factor seems to be the major difficulty in the children from the inner city, a program must be found that will carry its own intrinsic motivation.

It seems fairly clear now that none of the preschool remedial programs being proposed in the traditional schools are powerful enough to overcome the psychologically inappropriate atmosphere of the elementary school. A revolutionary overhaul of the educational system and its goals is mandatory for two reasons: first, to assure an overall healthy development of the child and, second, to avoid the present failures in learning.

The philosophy of the School for Thinking is primarily directed to the first point, the intellectual health of the child. To reach this goal an emphasis on reading and other academic subjects is insufficient. A child who makes satisfactory progress in a traditional elementary school is not by this fact alone laying a sound foundation for a healthy intellectual life. He may do so, but then this is primarily due to experiences he has outside the school and not to school activities. Our school accepts as a desirable secondary goal the teaching of reading, math, and other subject matters. But as the main goal we emphasize overall intellectual health and the necessity of keeping the children and teachers free from the premature pressure for standardized performance. Thus the individual variabilities of the child can be respected and the child does not see himself as a failure.

Tyler School is presented as an illustration of what was suitable and feasible in one particular case. We expect that other schools wishing to embrace the Thinking School philosophy will work out a model that takes into account the particular development and interest of their children. On the basis of Piaget's theory, as interpreted in these pages, we are fully convinced that a school must intentionally and purposefully emphasize the development of thinking in the child. Otherwise it will not be able to avoid learning failures and, in addition, an even greater number of children who will lose the creative curiosity that is part of all children's natural equipment.

## Preprimary education

Would not thinking activities be important for a younger age group, for children in preschool, in day-care centers, or at home? Of course our general philosophy is applicable at all ages, but the particular character of a thinking atmosphere is developmentally most appropriate within the four and a half to ten years age range of the growing child. While we recognize great individual variability at all ages and see no harm if occasionally some specific thinking games are presented at age four—particularly if the children themselves appear to enjoy them—generally the knowledge of the four-year-old child is not yet anchored to a self-consistent framework and so his world is naturally full of "childish" misconceptions. Piaget's theory describes this condition as a normal developmental stage of transition from the sensorimotor period of the preverbal infant to the concrete operations period of the school-age child. The three to four-year-old child is easily fascinated by simple events in everyday life but is not ready for reflective explanations; he is interested in representative play rather than in the rules that underlie the play; he is intent on building a pretty house of blocks and not on a conscious reflection on the mathematical relationships implicit in the various sizes and shapes of the blocks; he is more likely to play alongside friends than play and cooperate with them on a common task.

The School for Thinking philosophy, in agreement with Piaget, accepts the child's spontaneous developmental stage. We do not want to push children beyond their stage-characteristic pattern of thinking because we are too much convinced of the importance of the inner forces and motivation that guide and direct a child's development. The distinction between providing psychologically appropriate opportunities and insisting on adult imposed specific performance can make the difference between an intellectually healthy and unhealthy atmosphere.

We recognize that children in the primary grades are just beginning to enter the stage of concrete operations, that is, they are beginning to develop the first self-consistent structures of thinking which enable them to have stable concepts and to become aware of internal rules of knowing. Precisely because the children are close to attaining this first mature capacity for thinking, a full day of structured games that focus on this new thinking capacity is appropriate at the age of five or six and not much earlier. These children enjoy becoming aware of this intellectual capacity. Hence there is no boredom in exploring causal explanations for certain events, in playing permutation games, social drama, or visual perspective: The children are ready for this and enjoy the opportunity of using their newly found intellectual powers.

## Postprimary education

The goal of a primary School for Thinking is to help develop a child whose intelligence and personality are sufficiently mature and articulated so that he becomes capable of reading-based learning. By the time a child is eleven years old, his general intellectual capacities should be well developed and exercised. He should now be able to concentrate on learning and performing on certain subject matters without undue psychological stress or risk of an unbalanced development. Moreover, by this time the child's developed capacity of thinking enables him to use the difficult medium of the verbal language in an intelligent fashion. At earlier ages a child's thinking is invariably at a higher level than what he can express or comprehend verbally; when such a child is preoccupied with verbal material, he is not likely to be engaged in high-level challenging thinking.

We believe that there is and should be an important difference between the main goal of early education and the goal of the postprimary school. While the goal of the primary school ought to be development and not learning, once the child has reached an advanced stage of intellectual development the goal of the postprimary school can be learning based on reading. Of course, whatever content matter is presented for learning, it should be done so that content is continually assimilated to thinking, or more precisely, to high-level thinking. The child in the middle school and above should experience learning as an extension of his developed capacities of thinking and realize that his intelligence is essentially an open-ended instrument that is ever eager toward new explorations and discoveries.

As the child grows older, his unique individual capacities and talents come increasingly to the fore and will be reflected in the areas of specialization to which he devotes his learning efforts. Traditional academic subject matters, various physical skills, mechanical, artistic, and social abilities—all are partially dependent on a developed general intelligence. The knowledgeable teacher will know this and not expect premature performance in any of these abilities. If the child himself shows a spontaneous and exceptional talent and interest in a special field, this in itself usually indicates that the activity is psychologically appropriate. But generally speaking, learning from books is suitable and fruitful from postprimary school onward and not earlier.

Here is the place to answer a possible objection to a primary School for Thinking that claims to develop the general intelligence on which the school work of subsequent education is based. Will the graduates of a Thinking School not be handicapped if they continue education in a traditional high school? All available evidence points to general mechanisms of thinking as providing powerful instruments of learning, and the mere idea of these mechanisms interfering with learning is almost a contradiction in terms. The only thing that high-level thinking can possibly disturb is the meaningless memorizing of unconnected material. Even when it comes to situations other than intellectual accomplishments, there is no reasonable evidence to show that intelligent thinking is harmful for adjustment. Critical as we have to be about existing schools, we do not imagine them to be in such a state that thinking would be a serious hindrance to educational success.

However, the positive advantage of a primary School for Thinking is more crucial and has been assumed throughout these pages. We are convinced that the habit of creative thinking, firmly exercised during the primary school years, will have beneficial effects in the learning of specific subject matters in the years to come. Positive transfer effects of this type have not shown up in past educational studies that probed possible transfer effects from one subject matter to another. For example, the claim that the study of Latin improves a person's logical thinking has not been substantiated. Such conclusions strengthened the idea that all there was to a person's knowledge was the sum of separately acquired knowledge.

Today educators are no longer quite so confident in the correctness of this conception. Increasingly, educational articles are written on the necessity of teaching learning-how-to-learn rather than isolated facts of a subject. This trend recognizes that schools cannot possibly teach all the facts that could be included in the many different domains of desirable knowledge. We fully support this tendency and welcome the modern approaches to learning. But we believe that only a strong theory of the development of thinking provides sufficiently powerful concepts to counteract the mere learning of facts. The learning-to-learn postulate has led to a search for suitable learning strategies and educational applications that have never gone beyond setting up improved curricula for specific subject matters. Learning strategies and thinking are not synonymous concepts because the strategies are still tied to the presentation of specific subject matter whereas thinking is not. Moreover, learning-to-learn still assumes that learning and development are basically similar processes, whereas Piaget's theory has shown them to be different: According to Piaget, children do not "learn" to think, children think. And as they think— at a high-developmental level—they develop more advanced thinking mechanisms. For these reasons one can expect that a systematic emphasis on thinking over a prolonged period will make its impact, whereas a preoccupation with learning or learning strategies may fail to show transfer effects.

## Special education

It is more than a coincidence that many modern ideas in education have been introduced into the profession in connection with attempts to teach children who have a special disabling condition. These children fall into categories such as mental retardation, hearing or sight impairment, neurological damage (including cerebral palsy), and learning disorder. When children lack bodily or mental abilities which the traditional educational process assumes as a prerequisite, traditional methods are bound to be questioned.

While this is not the place to go into the special educational problems of profoundly blind or deaf children, the development of these sensorially deprived children into intelligent adults has implications for theories of education. If a child can develop without the benefit of visual experience or without society's verbal language, current opinions concerning their assumedly pivotal role in development and learning are challenged.

As for mentally retarded children, it is only too well known that the greatest number fall into the borderline class. Moreover, persons classified as borderline retarded do not appear to differ significantly from other persons in terms of social and work adjustment, in spite of the fact that they have difficulties in coping with the demands of the school system. Much the same thing can be said about children with minimal brain damage or learning disorders: They cannot be called retarded because their measured IQ score is within the normal range, but they fail in school nonetheless. Sometimes there is satisfactory evidence for a clear neurological impairment, but in the majority of cases there is only one objective reason for the diagnosis of brain damage or learning impairment, namely, poor school performance. In other words, school performance explains the disorder and the disorder explains school performance.

Within the framework of a School for Thinking it is possible to break away from the circularities of this explanation. If the diagnostic categories of borderline retardation, minimal brain damage, and, particularly, learning disorder hinge upon failure to meet the demands of the school, a change in the demands of the school could modify or even do away with these categories. This is exactly what a School for Thinking promises. We hold that these categories of a child's deficiency were invented largely in order to explain failures in school. Without failures there would be no need for these categories.

In fact, our project at Tyler included a number of activities that are used successfully in remedial reading programs with children who may be clasified by one or another of the labels mentioned above. We think it unreasonable to let children first become failures and only then do appropriate activities that should have been done in the first place. But we also found that these activities were not simply remedial but primarily developmental and therefore useful not merely for children who potentially fail but for all children. Here then is a clear case where activities originally designed for special children, such as body and sense thinking, are appropriately incorporated into an innovative program.

Unfortunately, the prevailing attitude toward children who have difficulties in school is ambiguous and devaluative. This classroom "may be fine for those kids, but not for my children," one parent at the Tyler School once said. However, if a School for Thinking prevents learning disorders it is therefore an ideal setting for *all* children, both "normal" and those who in a traditional school would be labeled as afflicted with learning disorders. (At the end of the year this parent had changed his mind and wished that all of his children had gone to a School for Thinking).

The theoretical base for the claim that a School for Thinking is as appropriate for all as it is for special children—whether they are "really" special, e.g., deaf, blind, or neurologically impaired, or "apparently" special, e.g., children with learning disorders—is Piaget's theory of development on which the School is founded. Human development, as described by Piaget, is characterized by its transcendence of special modalities. Although intelligence cannot develop without physical and social experience, it is not vitally dependent on *particular* modalities or *particular* experiences, and it is certainly not dependent on those experiences that children in special education lack. The development of thinking in these children proceeds in the same fashion as in nonspecial children. Contrast this with other theories that base development on specific body and sense modalities or verbal language and one can see at once that Piaget's theory is uniquely positive and accepting of what is healthy and strong in a special child rather than focusing on what is weak and lacking in him.

The School for Thinking puts this positive theory into practice and thereby gives the special child the same occasions for success that it gives other children. It does not teach "to the disability," it has no frantic need for diagnostic testing to find out in which exact area the child is deficient. As the School for Thinking occupies the special child with an abundance of challenging and successful activities, it is less inclined to rely on stereotypic thinking about a disabling condition. As an illustration, to help a profoundly deaf child acquire verbal skills is certainly a worthwhile effort; but the absence of verbal skills is no reason for neglecting math, science, creative and social thinking, and the remaining developmentally worthwhile activities. In other words, it is stereotypic thinking that makes educators blind to the manifold opportunities open to all children, both special and nonspecial. This is, of course, not so different from the world of work where disabled persons are most forcibly handicapped by prevailing rigid stereotypic notions that allow little room for creative imagination.

We would not deny that in many cases special educational attention must be given to a specific disability. But regardless of this particular need, all young children have the primary need for acceptance of self and for successful development. A School for Thinking can fulfill these needs in full measure in a manner that is self-evident from the school's ongoing activities. Moreover, its goal surpasses by far the narrow goal of scholastic success. It indicates to a child who may be truly disabled in respect to competitive success in certain academic subjects, that there are many different areas in which he can succeed in everyday life and eventually in the world of work.

## Outlook

The preparation and the training of teachers is the most important area as far as long-lasting educational change is concerned. The beginning of an elementary School for Thinking should be found in the atmosphere of thinking prevailing in schools of education across the country. Where are these schools? And at the same time where are the departments of psychology that teach a psychology of the thinking and feeling human child? And where are the other departments of the social sciences, of the physical sciences, and of the humanities that foster respect for the developing child and the thinking person? And what about industry, business, government, churches, and other institutions? What is it that makes high-level thinking a most important psychological process in every young child and a rare event in the life of adults?

Perhaps a School for Thinking is not for a world that has all but unlearned to think. Perhaps—but perhaps there is a way to counteract this unlearning of thinking and to attack this problem at its institutional source. Perhaps if the primary school gave all entering children four solid years in which to expand the spontaneous development of thinking, a critical mass of internal controls and initiatives might thereby be made available to the child on the threshold of adolescence. A sufficiently strong orientation toward thinking that is part of the child could then carry over into adolescence and adulthood.

Basically there are two ways to assure that a child acquires the desirable knowledge and customs within a society. There is the direct imparting of knowledge as a ready made product and there is the possibility of leaving the child free to construct knowledge on his own. The two ways are not necessarily opposed but in emphasis they are decidedly different. Each has advantages as well as carries grave risks. When adults are sure of their values and when there is a close structure of the family and community that gives love and acceptance to the child, the way of imparting ready made knowledge can work and has worked quite well, as we see around us. However, that this sort of education also has been partly responsible for a lot of human failure in terms of mental disease, guilt, fear, hypocrisy, delinquency, crime, and destructiveness, can scarcely be questioned.

The way of freedom is still an ideal and one can hardly point to any educational system that espouses it wholeheartedly. But this is the direction mankind is going, if only because freedom and education go hand in hand and in the long run point to similar goals. Consider the educational innovators, from Rousseau to Montessori, from Dewey to our present-day thinkers. They all speak of internal personal forces that freely move the child and the appropriate educational environment that must foster these forces as a gardener protects and nourishes a plant. Piaget stands in the long line of this liberating tradition; yet he stands apart from this tradition because, not being himself a teacher or a social reformer, he has been able to study the child's development of thinking in an analytic and detached fashion as no person can who is involved in everyday practice.

Consequently one will find the leading themes of the great educational thinkers of the past and the present incorporated in Piaget's theory. The absorbing mind of a Montessori, the organic reading of an Ashton-Warner, the experiential-pragmatic orientation of a Dewey, the freedom of inquiry of a Rogers, the openness of the British infant school, the feeling and awareness of Gestalt therapy, the bringing-to-consciousness of a Freire, and the deschooling of an Illich, as well as the programmed learning and the behavioral modifications of association theory—these and other ideas represent so many different aspects of the developing child, forcibly enunciated by involved persons. These themes need an all encompassing theory such as Piaget's to fall into place and to become available as a viable theory of development and learning for all schooling.

On the one hand, the problems of society are truly immense: peace and war, poverty, discrimination, justice, industrial pollution, the quality of life. On the other hand, the ideal of democracy is strong and universal and in spite of temporary deformations cannot be taken away just at the time when the ideal of freedom has become a part of mankind's accepted values. If we have optimism that society will find a way to work on these problems in a constructive manner, is this optimism justified and how can the work be done? Democracy is ultimately based on the reasonableness of individuals, on a belief that in the long run the more reasonable solution will be expressed through democratic processes. It has long been recognized that democracy cannot work well unless the individuals are educated to use their freedom in a responsible and critical manner.

We hold that educational failure is not merely a limited problem that involves the school and the individual. On the contrary, education for thinking is an important goal that has to be reached if democracy is really going to work. The optimism that is implicit in the democratic ideal must be extended to the educational process. We can no longer afford to put thinking aside during the formal period of schooling and then expect that individuals will participate freely and intelligently in the democratic process. In fact, Piaget's theory gives us a firmer base for optimism in the case of the child's development than the theories that inspired the optimism of those who initiated the ideal of democracy.

Social and educational reformers of the past appealed to reason, but based their arguments primarily on assumptions about personal human values; adherence to their beliefs was at least as much a matter of personal faith as of reasoned conviction. Piaget considers himself first and foremost the founder of a science of the nature of knowledge and its development. His theory of knowledge is open to the scientific scrutiny of methodical observation and critical interpretation. As a consequence the optimism that underlies a School for Thinking is more than a belief in certain human values. Piaget's scientific investigations demonstrate that the optimism implied by the ideal of personal freedom and social democracy is grounded in the psychological and biological nature of human knowledge itself.

# Notes

## Chapter 1

1. On the development of deaf children see: Hans G. Furth, *Thinking without language: Psychological implications of deafness*, New York: Free Press, 1966; *Deafness and Learning: A psychosocial approach*, Belmont, California: Wadsworth, 1973.

## Chapter 2

1. Special acknowledgment and tribute are gladly paid to Michelle Bossers, Marilyn Cavender, Frances Fuller, Eleanor Guthrie, Norma Taylor, and Kay Wingrove, and the PACE project (Program to Advance Creativity in Education) clinicians. Eleanor Sankowski diricted the PACE project. She together with Lorena Anderson and Marjorie Werner extended the original invitation.

2. Hans G. Furth. *Piaget for teachers*, Englewood Cliffs, New Jersey: Prentice-Hall, 1970.

## Chapter 4

1. One of the authors (HW) developed an *Inventory of Body and Sense Thinking Tasks* which was administered to the incoming children at Tyler School. This inventory provided a means of establishing the children's individual level in some aspects of body and sense thinking mentioned in Chapters 6 through 11. The Inventory is divided into seven sections: General movement thinking (8 items), Discriminative movement thinking (10 items), Visual thinking (5 items), Auditory thinking (4 items), Graphic thinking (7 items), Following verbal instructions (3 items), and Preference of hand (5 items). This series of tasks evolved over the past twenty years from clinical research of children both with or without cognitive disabilities. For preliminary standardization, see L. J. Vaughan, "The

construction and tryout of items for a screening test of perceptual motor skills," thesis, University of Pittsburgh, School of Education, 1973.

## Chapter 6

1. E. C. Seguin, *Idiocy and its treatment*, New York: Teachers College, Columbia University, 1907. This is a reprint of the original work entitled, *Idiocy, its diagnosis and treatment by the physiological method,* published 1864 in Albany, New York. Dr. Seguin was a pioneer in developing educational programs for mentally retarded persons in the United States in the middle of the nineteenth century. He called his method "physiological" in recognition of the basic importance of body and sense thinking much as we use the phrase in this book.

2. H. Wachs, "The primary function of all of the learning processes," *Journal of the American Optometric Association* 42 (1971), 362–63.

3. D. B. Harmon, *Notes on a dynamic theory of vision,* Austin, Texas: published by the author, 1958. As an educator Harmon related knowledge from various fields—physiology, psychology, anthropology, medicine, optometry, architecture—and developed important concepts on the influence of the physical condition of the classroom on body functions.

4. For a thorough understanding of the complicated crossing and inversion of the optic nerve fibers, the reader is referred to any basic ophthalmic neurology or physiology text.

5. For proper classroom architecture, see Harmon, *Notes on a dynamic theory of vision.*

6. G. N. Getman describes this activity in a detailed unit entitled *Eye-hand coordination exercises,* available through Teaching Resources, 100 Boylston Street, Boston, Massachusetts 02116. During the 1940's Getman worked with Arnold Gesell at Yale University. As a result of this collaborative research, Getman established important concepts of developmental optometry.

7. Bimanual circles on the chalkboard are mentioned by several well-known authorities, such as Harmon, Getman, and Kephart. A convenient compilation is found in G. N. Getman and D. B. Harmon, *Proper chalkboards, properly used . . . ,* Chicago Heights, Illinois: Weber Costello, 1964.

8. Plus lenses are commonly used to compensate for hyperopia (farsightedness) or presbyopia (inability to focus properly for near-vision). While presbyopia is associated with an aging vision process, some children can be found with near-vision problems

that are alleviated by plus lenses or bifocals. Harmon's research on the effect of plus lenses on body physiology supports A. M. Skeffington's clinical data on the value of plus lenses for the primary school age child published in various Optometric Extension Program Papers, Duncan, Oklahoma.

9. L. A. Cohen, "Mechanisms of perception: their development and function," in M. R. Sloan (Ed.), *Perceptual-motor foundations: a multidisciplinary concern*, Washington, D. C.: American Association for Health, Physical Education, and Recreation, 1969. D. B. Harmon, *The coordinated classroom*, Grand Rapids, Michigan, Seating Company, 1951. R. Held and A. Hein, "Movement-produced stimulation in the development of visually guided behavior," *Journal of Comparative and Physiological Psychology* 56 (1963), 872.

10. One of Harmon's important body alignment devices, the Harmon walking rail, can be purchased from Ideal School Supply Co., Oak Park, Illinois.

11. N. C. Kephart, *The slow learner in the classroom*, Columbus, Ohio: Merrill, 1960. This was one of the early texts that discussed body movement thinking games.

## Chapter 7

1. The vision problems of Eskimo children was reported in Young et al., "The transmission of refractive errors in Eskimo families," *American Journal of Optometry and Archives of American Academy of Optometry* 46, No. 9 (1969), 676–85.

2. An ocular tracking device that has proven quite successful for the game of keep looking at me (Chapter 7, Game 31) is available as *Spacesighters*, from McGraw-Hill, Webster Division, Manchester Road, Manchester, Missouri 63011. These are hand held paddles of durable material with an approximate one inch hole cut out of the center of the paddle.

3. This ball is commercially available as the *Marsden ball* through Keystone View Company, subsidiary of Mast Development Company, Davenport, Iowa.

4. This approach has been recommended by G. Baxter Swarthart, O.D.

5. This game was originally devised by A. J. Kirshner, O.D.

6. See also "Hands," in *Life*, December 17, 1971.

7. C. F. Jayne, *String figures and how to make them—A study of cat's-cradle in many lands*, New York: Dover Publications, 1962. Also Scout manuals or any text on simple knot-tying.

8. This game was originally devised by Anne Gray, speech pathologist, D. T. Watson Home for Crippled Children.

## Chapter 8

1. The screening focused on eight areas of visual functioning.
   (1) Distance visual acuity—right, left, both eyes. (Materials: Illiterate "E" Cube by Ophthalmix, H.O.V. Optical Co., Inc. 137 N. Wabash Ave., Chicago, Ill.)
   (2) Near visual acuity—right, left, both eyes. (Materials: Illiterate "E" Card by G. Guibar, Austin Belgard, Inc., Opticians Distributors, London, England.)
   (3) Excessive hyperopia (farsightedness). (Materials: A pair of glasses with two +1.50 lenses.)
   (4) Beginning myopia (Nearsightedness). (Materials: A pair of glasses with two +.75 lenses.)
   (5) Ocular tracking and ocular convergence. (Materials: A cat bell suspended from a string.)
   (6) Vertical coordination—Are the eyes stable or does one tend to move away from the other in an up-down direction? (Materials: Basic Binocular Series No. 4, Keystone View Co., subsidiary of Mast Development Co., 2212 E. 12th St., Davenport, Iowa.)
   (7) Lateral coordination—Are the eyes stable laterally or does one eye tend to move toward or away from the other in a horizontal direction? (Materials: Basic Binocular Card No. 2.)
   (8) Stereopsis—Can the child synchronize simultaneous function of both eyes to elicit a three-dimensional effect from pictures on a flat surface? (Materials: Basic Binocular Card No. 12.)
   For a more detailed analysis of the procedures, reference is made to J. R. Evans, H. Wachs, and J. M. Borger, "A survey of visual skills of institutionalized retarded patients," *American Journal of Mental Deficiency* 76, No. 5 (1972), 555–60. This screening for vision defects was a simple 10 minute survey and in no way was considered as a substitute for a professional vision analysis. Standards for referral were arbitrarily established, and students not meeting these standards were referred to local vision doctors. Occasionally one of the authors (HW) was requested to administer a cursory evaluation and offer a professional opinion as to whether or not referral was indicated.

2. In various seminars on the Thinking School philosophy, a general outline applicable to most sense thinking aspects received favorable comments. This outline was based on the commonality and overlapping of body and sense thinking as discussed on p. 71 through 208. The following developmental sequence of visual thinking activities can be applied to most games of visual thinking, hand thinking, and, in a broad sense, auditory thinking.
   (1) Same-not-same. The knowledge that an input has or has not changed is basic to all discrimination. See Chapter 6, note 2.

(2) Stacking blocks—broad and narrow (Game 61). This and the following step is more applicable to hand and visual thinking rather than auditory thinking.

(3) Building a bridge (Game 61).

(4) Actual match (Game 61). (a) The child to the best of his ability reproduces an exact duplication of a model that has been presented. The model could be a visual pattern, a sound, a pattern inside the feel-and-find box, or a graphic pattern. (b) Take-away (Game 62). (c) Add-on (Game 62). In auditory thinking a nonsense sound is presented and the child is asked to produce it with a specific part of that sound removed or another added or substituted. Hand and graphic thinking games are played the same as visual games. (Chapter 9, Game 105).

(5) Picture match (Game 63). (a) Juxtaposition. (b) Locations in space. At this step the child develops the knowledge that a sign of a thing represents the thing. In auditory thinking this is the step where the child utilizes a code of written or concrete object signs for the sound presented. Hand thinking games are played the same as visual games.

(6) Outline (Game 65). (a) With demarcations. (b) Without demarcations. This is a parts-whole concept, and has similar application in visual and hand thinking. In auditory thinking this step introduces temporal order, i.e., recognition and manipulation of beginning, middle and end sounds (Chapter 9, Games 105 and 108).

(7) Separation (Game 61). The concept of pause or separation is common to all sense thinking.

(8) Memory (Game 64). Its application to all sense thinking is obvious.

(9) Reversals (Game 66). (a) Horizontal axis. (b) Vertical axis. (c) "Z" (transverse) axis. (c) Diagonal rotations. Again, its application to all sense thinking is obvious, e.g., auditory—repeating numbers, letters, or sounds in reverse.

(10) Perspective (Game 68). This game of spatial knowledge helps the child develop the know-how of "how it would look from there." It plays a role in hand thinking development but less in auditory thinking.

(11) Integration with other sense inputs. At this step auditory, visual, and hand thinking are integrated. The auditory decoding games (Chapter 9, Games 96 through 103) that employ a written symbol coordinate visual and auditory thinking. In Game 111, What am I where, the child integrates visual and hand thinking when he matches inside the box the pattern of a picture placed on top of the box.

(12) Integration with time perception. (a) How long will it take (Game 69). (b) How much can be done in a limited time (Game 69). (c) How fast can it be recognized on a momentary exposure (Tachistoscope Games 75 to 85). Time limitations enhance the child's knowledge of any act and develop a high level of efficiency. This step can be applied to all sense thinking activities.

(13) Minimum clue (Game 80). The game of "flash fog" enhances visual thinking by providing the minimal stimulus to evoke successful interpretation and understanding. An auditory thinking game can be played by the gradual emergence of a spoken work on a tape recorder. This can be accomplished by the slowing down of the tape recorder's speed and gradually increasing the speed until the voice can be legible. This step is difficult to apply to hand thinking.

(14) Noise-on-the-circuit. In this step the child extracts meaningful information from confusing stimuli and thereby enhances the development of all sense thinking (Games 88, 110, 128).

(15) Chalkboard presentation of design (Game 67). Instead of the model being drawn on paper beside the child's work area, the model is drawn on the chalkboard. This game is applicable to hand as well as auditory thinking.

(16) Communication (Game 70). This step applies to all sense thinking. (a) Nonverbal (Nonlanguage): Gesture (mainly movement thinking), drawing (mainly graphic thinking). (b) Verbal (language): vocal (mainly auditory thinking), written (mainly visual thinking).

3. The game of Camouflage was manufactured by Milton Bradley Company, East Long Meadow, Mass.

4. The game of fit-a-space is available commercially through Lauri Enterprises, Haverhill, Mass.

5. A set of size blocks of specific dimensions can be purchased from the Child-Care Company, P.O. Box 366, Loveland, Colo. 80537.

## Chapter 11

1. An easily understandable diagram and explanation of postural set during graphic activities is found in the booklets *The coordinated classroom* (see Chapter 6, note 9) and *Proper chalkboards, properly used* (see Chapter 6, note 7).

2. Suitable templates are available through McGraw Hill, Webster Division, Manchester, Missouri 63011; or the Instructo Corporation, Paoli, Pa. 19301.

3. The game of *Shaky Jake* is available through Cadaco Inc., Chicago, Illinois.

4. The *School skill tracing board* is available with completely revised

and updated Teachers' Manual from the C-Faster Corporation, 2127 Marshall Ave. Saint Paul, Minnesota 55108.

5. Graphic puzzles are commercially available as *The Grofman visual tracing program* through Keystone View Company, subsidiary of Mast Development Company, Davenport, Iowa.

6. N. C. Kephart describes similar techniques in the reference cited in Chapter 6, note 11 and also in worksheet reprints from Purdue Child Achievement Center, Purdue University, Lafayette, Indiana.

## Chapter 13

1. This section was written by Carol Even. A specialist in experience drama, she did not participate in the Charleston project but generally cooperated with the authors in the conception of the School for Thinking.

2. Viola Spolin, *Improvisations for the theater*, Evanston, Illinois: Northwestern University Press (1963).

3. Inexpensive cameras which are able to be handled by children are available from Snap Shooter Camera Company, 9810 Ashton Road, Philadelphia, Pennsylvania 19114.

## Chapter 14

1. Many readers will undoubtedly be disappointed that we report only qualitative and no controlled quantitative results of the Charleston project—and so are we. As we point out in the text, we mounted the project as a four year plan and were willing and eager to be evaluated on standard norms at the end of the period. However, this project was very small in size and together with its sponsoring Pace project was prematurely discontinued after only a year and a half. We all must learn to resist the unreasonable pressure for quick performance results. It is an illusion to conceive of the educational process, particularly at the primary school age, as a cumulative addition of learned performances that can be programmed and controlled at will. Development of the thinking child takes time, and our research and educational policies must reflect this fact under pain of turning out result after result that may have statistical but no psychological significance.

# Index